In accordance with the latest syllabus prescribed by the Central Board of Secondary Education, New Delhi, for Class XII Examination.

CBSE

A TEXT BOOK OF

LEGAL STUDIES

For Class XII

By

Vibbhaa. S. Kumar
B.A., LL.B, LL.M

Praveen Tripathi
B.A., LL.B, LL.M
Assistant Professor of Law
National Law School of India University, Bangalore

OSWAL PUBLISHERS

1/12, Sahitya Kunj, M. G. Road, Agra-282 002

Edition : 2020

Price : 311 /-

ISBN : 978-93-88623-96-4

OSWAL PUBLISHERS

Head office   : 1/12, Sahitya Kunj, M.G. Road, Agra-282 002
Phone   : (0562) 2527771– 4, +91 75340 77222
E-mail   : contact@oswalpublishers.com, sales@oswalpublishers.com
Website   : www.oswalpublishers.com
Facebook link   : https://www.facebook.com/oswalpublishersindia
Available at   : amazon.in, Flipkart, snapdeal, paytm

Preface

Laws are rules, regulations and restrictions that apply to all members of the society. Laws define how people should behave or conduct themselves, and provide sanctions and deterrents against improper and destructive behaviour. They help to organise our societies, maintain order, ensure our safety and prevent infringements of our rights. Without laws, societies would descend into lawlessness, anarchy and violence. In a democratic society, laws are created by representatives of the people (parliaments) and independent judges and magistrates (courts).

The importance of learning about the essential nature of law and the concerned legal systems cannot be overstated. Familiarity with law enhances one's understanding of public affairs and provides a clearer idea about one's rights and obligations as a citizen. Another advantage is that an understanding of law can undoubtedly encourage talented students to pursue a career in law-an objective which is laudable in its own right.

The syllabus of this course as well as the content of this book is framed in a way that has objectives beyond aspiring one to undertake a formal law degree upon graduating from Grade XII. The materials presented offers basic background on what law is all about both in domestic as well as international contexts and serves to benefit those interested in pursuing a law degree.

The complex legal materials had to be selected and simplified enough for the general understanding of students. This may sometimes lead to the ongoing criticisms of less or over simplification and omitting many other relevant areas and issues. However, there are instances where information and analysis are inseparable. All sources referred to in this work have been attributed at the end of every section. Finally, the process is continuous; there is an ongoing evaluative mechanism in place to help us revise, update and re-work this effort to ensure we continue to respond to the needs of the students,teachers and others alike.

I consider it my most humble privilege to have been able to work on this book which has been one of the most enriching experience of my life and has also endowed me with an empirical and empathetic perspective towards the subject. I'd like to extend my heartfelt thanks to the people who have rendered this project a reality.

I would take this privilege to thank the editorial team at Oswal Publishers for their unwavering and unconditional support without which this book would not have been feasible. I would also like to express my earnest gratitude to my teachers, parents and my husband and every person without whose help, support and guidance, and in fact mere presence, this book would never transform from strands and traces of mere thoughts into tangible black and white reality.

Authors

SYLLABUS

Legal Studies (Code 074)

| One Paper | Times : 3 hours | Marks : 100 |

Units	Periods	Marks
1. Judiciary	35	10
2. Topics in Law	35	20
3. Arbitration, Tribunal Adjudication and Alternate Dispute Resolution	35	10
4. Human Rights in India	35	10
5. Legal Profession in India	35	10
6. Legal Services	35	10
7. International Context	10	10
8. Project (Based on Syllabus)		20
Total	**220**	**100**

Course Contents :	Periods
1. Judiciary Structure and Hierarchy of Courts and Legal Offices in India Constitution, Roles and Impartiality Appointments, Trainings, Retirement and Removal of Judges Courts and Judicial Review	35
2. Topics in Law Law of Property Law of Contracts Law of Torts Introduction of Criminal Laws in India Administrative Law	35
3. Arbitration, Tribunal Adjudication and Alternative Dispute Resolution Adversarial and Inquisitorial System Introduction to Alternative Dispute Resolution Types of ADR—Arbitration and Administrative Tribunals Mediation and Conciliation Lok Adalats Ombudsman Lokpal and Lokayukta	35
4. Human Rights in India Introduction—History and International Context Constitutional framework and Related laws in India Complaint Mechanisms of Quasi Judicial Bodies	35
5. Legal Profession in India Introduction History of Legal Profession in India—Classification of lawyers, Advocates Act, 1961, Bar Council of India, professional ethics and advertising by lawyers, legal education in India, liberalisation of profession Legal Profession in other jurisdictions	35

6.	**Legal Services**	
	Introduction	
	Brief History of legal services	
	Legal background—International law, Indian legal system, Criminal law, efforts by the State, Indian Constitution, NALSA Regulation	35
	Criteria for giving free Legal Services—Legal Services	
	Hierarchy of Legal Aid Service Authorities—Central Authority, State Authority and District Authority and Taluk Committee, Lok Adalat and Permanent Lok Adalat	
	Legal aid in context of social justice and human rights	
	Funding	
7.	**International Context**	
	Introduction to International Law—History and types of International Law	
	Sources of International Law—Treaties, Customs and ICJ Decisions	10
	International Institutions	
	International Human Rights	
	Customary International Law	
	International Law and Municipal Law	
	International Law and India	
	Dispute Resolution—ICJ, ICC and other mechanisms	
8.	**Project (Based on Syllabus)**	
	A detailed analysis of any case law pertaining to any unit from the curriculum. It will be preferred to pick any case law mentioned in the book. E.g. : Maneka Gandhi vs UoI or Kesavananda Bharati case. However, it is open to go beyond the textbook as long as the case elucidates a concept of the book.	
	The project should speak of the facts, issue, relevant legislation and discussed precedents and the decision of the case along with a conclusion which shows how well the concept has been understood.	
	A viva along with file will be assessed in the following format :	
	Presentation and preparation of file—2 marks	
	Research—3 marks	
	Application of the understanding of legal context—5 marks	
	Legal reasoning and logic—5 marks	
	Viva—5 marks	

CONTENTS

★★★★★

Judiciary

INTRODUCTION

Judiciary in Ancient India

According to the Arthashastra of Kautilya, who is generally recognised as the Prime Minister of the first Maurya Emperor (321-298 B.C.), the realm was divided into administrative units called Sthaniya, Dronamukha, Khrvatika and Sangrahana (the ancient equivalents of the modern districts, tehsils and Parganas). Sthaniya was a fortress established in the center of eight hundred villages, a dronamukha in the midst of 400 villages, a kharvatika in the midst of 200 villages and a sangrahana in the center of ten villages. Law courts were established in each sangrahana and also at the meeting places of districts (Janapada-sandhishu). The Court consisted of three jurists (dhramastha) and three ministers (amatya).

This suggests the existence of circuit courts, for it is hardly likely that three ministers were permanently posted in each district of the realm. The great jurists, Manu, Yajn-valkya, Katyayana, Brihaspati and others and in later times commentators like Vachaspati Misra and others, described in detail the judicial system and legal procedure which prevailed in India from ancient times till the close of the Middle Ages.

Law in British-Ruled India

The common law system – a system of law based on recorded judicial precedents- came to India with the British East India Company. The company was granted charter by King George I in 1726 to establish Mayor's Courts in Madras, Bombay and Calcutta (now Chennai, Mumbai and Kolkata respectively). Judicial functions of the company were expanded substantially after its victory in Battle of Plassey and by 1772 company's courts were expanded out from the three major cities. In the process, the company slowly replaced the existing Mughal legal system in those parts.

Following the First War of Independence in 1857, the control of company territories in India passed to the British Crown. Being part of the empire the law system saw the next big shift in the Indian legal system. Supreme courts were established replacing the existing mayoral courts. These courts were converted to the first High Courts through letters of patents authorised by the Indian High Courts Act passed by the British Parliament in 1862. Superintendence of lower courts and enrollment of law practitioners were deputed to the respective high courts.

During the Raj, the Privy Council acted as the highest court of appeal. Cases before the council were adjudicated by the law lords of the House of Lords. The state sued and was sued in the name of the British sovereign in her capacity as Empress of India.

During the shift from Mughal legal system, the advocates under that regimen, vakils, too followed suit, though they mostly continued their earlier role as client representatives. The doors of the newly created Supreme Courts were barred to Indian practitioners as right of audience was limited to members of English, Irish and Scottish professional bodies. Subsequent rules and statutes culminating in the Legal Practitioners Act of 1846 which opened up the profession regardless of nationality or religion.

Coding of law also began in earnest with the forming of the first Law Commission. Under the stewardship of its chairman, Thomas Babington Macaulay, the Indian Penal Code was drafted, enacted and brought into force by 1862. The Code of Criminal Procedure was also drafted by the same commission. Host of other statutes and codes like Evidence Act (1872) and Contracts Act (1872).

The Judicial System Today

The Indian Judicial System is one of the oldest legal systems in the world today as the part of the inheritance India received from the British after more than 200 years of their Colonial rule, and the same is evident from the many similarities the Indian legal system shares with the English Legal System. The frame work of the current legal system has been laid down by the Indian Constitution and the judicial system derives its powers from it.

The Constitution of India is the supreme law of the country, the fountain source of law in India which came into effect on 26 January, 1950 and is the world's longest written constitution. It not only laid the framework of Indian judicial system, but has also laid out the powers, duties, procedures and structure of the various branches of the government at the Union and State levels. Moreover, it also has defined the fundamental rights and duties of the people and the directive principles which are the duties of the State.

Inspite of India adopting the features of a federal system of government, the Constitution has provided for the setting up of a single integrated system of courts to administer both Union and State laws. The Supreme Court is the apex court of India, followed by the various High Courts at the state level which cater to one or more number of states. Below the High Courts exist the subordinate courts comprising of the District Courts at the district level and other lower courts.

Salient Features of Indian Judiciary

Judiciary in India acts as the guardian protector of the Constitution and the fundamental rights of people. Some of its features are :

1. India as a Common Law Jurisdiction–An important feature of the Indian Judicial System, is that it's a 'common law system'. In a common law system, law is developed by the judges through their decisions, orders or judgements. These are also referred to as precedents. Unlike the British legal system which is entirely based on the common law system, where it had originated from, the Indian system incorporates the common law system along with the statutory law and the regulatory law.

2. Adversarial Model of Dispute Resolution–Another important feature of the Indian Judicial System is that our system has been designed on the pattern of the adversarial system. Adversarial system is where two advocates represent their parties' positions before an impartial person or group of people, usually a **jury** or **judge**, who attempt to determine the truth of the case. This is to be expected since courts based on the common law system tend to follow the adversarial system of conducting proceedings instead of the inquisitorial system. In an adversarial system, there are two sides in every case and each side presents its arguments to a neutral judge who would then give an order or a judgment based upon the merits of the case.

3. Judicial Review– Indian judicial system has adopted features of other legal systems in such a way that they do not conflict with each other while

benefiting the nation and the people. For example, the Supreme Court and the High Courts have the power of judicial review. According to the concept of judicial review, the legislative and executive actions are subject to the scrutiny of the judiciary and the judiciary can invalidate such actions if they are *ultra vires* of the Constitutional provisions.

Constitution of Supreme Court

On the 28th of January, 1950, two days after India became a Sovereign Democratic Republic, the Supreme Court came into being. The inauguration took place in the Chamber of Princes in the Parliament building which also housed India's Parliament, consisting of the Council of States and the House of the People. It was here, in this Chamber of Princes, that the Federal Court of India had sat for 12 years between 1937 and 1950. This was to be the home of the Supreme Court for years that were to follow until the Supreme Court acquired its own present premises.

The original Constitution of 1950 envisaged a Supreme Court with a Chief Justice and 7 puisne Judges– leaving it to Parliament to increase this number. In the early years, all the Judges of the Supreme Court sat together to hear the cases presented before them. As the work of the Court increased and arrears of cases began to cumulate, Parliament increased the number of Judges from 8 in 1950 to 11 in 1956, 14 in 1960, 18 in 1978, 26 in 1986 and 31 in 2008 (current strength). As the number of the Judges has increased, they sit in smaller Benches of two and three - coming together in larger Benches of 5 and more only when required to do so or to settle a difference of opinion or controversy.

The Supreme Court of India comprises the Chief Justice and not more than 30 other Judges appointed by the President of India. Supreme Court Judges retire upon attaining the age of 65 years. In order to be appointed as a Judge of the Supreme Court, a person must be a citizen of India and must have been, for atleast five years, a Judge of a High Court or of two or more such Courts in succession, or an Advocate of a High Court or of two or more such Courts in succession for at least 10 years or he must be, in the opinion of the President, a distinguished jurist. Provisions exist for the appointment of a Judge of a High Court as an Ad-hoc Judge of the Supreme Court and for retired Judges of the Supreme Court or High Courts to sit and act as Judges of that Court.

Supreme Court Rules, 1966 are framed under Article 145 of the Constitution to regulate the practice and procedure of the Supreme Court.

"As per Article 348 of Constitution of India, the proceedings of Supreme Court are conducted in English only. the Parliament has the power to alter the official language under Article 348 but till now it has not altered the official language of Supreme Court. Recently, the orders of Supreme Court are available on Supreme Court official website in regional languages."

NATURE OF INDIAN LEGAL SYSTEM

1. Common Law– The Common Law is a body of law derived from judicial decisions known as case laws, rather from statutes. This system of jurisprudence initially originated in England. It includes those rules of law which derive their authority from the statement of principles found in the decisions of courts. This system of law includes tradition, custom and usage, fundamental principles and modes of reasoning. It is the embodiment of broad and comprehensive unwritten principles, which were derived out of natural reasoning and innate sense of justice. The common law is quite different from codified law as it follows the judgment while the codified law precedes it. Therefore it can be said that it is a system of rules and declarations of principles from where the judicial ideas and legal definitions are derived. This law is ever changing as its principles are influenced by the changing conditions and requirements of the society.

Does it Apply in India ?

The application of Common Law has been overarching in the Indian context; it has been enshrined in the Indian legal system over the space of two centuries by the English to the point that one can't allocate an individual identity to Indian jurisprudence. Thus it can be said that Common Law has been applicable here though in a different format than that of England as the needs and demands of the Indian society were different from that of the English. It is to be found out that much of the law compiled in codes we have today were primarily derived from the Common Law principles. The basic statutes governing civil and criminal justice are the Indian Penal Code, 1860, Indian Evidence Act, 1872, the Code of Criminal Procedure, 1973 and the Code of Civil Procedure, 1908. It has already been discussed how these laws came into being, one thing can be said about these legislations is that they have stood the test of time with minimal amendments. Codification of laws made the law uniform throughout the country and fostered a kind of legal unity in fundamental laws. The Codes apply uniformly throughout the nation.

The system of Precedents derived from the Common Law too has wide application within the Indian legal system, a precedent in Common Law parlance means a previously decided case which establishes a rule or principle that may be utilised by the court or a judicial body in deciding other cases that are similar in facts or issue. Initially the English judges and barristers presiding and practicing in the Indian courts followed the decisions of the courts in England, thus slowly the concept of precedents came to be ardently followed within the Indian courts. This law has been carried forward in the present day Legal system as in regard to the judgments of the Supreme Court of India, the Indian Constitution provides that "The law declared by the Supreme Court shall be binding on all courts within the territory of India." Hence it can be said unequivocally that Common Law has wide application within the Indian Legal fold as many of the features of this system have been adopted and further developed from that of The English Common Law System, even though its application hasn't been discussed in entirely and only the major principles derived from it have been discussed.

Thus it can be said that common law traces back its origins to England and is primarily a method of administering justice, which has incorporated different aspects of the legal pedagogy and practice with the help of deliberations of laymen and the learned over the course of time. In the Indian context the Common Law initially was applied for the convenience of the English, so they could govern their territories properly but, as they became the overlords of India the common law became common for Indians. There developed a symbiotic relationship between the Indian customary law and the common law which gave birth to the modern day Indian legal system. Hence we can say India has an organic law as a consequence of the common law system.

2. Adversial System of Law–Another contribution to Indian legal system by Common Law has been the adversarial system of trial. In this system the accused is presumed to be innocent and the burden is on the prosecution to prove beyond reasonable doubt that he is guilty. The accused also enjoys the right to silence and cannot be compelled to reply. The truth is supposed to emerge from the respective versions of the facts presented by the prosecution and the defence before a neutral judge. Both the parties have a right to question their witnesses and the opposing side has a right to test their testimony by questioning them. The judge acts like an umpire to see whether the prosecution has been able to prove the case beyond reasonable doubt and gives the benefit of doubt to the accused, his ultimate duty being to pronounce the judgment regarding the matter.

3. Due Process of Law–Due process of law doctrine not only checks if there is a law to deprive the life and personal liberty of a person, but also see if the law made is fair, just and not arbitrary. If SC finds any law as unfair, it will declare it as null and void. This doctrine provides for more fair treatment of individual rights. Under due process, it is the legal requirement that the state must respect all of the legal rights that are owed to a person and laws that states enact must confirm to the laws of the land like – fairness, fundamental rights, liberty etc. It also gives the judiciary to access the fundamental fairness, justice, and liberty of any legislation.

4. Procedure Established by Law– It means that a law that is duly enacted by legislature or the concerned body is valid if it has followed the correct procedure. Following this doctrine means that, a person can be deprived of his life or personal liberty according to the **procedure established by law.** So, if Parliament pass a law, then the life or personal liberty of a person can be taken off according to the provisions and procedures of the law. This doctrine has a major flaw. What is it ? It does not seek whether the laws made by Parliament is fair, just and not arbitrary. Procedure established by law means a law duly enacted is valid even if it's contrary to principles of justice and equity. Strictly following procedure established by law may raise the risk of compromise to life and personal liberty of individuals due to unjust laws made by the law making authorities. It is to avoid this situation, SC stressed the importance of due process of law.

The difference in Layman's terms is as below :

Due Process of Law = Procedure Established by Law + The procedure should be fair and just and not arbitrary.

STRUCTURE HIERARCHY AND LEGAL OFFICES IN INDIA

Legal systems are among the most imperative requisites of a country to ensure that it remains a safe & peaceful place to live. The Indian legal system hierarchy or simply saying the Indian Judicial system is partially the British legal system's continuation, the system which was established in the mid era of the 19th century by English government.

The Indian Judicial system has a systematic arrangement of all types of courts that exist and run in India currently. Broadly saying this gets divided into 3 levels. The Indian legal system hierarchy is briefly explicated as below in chronological order means starting with the highest level court of the hierarchy and ending with the lowest one :

1. Supreme Court

The Indian legal hierarchy system, the Supreme Court is at the top level of the Indian court system. The Supreme Court is the utmost authority holder court system in India whose decision can't be challenged by any other Indian court. If someone wishes to challenge it, he/she has to file a letter to President or Prime Minister of India to do so.

Indian legal system has only one Supreme Court and that is in Delhi, the national capital of India. The Supreme Court came into existence in the year 1950 on 28th of January, soon 2 days after the constitution of India came into continuation. Ever since that time, this highest court has been in Delhi.

Supreme Court Registry

The Registry of the Supreme Court is headed by the *Secretary General* who is assisted in his work by seven Registrars, and twenty one Additional Registrars etc. Article 146 of the Constitution deals with the appointments of officers and servants of the Supreme Court Registry.

Attorney General of India

The Attorney General for India is the Indian government's chief legal advisor and its primary lawyer in the Supreme Court of India. He is appointed by the President of India under Article 76(1) of the Constitution and holds office during the pleasure of the President. He must be a person qualified to be appointed as a Judge of the Supreme Court, also must have been a judge of some high court for five years or an advocate of some high court for ten years or an eminent jurist, in the opinion of the President and must be a citizen of India. The 15th and current Attorney General is K.K. Venugopal. He was appointed by Pranab Mukherjee, the President of India of that time. He has been formally appointed as Attorney General of India with effect from 30 June 2017 and shall have a tenure of 5 years.

Supreme Court Advocates

There are three categories of Advocates who are entitled to practice law before the Supreme Court of India :

(i) Senior Advocates–These are Advocates who are designated as Senior Advocates by the Supreme Court of India or by any High Court. The Court can designate any Advocate, with his consent, as Senior Advocate if in its opinion by virtue of his ability, standing at the Bar or special knowledge or experience in law the said Advocate is deserving of such distinction. A Senior Advocate is not entitled to appear without an Advocate-on-Record in the Supreme Court or without a junior in any other court or tribunal in India. He is also not entitled to accept instructions to draw pleadings or affidavits, advise on evidence or do any drafting work of an analogous kind in any court or tribunal in India or undertake conveyancing work of any kind whatsoever but this prohibition shall not extend to settling any such matter as aforesaid in consultation with a junior.

(ii) Advocates on Record–Only these Advocates are entitled to file any matter or document before the Supreme Court. They can also file an appearance or act for a party in the Supreme Court.

(iii) Other Advocates–These are Advocates whose names are entered on the roll of any State Bar Council maintained under the Advocates Act, 1961. They can appear and argue any matter on behalf of a party in the Supreme Court but they are not entitled to file any document or matter before the court.

Role of Supreme Court

The role and position of the Supreme Court is vital in the judicial and political system of India. The primary duty of the Supreme Court is to ascertain whether the laws are executed and obeyed properly and to see to it that no person is deprived of justice in any court of law. With this purpose in view, the Supreme Court occupies the highest place in our unitary judicial system. Attempt has been made, as far as possible, to ensure its independence and achieve the goal of ensuring justice.

The Supreme Court has been equipped with enormous powers. By virtue of its place at the apex of the judicial pyramid, the Supreme Court acts as a great unifying force. We have seen that its decisions and verdicts are binding on any court in India. As a result, there is a good possibility of integration, consistency and cohesion in the entire judicial system of the country.

The role and functions of the Supreme Court in our judicial and political system are explained further below :

As a Federal Court–Supreme Court is the Federal Court of India, India being a federation; powers are divided between the Union and State governments. The Supreme Court of India is the final authority to see to it that the division of powers as specified in the constitution is obeyed by both the Union and the State governments. So, Article 131 of the Indian Constitution vests the Supreme Court with original and exclusive jurisdiction to determine the justiciable disputes between the Union and the States or between the States.

Interpreter of the Constitution and Law–The responsibility of interpreting the constitution rests on the Supreme Court. The interpretation of the constitution which the Supreme Court shall make must be accepted by all. It interprets the constitution and preserves it. Where a case involves a substantial question of law as to the interpretation of the constitution either certified by the High Court or being satisfied by the Supreme Court itself, an appeal shall lie to the Supreme Court for interpretation of the question of law raised.

As a Court of Appeal–The Supreme Court is the highest court of appeal from all courts in the territory of India. An appeal lies to the Supreme Court of the cases involving interpretation of the constitution. Appeals in respect of civil and criminal cases also lie to the Supreme Court irrespective of any constitutional question.

The appellate jurisdiction of the Supreme Court can be invoked by a certificate granted by the High Court concerned under Article 132(1), 133(1) or 134 of the Constitution in respect of any judgement, decree or final order of a High Court in both civil and criminal cases, involving substantial questions of law as to the interpretation of the Constitution. Appeals also lie to the Supreme Court in civil matters if the High Court concerned certifies :

● that the case involves a substantial question of law of general importance

● that, in the opinion of the High Court, the said question needs to be decided by the Supreme Court. In criminal cases an appeal lies to the Supreme Court if the High Court.

● has on appeal reversed an order of acquittal of an accused person and sentenced him to death or to imprisonment for life or for a period of not less than 10 years,

● has withdrawn for trial before itself any case from any Court subordinate to its authority and has in such trial convicted the accused and sentenced him to death or to imprisonment for life or for a period of not less than 10 years,

● certified that the case is a fit one for appeal to the Supreme Court. Parliament is authorised to confer on the Supreme Court any further powers to entertain and hear appeals from any judgement, final order or sentence in a criminal proceeding of a High Court

Advisory Role–The Supreme Court has an advisory jurisdiction in offering its opinion any question of law or fact of public importance as may be referred to it for consideration by the President.

Guardian of the Constitution–The Supreme Court of India is the guardian of the constitution. There are two points of significance of the Supreme Court's rule as the protector and guardian of the constitution.

(i) First, as the highest Federal Court, it is within the power and authority of the Supreme Court to settle any dispute regarding division of powers between the Union and the States.

(ii) Secondly, it is in the Supreme Court's authority to safeguard the fundamental rights of the citizens.

In order to discharge these two functions it is sometimes necessary for the Supreme Court to examine or review the legality of the laws enacted by both the Union and the State Governments. This is known as the power of Judicial Review. Indian Supreme Court enjoys limited power of Judicial Review.

Curative Petition–Supreme Court can entertain a curative petition and reconsider its judgment/order and exercise of its inherent powers in order to prevent abuse of its process to cure gross miscarriage of justice.

Writ Jurisdictions–Under Article 32 of the constitution, Supreme Court can issue writs for the enforcement of fundamental rights. These writs are in the nature of Habeas Corpus, Mandamas, Prohibition, Quo-warranto and Certiorari.

Contempt Jurisdiction–Under Articles 129 and 142 of the Constitution the Supreme Court has been vested with power to punish for contempt of Court including the power to punish for contempt of itself.

Public Interest Litigation (Janhit Yachika)–Although the proceedings in the Supreme Court arise out of the judgments or orders made by the Subordinate Courts including the High Courts, but of late the Supreme Court has started entertaining matters in which interest of the public at large is involved and the Court can be moved by any individual or group of persons either by filing a Writ Petition at the Filing Counter of the Court or by addressing a letter to Hon'ble the Chief Justice of India highlighting the question of public importance

for invoking this jurisdiction. Such concept is popularly known as 'Public Interest Litigation' and several matters of public importance have become landmark cases. This concept is unique to the Supreme Court of India only and perhaps no other Court in the world has been exercising this extraordinary jurisdiction. A Writ Petition filed at the Filing Counter is dealt with like any other Writ Petition and processed as such. In case of a letter addressed to Hon'ble the Chief Justice of India the same is dealt with in accordance with the guidelines.

PIL came for the first time before the Supreme Court in India in the case of Hussainara Khatoon v. State of Bihar. A lawyer filed this case depicting the inhuman conditions of the prisoners in the Bihar Jail. A Supreme Court bench headed by Justice P.N. Bhagwati considered this case as Public Interest Litigation. The Bench declared the right for free legal aid for those prisoners and ordered expeditious trial of them. Guidleines are laid down by the Apex Court in different cases for filing PIL. Currently Supreme Court accepts PIL through online mode on their official website.

Frivolous Public Interest Litigation (PIL) has increased a lot in recent times. It is not allowed at all and dealt with seriously by Supreme Court and High Courts. In several judgments, the Supreme Court and High Courts have warned litigants for filing frivolous and malicious PIL as it would defeat the noble objective of PIL.

AMICUS CURIAE (Friend of Court)–If a petition is received from the jail or in any other criminal matter if the accused is unrepresented then an Advocate is appointed as amicus curiae by the Court to defend and argue the case of the accused. In civil matters also the Court can appoint an Advocate as amicus curiae if it thinks it necessary in case of an unrepresented party; the Court can also appoint amicus curiae in any matter of general public importance or in which the interest of the public at large is involved.

Election Petitions under Part-III of the Presidential and Vice Presidential Election Act, 1952 are also filled directly in the supreme court.

2. High Court

The State Courts come direct under the Supreme Court of India in the Indian legal system hierarchy. Every state of India is provided with a court that has the utmost power of judicial system employed in that state only. This state court is termed as High Court and is usually in the capital of that particular state.

The final decisions for that state's cases are judged by that court and only Supreme Court has the power & authority to challenge the verdicts that come from High Court decisions.

Role of High Court

The powers and functions of High Courts have not been described in detail in the constitution. Before the present constitution was adopted, the High Courts with well-defined powers, were functioning in different states. Thus, the framers of the Constitution did not feel the need for describing the jurisdiction of High Court in detail. On the other hand, the Supreme Court, being a new creation, required a dear definition of its powers and jurisdiction. The powers and functions of High Courts may be discussed under the following five heads :

1. Original Jurisdiction–In some matters cases can be directly filed in the High Courts.

(i) Fundamental Rights–Our Constitution has given fundamental rights to citizens. In any democracy, fundamental or basic rights have a special place and it is the duty of the state to ensure that the citizens enjoy fundamental rights without any fear or danger.

Under Article 226, the High Court shall have the power to issue any person or authority, directions, orders or writs in nature of Habeas Corpus, Mandamus, Prohibition, Quo Warranto and Certiorari or any of them for the enforcement of any of the fundamental rights and for any other purpose. The High Court is empowered to entertain any petition for the redressal of any injury even if, by or under any law, remedy for such redressal has been provided for. Election cases are entertained by the High Court through this power.

According to D. D. Basu, the High Court has larger jurisdiction than the Supreme Court in respect of issuing writs. The Supreme Court, under Article 32, can issue writs only where a fundamental right has been infringed upon. But a High Court, under Article 226, can issue them not only in such cases, but also where an ordinary legal right has been infringed upon, provided a writ is a proper remedy in such cases.

(ii) Election Cases–Cases relating to elections can be directly filed in the High Court.

(iii) Marriage and Divorce–Cases relating to marriage/divorce can be directly entertained by the High Court.

2. Appellate Jurisdiction–The High Court has appellate jurisdiction over both civil and criminal cases. It can hear appeal on civil cases tried by the Courts of Munsifs and District Judges. In criminal cases, the jurisdiction extends to cases tried by the Sessions and Additional Sessions Judges. An appeal can be filed against the decision of a Session Judge if the accused has been sentenced for 7 years or more. Capital punishment given by a session's judge cannot be executed unless it is confirmed by the High Court.

3. Supervisory Jurisdiction–The High Court, under Article 227, has the power of superintendence over all the Courts and Tribunals except those which deal with Armed Forces located in the state. The High Court has the power to :

- Call for return from such courts;
- Make and issue general rules and prescribe forms for regulating the practice and proceeding of such courts and
- Prescribe forms in which books, entries and accounts are to be kept by the officers of such courts.

The power of superintendence, vested in the High Court, is judicial as well as administrative in nature. The High Court is thus in charge of the administration of justice in the state. It is important to note that the Supreme Court has no similar power vis-a-vis the High Courts.

4. Administrative Jurisdiction–The officers and servants (employees) of the High Court are under its total control. They are appointed by the Chief Justice or any other Judge or officer of the High Court, as he may direct (Article 229). However, the High Court may be required by the Governor of the state to consult the Public Service Commission while appointing the officers and staff of the High Court.

The Chief Justice has the power to suspend or dismiss any of the officers or servants of the High Court. He or any other Judge of the High Court authorized by him, shall determine the service conditions of its officers and staff subject to any act of the state legislature.

The administrative expenses of the High Court are charged upon the Consolidated Fund of the State. These are non-votable.

5. Power to Transfer cases from Subordinate Courts–If the High Court is satisfied that a case pending in a Subordinate Court involves a substantial question of law as to the interpretation of the constitution, it may withdraw the case to itself and do either of the following two :

(i) It will dispose of the case; or

(ii) It will determine the question of law and return the case to the concerned court along with its judgment and direct that court to dispose of the case in conformity with this judgement.

The exercise of this power by this High Court serves a good purpose. It prevents multiple and conflicting interpretations of tile constitutions by Subordinate Courts. The High Court has also the power to call for any records from any Subordinate Court to examine the orders passed by them. In exercising this power, the High Court seeks to ensure that the orders passed by the Subordinate Courts are legal and correct.

6. A Court of Record–The High Court is a Court of Record.

Its decisions are binding for all Subordinate Courts. The decisions and proceedings of the High Court have evidentiary value and no Subordinate Court can challenge them.

7. Miscellaneous Powers–

(i) The High Court has the power to send for the judgment of lower court. By exercising this power, the High Court can examine the legal validity of this judgment.

(ii) The High Court can punish any person or institution for contempt of court.

3. District Court

Every state of India further incorporates some lower courts that are lower in terms of power and authority than the High Court of that state. These courts are in terms of district means every district of a state has a court that employs maximum government judicial power in that district only.

The highest court in each district is that of the District and Sessions Judge. This is the principal court of civil jurisdiction. This is also a court of Sessions. Sessions-trial cases are tried by the Sessions Court. It has the power to impose any sentence including capital punishment. There are many other courts subordinate to the Court of District and Sessions Judge.

There is a three tier system of courts. On the civil side, at the lowest level is the court of Civil Judge (Junior Division). On criminal side the lowest court is that of the Judicial Magistrate. Civil Judge (Junior Division) decides civil cases of small pecuniary stake. Judicial Magistrates decide criminal cases which are punishable with imprisonment of up to five years. At the middle of the hierarchy there is the Court of Civil Judge (Senior Division) on the civil side and the Court of the Chief Judicial Magistrate on the Criminal

side. Civil Judge (senior division) can decide civil cases of any valuation. There are many additional courts of Additional Civil Judge (senior division). The Jurisdiction of these addition courts is the same as that of the principal court of Civil Judge (Senior Division). The Chief Judicial Magistrate can try cases which are punishable with imprisonment for a term up to seven years. Usually there are many additional courts of Additional Chief Judicial Magistrates. At the top level there may be one or more courts of additional district and session's judge with the same judicial power as that of the District and Sessions judge. Besides these Courts, there are Courts of Assistant judges, Sub-Judges, Munsifs and Courts of small causes.

Role of Lower Courts

The **District Courts** of India are presided over by a judge. They administer justice in India at a district level. These courts are under administrative and judicial control of the High Court of the State to which the concerned district belongs.

Judicial independence of each court is the characteristic feature of the district judiciary. In each district there is a strong bar which ensures that courts decide cases according to law and without fear or favour. The greatest problem of district courts is that of huge backlog of cases leading to undue delay in deciding cases.

4. Tribunals

Aside from these legal bodies, Indian judiciary is likewise described by various semi-judicial bodies required in dispute resolution. These bodies run as semi or quasi-judicial bodies since they may comprise of authoritative officers or judges without a legitimate foundation. However they work in their legal limit and listen significant legitimate matters and settle claims between the gatherings. Tribunals have been constituted under particular sacred command revered in the Constitution of India or through legitimate authorisations, *e.g.,* a law went by the governing body. Their creation goes for expanding proficiency in determining debate and lessening the weight on courts. Case of some of these tribunals include :

- Central Authoritative Tribunal (CAT) for determining the grievances and debate of focal government representatives.
- State Administrative Tribunals (SAT) for state government representatives.
- Telecom Dispute Settlement Appellate Tribunal (TDSAT) for determining question in the telecom part in India.

National Green Tribunal (NGT) for question including natural issues. Some of these tribunals capacity with controllers. Controllers are specific government organisations that regulate the law also, arrange consistence in the significant government areas. For instance, one of the tribunals TDSAT capacities close by the controller, TRAI (Telecom Regulatory Power of India) in figuring laws and arrangement for determining telecom debate in India. In this manner these tribunals supplement and supplement the part of courts in keeping up law and equity in the general public.

ATTORNEY GENERAL OF INDIA AND LAW OFFICES IN INDIA

Attorney General–The discourse on the structure of Indian legal would stay deficient without a clarification of law workplaces and officers delegated by the Centre and State Governments in India. Certain law workplaces at the Union and State level exist to exhort the official wing of the legislature. These law officers are taken up by law officers, who get their order either from the Constitution or other statutory authorisations. The Attorney General is the primary legitimate officer of the nation. The Attorney General of India is selected by the President of India under Article 76 of the Constitution, which expresses that he can hold the workplace amid the delight of the President. The Attorney General must be a man qualified to be selected as a Judge of the Supreme Court, having sufficient lawful practice or have served as a judge for an imperative length as commanded by the Constitution. It is the obligation of the Attorney General for India to offer guidance to the Government of India upon lawful matters and to perform different obligations of lawful character as might be given to him by the President. In the execution of his obligations, he has the privilege to show up in the Courts. This is known as a privilege to gathering of people given to the Attorney General. He may likewise partake in the procedures of the Parliament without a privilege to vote. In release of his capacities, the Attorney General is helped by a Solicitor General and four Additional Solicitors General. The position of the Solicitor General and Extra Solicitors General is not perceived in the Constitution. Be that as it may they are administered through principles instituted by the Parliament.

Law Offices–Like the Attorney General of India, the position of Advocate General exists at the state level. An Advocate General is a senior law officer who goes about as a lawful consultant to the State Government. As indicated by Article 165 of the Constitution, Advocate General is delegated by the Governor of the individual state. The Advocate General is the boss legitimate counsel of the State and performs obligations of a lawful character including speaking to the State before the courts either through himself/herself or through the law officers or pleaders selected by the State. The capability required for arrangement as an Advocate General is like that of a judge of a High Court. The office of an Advocate General is held amid the delight of the Governor, who too decides the way of compensations for the Advocate General. Extra Advocate Generals are additionally designated to help the workplace of the Advocate General.

CONSTITUTION AND IMPARTIALITY

Independence of Judiciary

Indian Constitution has given high importance to the Independence of Judiciary System. Every democratic country puts a great store on the independence of the judiciary as a guarantee of individual freedom.

What is the meaning of Independence of Judiciary or Judicial Independence ?

Judicial Independence or Independence of Judiciary refers to an environment where judges are free to make decisions or pass judgment without any pressure from the government or other powerful entities.

Independence of Judiciary means that the judiciary as an organ of the government should be free from influence and control of the other two organs *i.e.*, the executive and the legislature of government.

Why is Judicial Independence important ?

Courts are expected to act as protectors of the law who independently exercise their judicial powers without functional or individual interference. Such intereference comes from legislative, executive, political parties, criminal groups and judicial hierarchy itself.

Judicial independence play an important role in maintaining the democratic set-up of any country. An impartial and independent judicial system alone can protect the rights of the citizens against the arbitrary powers of the executive or legislature. Freedom from the influence and control of the executive is of crucial importance. It is important for individual freedom that the judges give their verdict without fear or favour. It refers to an environment where the judge can pass impartial judgment.

Independence of Judiciary in India

1. Provisions Relating to the judges

The constitution of India adopts diverse devices to ensure the independence of the judiciary in keeping with both the doctrines of constitutional and Parliamentary sovereignty. Elaborated provision are in place for ensuring the independent position of the Judges of the Supreme Court and the High Courts.

(i) The judges of the Supreme Court and the High Courts have to take an oath before entering office that they will faithfully perform their duties without fear, favour, affection, ill-will, and defend the constitution of India and the laws. Recognition of the doctrine of constitutional sovereignty is implicit in this oath.

(ii) The process of appointment of judges also ensures the independence of judiciary in India. The judges of the Supreme Court and the High Courts are appointed by the President. The constitution of India has made it obligatory on the President to make the appointments in consultation with the highest judicial authorities. He of course takes advice of the Cabinet. The constitution also prescribes necessary qualifications for such appointments. The constitution tries to make the appointments unbiased by political considerations.

(iii) The Constitution provides for the security of tenure of Judges. The judges of the Supreme Court and the High Court's serve **during good behavior** and not during the pleasure of the President, as is the case with other high government officials. They cannot be arbitrarily removed by the President. They may be removed from office only through impeachment. A Judge can be removed on the ground of proved misbehaviour or incapacity on a report by both Houses of Parliament supported by a special majority.

(iv) Their salaries and allowances are charged upon the Consolidated Fund of India. Further, the salaries and allowances of Judges of Supreme court and High courts cannot be reduced during their tenure, except during a financial emergency under Article 360 of the constitution.

(v) The activities of the Judges cannot be discussed by the executive or the legislature, except in case of removal of them.

(vi) The retirement age is 65 years for Supreme court judges and 62 years for High Court judges. Such long tenure enable the judges to function impartially and independently.

(vii) A retired Supreme Court judge cannot practice engage in legal practice in any court in India. However, a retired High Court judge can practice law in a state other than the state in which he served as a High Court judge. These restrictions ensure that a retired judge is not able to influence the decision of the courts.

Independence and Impartiality of Judiciary

At the time of framing the Indian Constitution, the framers were concerned about the kind of judiciary our country should have. This concern of the members of the constituent assembly was responded by Dr. B. R. Ambedkar in the following words : *"There can be no difference of opinion in the House that our judiciary must be both independent of the executive and must also be competent in itself. And the question is how these two objects can be secured."*

The question is about providing the separate entity to the judiciary and making itself competent. The answer to this question lies in the very basic understanding that so as to secure the stability and prosperity of the society, the framers at that time understood that such a society could be created only by guaranteeing the fundamental rights and the independence of the judiciary to guard and enforce those fundamental rights. Also in a country like India, the independence of the judiciary is of utmost importance in upholding the pillars of the democratic system hence ensuring a free society.

It is not enough for the judiciary, as an institution, to be independent - individual judges must be seen to be objective and impartial. In their personal lives, judges must avoid words, actions or situations that might make them appear to be biased or disrespectful of the laws they are sworn to uphold. They must treat lawyers, clients and witnesses with respect and must refrain from comments that suggest they have made up their minds in advance. Outside the courtroom, judges do not socialize or associate with lawyers or other persons connected with the cases they hear, or they may be accused of favoritism. Judges typically declare a conflict and withdraw from a case that involves relatives or friends. The same is true if the case involves a former client, a member of the judge's former law firm, law partners or a former business associate, at least until a year or two has passed since the judge was appointed and those ties were severed.

Judges often choose to avoid most forms of community involvement. A judge may undertake community or charitable work but cannot offer legal or investment advice. Judges cannot take part in politics, either as a party member, fund-raiser or donor and many choose to relinquish their right to vote. While judges have been more willing in recent years to make public speeches or agree to media interviews, they refrain from expressing opinions on legal issues that could come before them in a future case. Judges are forbidden from being paid to do anything other than their judicial duties, but can accept appointments to serve on royal commissions, inquiries and other official investigations.

Need for the Independence of the Judiciary

The basic need for the independence of the judiciary rests upon the following points :

To check the functioning of the organs– Judiciary acts as a watchdog by ensuring that all the organs of the state function within their respective areas and according to the provisions of the constitution. Judiciary acts as a guardian of the constitution and also aids in securing the doctrine of separation of powers.

Interpreting the provisions of the constitution– It was well known to the framers of the constitution that in future the ambiguity will arise with the provisions of the constitution so they ensured that the judiciary must be independent and self-competent to interpret the provision of the constitution in such a way to clear the ambiguity but such an interpretation must be unbiased *i.e.* free from any pressure from any organs like executive. If the judiciary is not independent, the other organs may pressurise the judiciary to interpret the provision of the constitution according to them. Judiciary is given the job to interpret the constitution according to the constitutional philosophy and the constitutional norms.

Dispute reffered to the judiciary– It is expected of the Judiciary to deliver judicial justice not partial or committed justice. By committed justice we mean to say that when a judge emphasises on a particular aspect while giving justice and not considering all the aspects involved in a particular situation. Similarly judiciary must act in an unbiased manner.

2. Provisions Relating to the Institution of Judiciary

Many provisions are provided in our constitution to ensure the independence of the judiciary. The constitutional provisions are discussed below :

Security to the tenure– The judges of the Supreme Court and High Courts have been given the security of the tenure. Once appointed, they continue to remain in office till they reach the age of retirement which is 65 years in the case of judges of Supreme Court (Art. 124(2)) and 62 years in the case of judges of the High Courts (Art. 217(1)). They cannot be removed from the office except by an order of the President and that too on the ground of proven misbehavior and incapacity. A resolution has also to be accepted to that effect by a majority of total membership of each House of Parliament and also by a majority of no less than two third of the members of the house present and voting. Procedure is so complicated that there has been no case of the removal of a Judge of Supreme Court or High Court under this provision.

Salaries and allowance–The salaries and allowances of the judges is also a factor which makes the judges independent as their salaries and allowances are fixed and are not subject to a vote of the legislature. They are charged on the Consolidated Fund of India in case of Supreme Court judges and the Consolidated Fund of state in the case of High Court judges. Their emoluments cannot be altered to their disadvantage [Art. 125(2)] except in the event of grave financial emergency.

Powers and Jurisdiction of Supreme Court– Parliament can only add to the powers and jurisdiction of the Supreme Court but cannot curtail them. In the civil cases, Parliament may change the pecuniary limit for the appeals to the Supreme Court. Parliament may enhance the appellate jurisdiction of the Supreme Court. It may confer the supplementary powers on the Supreme Court to enable it work more effectively. It may confer power to issue directions, orders or writs for any purpose other than those mentioned in Art. 32. Powers of the Supreme Court cannot be taken away making judiciary independent.

No discussion on conduct of Judge in State Legislature / Parliament–Art. 211 provides that there shall be no discussion in the legislature of the state with respect to the conduct of any judge of Supreme Court or of a High Court in the discharge of his duties. A similar provision is made in Art. 121 which lays down that no discussion shall take place in Parliament with respect to the conduct of the judge of Supreme Court or High Court in the discharge of his duties except upon a motion for presenting an address to the President praying for the removal of the judge.

Power to punish for contempt–Both the Supreme Court and the High Court have the power to punish any person for their contempt. Art. 129 provides that the Supreme Court shall have the power to punish for contempt of itself. Likewise, Art. 215 lays down that every High Court shall have the power to punish for contempt of itself.

Separation of the Judiciary from the Executive– Art. 50 contains one of the Directive Principles of State Policy and lays down that the state shall take steps to separate the judiciary from the executive in the public services of the state. The object behind the Directive Principle is to secure the independence of the judiciary from the executive. Art. 50 says that there shall be a separate judicial service free from executive control.

COMPOSITION, APPOINTMENT, QUALIFICATION, TENNURE AND REMOVAL OF JUDGES

1. Supreme Court

The Supreme Court is the highest court in India. The appointment of judges of Supreme Court is currently made on the decisions evolved in Three Judges Case. The First Judges Case was S P Gupta Vs. Union of India and Ors., 1981 where Supremacy of Executive was ensured. The Second Judges Case was Supreme Court Advocates on Record Association Vs. Union of India, 1993 where Judicial Supremacy replaced Supremacy of Executive. Third Judges Case was In Re Special Reference Case, 1999 where Judicial Supremacy was reinstated. As per the second and third judges case, the collegium of judges was reconstructed and it includes Chief Justice of India and four other seniormost puisne judges of the Supreme Court. It was held in third judges case that the recommendation made by the Chief Justice of India on appointment of Judges of Supreme Court and High Court by not following consultation process are not binding on the government.

Composition–It consists of the Chief Justice and not more than 25 judges. The President may appoint an adhoc judge at the request of the Chief Justice.

Appointment–`Every judge of the Supreme Court is appointed by the President of India after consultation with such judges of the Supreme Court and the High Courts of States as the President may deem necessary for the purpose. However, in the matter of appointment of a judge other than the Chief Justice, consultation of the Chief Justice of India by the President is obligatory.

Qualifications–To be a judge of the Supreme Court, one must be

- a citizen of India.
- a judge of a High Court at least for five years; or
- an advocate of a High Court for at least ten years.
- a distinguished jurist in the opinion of the President.

Tenure–A judge of the Supreme Court retires at the age of 65 years. He may also resign from his office.

Removal–A judge of the Supreme Court can also be removed by the President from his position only on the ground of proved misbehaviour or incapacity if a resolution in this regard is passed by the Parliament supported by two-thirds of the members present and voting in each House and the majority of the total membership of each House. This process is known as Impeachment.

2. High Court

The Constitution provides for a High Court in every State which works under the Supreme Court of India. But in some cases, one High Court serves more than one State. For example, the Gauhati High Court serves not only Assam but also the other States of the North-Eastern region.

Composition–The High Court consists of a Chief Justice and other judges. There is no fixed number regarding the judges of the High Courts. The President may also appoint a qualified person as an additional judge in a High Court for two years.

Appointment–The judges of the High Court are appointed by the President of India. The President appoints the Chief Justice of a High Court after consultation with the Chief Justice of India and the Governor of the State.

Qualifications–To be a judge of a High Court one must :

- be a citizen of India
- have held for, at least ten years a judicial office in the territory of India
- have been for, at least, ten years an advocate of a High Court.

Tenure–A judge of a High Court retires at the age of 62 years. He may also resign from his office at any time.

Removal–The President may remove a judge of a High Court on the ground of 'proved misbehaviour' or 'incapacity'.

3. Subordinate Courts

The High Court has been given control over District Courts and courts subordinate thereto including the posting and promotion of and the grant of leave to persons belonging to the judicial service of a State and holding any post inferior to the post of District Judge.

The procedure for appointment for the district and sub-ordinate Courts or the lower judiciary in

India is discussed in Article 233 of the Constitution. Appointment of district judges in any State shall be made by the Governor of the State in consultation with the High Court exercising jurisdiction in relation to such State. The qualifications for appointment as District Judge include :

● Member of judicial service of the State; or

● Any person who has had a minimum of seven years of practice as a lawyer at bar.

Judicial Training

National Judicial Academy is an Indian government-funded training institute primarily for Judicial Officers, working in the Supreme Court and the High Courts, during their service. The institute was registered on 17 August, 1993 under the Societies Registration Act of 1860. It has a registered office in Delhi. The President of India inaugurated the institute building on September 5, 2002. Established with the objectives of "Judicial Reform and Policy Development as well as Research Support Services for greater efficiency, fairness, access and productivity. It also includes improvements in court administration and management for a litigant friendly justice system", the institute has been functioning as a "centre of excellence in judicial education, research and training".

The National Judicial Education Strategy (NJES) was established by the Institute in September, 2006, as a national level system for judicial education, with which it hopes to achieve its objectives in technical education. The courses offered here follow the same system. Instead of a 'teacher - student' setting found usually in academic institutions, the institute follows a 'solution driven' approach instead, working to eliminate the obstacles faced by the judges participating in a programme by identifying them over discussions in portals. Based on this, the institute offers 6 types of programmes to its three categories of candidates, High Court Justices, District Judiciaries and State Judicial Academics.

COURTS AND JUDICIAL REVIEW

Judicial Review

Judicial review is a special power of the Supreme Court and the High Courts in India to scrutinize whether a law passed by the legislature or an action taken by the executive is in accordance with the provisions of the Constitution or not. If it is found that such a law or an action not in accordance with the Constitution, then it can declare them as invalid or unconstitutional. This means that the judiciary has to act as the guardian or custodian of the Constitution. In countries like the United States, France and Canada, under judicial review the court can cancel the law or the act of the legislature or the executive if they are found to be unconstitutional. In the United Kingdom, the courts do not have power to cancel legislation of the Parliament even if they are unconstitutional. But in U.K, the administrative actions can come under the purview of Judicial Review.

Origin–The concept of judicial review originated in the United States of America in the Marbury V.Madison case of 1803. The Chief Justice of the Supreme Court of America, John Marshall while delivering his judgment in this case used the famous 'Due Process of Law' clause of the American Constitution. According to this clause, 'due' means what is just and proper and 'law' means natural law. Justice Marshall said that as the Supreme Court had been made the protector of the Constitution and the rights of the people, so it had to perform its duty and give justice. While doing so, it would try to determine the exact meaning of law, to expand its details and apply the general principles of justice, equity and morality. The process, thus, initiated by justice Marshall has been continuing and the Supreme Court has been creating some new laws while deciding various cases. The power of judicial review has made the Supreme Court of America one of the strongest judiciaries in the world.

Judicial Review in India

In India, the Supreme Court while exercising its power of judicial review has to follow the principle of "procedure established by law." Article 21 of the Indian Constitution provides that "no person shall be deprived of his life or personal liberty except according to procedure established by law". Here, the term 'law' does not mean 'natural law' but it means 'State-made laws'. In other words, the court can only question the procedure and if the procedure is not followed, the court can declare any legislation made by the Parliament as unconstitutional. Further, the Supreme Court can declare any legislation as invalid if it violates the provisions of the Constitution. Thus, the Supreme Court of India has limited power of judicial review. Still, it has been able to exercise this power effectively in many cases and interpret and protect the provisions of the Constitution.

Judicial review is one of the basic structures of the Indian Constitution and it cannot be amended. It has helped to preserve the constitutional principles and values and the constitutional supremacy. As per

B.R. Ambedkar, Article 32 is the heart and soul of Indian Constitution. The Supreme Court has the power to review any legislative and executive action under Article 32 of Constitution of India. Largely, this power has been applied for the protection and enforcement of fundamental rights provided in the Constitution. To a lesser extent, judicial review has also been used in matters concerning the legislative competence with regards to the Centre-State relations. With respect to judicial review on matters of executive or administrative actions, courts have employed doctrines such as 'proportionality', 'legitimate expectation', 'reasonableness' and the 'principles of natural justice'.

Essentially, the scope of judicial review in courts in India has developed with respect to three issues :

(i) Protection of fundamental rights as guaranteed in the Constitution

Art. 13 of constitution incorporates "Judicial Review of Post constitution and Pre-constitutional laws". Article 13 provides for the 'judicial review' of all the legislations in India, past as well as future. This power has been conferred on the Supreme Court of India and the High Courts under Art. 32 and 226 which can be declare a law unconstitutional if it is inconsistent with any of the provisions of PART III of the Constitution. Under Article 32 and 226, the Supreme Court of India and High Courts have the power to issue directions or order or writs in the nature of: 1) habeas corpus, i.e., to order the release of person is unlawfully detained; 2) mandamus, i.e., to order to a public authority to do its duty; 3) prohibition, i.e., to prevent a subordinate court from continuing on a case; 4) quo warranto, i.e., to issue directive to a person to vacate an office wrongfully occupied; and 5) certiorari, i.e., to remove a case from a subordinate court and get the proceedings before it.

In India, the judiciary has been given the power to protect the Constitution and to preserve the Fundamental Rights of the people. It has been empowered by the authority of judicial review and in that capacity it has been exercising its power in recent years which is dubbed as judicial activism. Under judicial activism, the court has begun to intervene in and question the activities of the executive and the legislature, reminding them, from time to time, of their duties and responsibilities to the society. The beginning of judicial activism in India could be traced back to 1985 when the then Chief Justice of India, Justice P.N. Bhagavati converted a letter written to him on a post card by an aggrieved person into a Public Interest Litigation. By the middle of the 1990s, judicial activism became more and more pronounced. The activism of the Supreme Court became visible in terms of sensitizing the Central Intelligence Agency to discharge their constitutional obligations in the hawala cases in which top level political personalities were involved. It has passed landmark judgments over environmental degradation, pollution control, preservation of historical monuments, eviction of unauthorized occupation of government buildings, etc. In this way, the judiciary has become over-whelmingly busy with cases brought before it from various quarters of the society and the activism of the Indian Judiciary has benefited the common people in terms of addressing their grievances to a large extent.

(ii) Matters concerning the legislative competence between the centre and states

Art. 245 and 246 of the Indian constitution gives legislatives powers to Parliament to make laws with respect to matters itemised in the 'Union List' (List 1 of the Seventh Schedule of the Constitution) and the 'Concurrent List' (List III of the Seventh Schedule of the Constitution). Whereas, it gives power to State legislature to make laws with respect to matters itemised in the 'State List' (List II of the Seventh Schedule) and the 'Concurrent List'. Here the Judiciary has the role to monitor on the powers of Central Government and the State Government so that they don't encroached into the powers of each other. The Supreme Court has supreme power under Art. 141 which incorporates 'Doctrine of Precedent' to implement its own view regarding any conflicted issue and it's also have binding force.

Supreme Court gives us some relevant observations through judicial decisions regarding the legislative actions of Parliament and State Legislatures. In S.P. Sampat kumar vs.Union of India it was held that the judicial review which an essential features of the constitution is can be taken away from the particular area only if an alternative effective institutional mechanism or authority is provided. Again in L. Chandra vs. Union of India, the Constitutional Bench unanimously held that "these provisions are to the extent they exclude the jurisdiction of the High Courts and Supreme Courts under Art.226/227 and 32 of the constitution are unconstitutional as they damage the power of judicial review. The power of judicial review over Legislative Actions vested in the High Courts and Supreme Court under Art. 226/227 and Art.32 is an integral part and it also formed part of its basic structure." In I.R. Coelho vs. State of Tamil Nadu, the Supreme court observed that "Judicial Review of legislative actions on the touchstone of the basic structure of the constitution"

(iii) Fairness in executive acts

"When the legislature confers discretion on a court of law or on an administrative authority, it also imposes responsibility that such discretion is exercised honestly, properly and reasonably" This view of 'DE Smith' clearly point out that discretion of administrative action should be used with care and caution. So, the abusive discretionary power of Administrative action must be review by judiciary. If judiciary founds any ground of illegality of any administrative action, it is the duty of the judiciary to maintain check and balance.

The doctrines of Principle of Natural Justice, proportionality, reasanobaleness and principle of legitimate excpectations are some doctrine which the Courts should take into account while deciding on any administrative or executive ation. All the parties should be given equal opportunity to be heard before the Court of Law in a judicial proceeding. The principle of audi altarem partem (means listen to the other side) should be implemented while deciding on any judicial proceeding. The judicial review of administrative action can be exercised on the following grounds :

Illegality– means that the decision maker must correctly understand the law that regulates his decision making power and must give effect to it.

Irrationality– means that the decision is so outrageous in its defiance of logic.

Moral Standard– accepted moral standards that no sensible person could have arrived at such a decision.

Procedural impropriety– means that the procedure for taking administrative decision and action must be fair, reasonable and just.

Proportionality– means in any administrative decision and action the end and means relation-ship must be rational.

Unreasonableness– means that either the facts do not warrant the conclusion reached by the authority or the authority or by the decision is partial and unequal in its operation.

In Maneka Gandhi v. Union of India, passport of Maneka Gandhi was confiscated by the governmental officials without giving her any chance of prior hearing. The Supreme Court invoked its power of judicial review and held that such executive action was unconstitutional as it was against the Right to Liberty guaranteed under Article 21 of Constitution of India. In the interest of the principles of natural justice, the party should be given the opportunity of hearing before confiscation of passport. A chance was given and her passport was returned to her.

Basic Structure

The Constitution of India does not explain the basic structure of the constitution. However, the Supreme Court of India, in its judgment on the Kesavananda Bharti Case said that every provision of the Constitution can be amended provided in the result the basic foundation and structure of the constitution remains the same. The basic structure may be said to consist of the following features:

(i)   Supremacy of the Constitution

(ii) Republican and Democratic Form of Government

(iii) Secular Character of the Constitution

(iv) Separation of powers between the Legislature, the Executive and the Judiciary

(v)   Federal Character of the Constitution.

(vi) Judicial Review.

"The above structure is built on the basic foundation, *i.e.*, the dignity and freedom of the individual. This is of supreme importance. This cannot by any form of amendment be destroyed".

Thus, the Constitution cannot be amended in a way as to destroy its basic structure.

Summary

Judiciary in Ancient India– In Ancient India , according to the Arthashastra of Kautilya , the realm was divided into the administrative units called Sthaniya, Drona-mukha, Khrvatika and Sangrahana.

Law in British Ruled India–A system of law based on recorded judicial precedents, called the common law system, came to India with the British East India Company.

Modern Indian Judiciary–Consists of the following points.

- India as a common law jurisdiction
- Adversial model of Dispute Resolution
- Judicial Review.

The Supreme Court–On the 28th of January1950, two days after India became a Sovereign Democratic Republic, the Supreme Court came into being.

Nature of Indian Legal System–Consists of the Common Law system ,Adversial System of Law, Due Process of Law and Procedure Established by Law.

Structure Hierarchy and Legal Offices in India– follows the integrated system of judiciary comprising of courts to administer both central and state laws.

- **The Supreme Court** located in New Delhi is the apex court of India.
- **The High Courts** at the state level which function for one or more number of states.
- **The District Court** known as the lower courts of India.
- **Tribunals** to adjudicate sector specific claims such as labour, consumer, service matter disputes.

Attorney General of India is the primary legitimate officer of the nation and selected by the President of India under Article 76 of the Constitution, which expresses that he can hold the workplace amid the delight of the President.

An Advocate General is a senior law officer who goes about as a lawful consultant to the state government.

Independence of Judiciary refers to an environment where judges are free to make decisions or pass judgement without any pressure from the government and the other powerful entities.

Need for the Independence of the Judiciary–To check the functioning of the organs, Interpreting the provisions of the constitution and dispute referred to the judiciary.

Provisions Relating to the Judges–Once appointed, judges are provided with a security of tenure till they reach a retirement age, Judges can not be easily removed from their office except for proven misbehaviour and incapacity. The salaries and allowances of judges are fixed and not subject to vote of the legislature. The judicial conduct of the judges has been kept immune from examination by other constitutional organs.

Provisions to ensure the Independence of the Judiciary–Security of tenure, Salaries and allowances, Powers and jurisdiction of Supreme Court, No discussion on conduct of judges in State Legislature or Parliament, power to punish for contempt, separation of the judiciary from the Executive

Role of Supreme Court–As a federal court, Interpreter of the Constitution and Law,As a court of Appeal, Advisory role, Guardian of the Constitution, Curative petition, Writ jurisdiction, Contempt Jurisdiction, Public Interest Litigation and Friend of Court.

Role of High Court–Original Jurisdiction, Appellate Jurisdiction, Supervisory jurisdiction, Administrative Jurisdiction, Power to transfer case from Subordinate Courts, court of record.

Retirement of Judges–The retirement age for a Supreme Court Judge is 65 years. Similarly , a high court 17 judges continue in his office, till the retirement age which is 62 years. The age of retirement of District court judges is determined by their respective state government under special service rules.

Removal of Judges–Judges of Supreme court and high court can be removed through a process called as 'Impeachment'. The grounds for removal include Proven misbehavior and Incapacity. This inquiry is done by a committee of three members of which two judges one from the Supreme Court and second is the Chief Justice of High Court. As to the removal of judges in the lower judiciary, a District judge or an Additional District Judge can be removed from his office by the State Government in consultation with the High Court.

Scope of Judicial Reveiw in India–Judicial review is a special power of the Supreme Court and the High courts in India to scrutinize whether a law passed by the legislature or an action taken by the executive is in accordance with the provisions of the constitution or not.

Salient Features of Judicial Review–Individual and group rights, Central and State relations, Judicial review of Administrative actions and Basic Structure.

Basic Structure–Supremacy of the constitution, Republican and Democratic Form of Government, Secular Character of the Constitution, Separation of powers between the legislature, the executive and the judiciary and federal character of the constitution.

Multiple Choice of Questions

1. The highest and final judicial tribunal of India.
   (a) President   (b) Parliament
   (c) Supreme Court   (d) Union Cabinet

2. Who of the following decides the number of judges of High Court ?
   (a) The President
   (b) Chief Minister of a State
   (c) The Parliament
   (d) Prime Minister

3. The Chief Justice and and other judges of the High Court are appointed by :
   (a) President
   (b) Chief Justice of Supreme Court
   (c) Governor of the concerned state
   (d) Attorney General of India

4. In India, the power to increase the number of Supreme Court judges lies with the :
   (a) The President of India
   (b) The Chief Justice of India
   (c) Union Ministry of Law
   (d) The Parliament of India

5. Disputes between states of India comes to the Supreme Court under :
   (a) Original Jurisdiction
   (b) Appellate Jurisdiction
   (c) Advisory Jurisdiction
   (d) None of the above

6. Which of the following statements are correct with respect to the reitired judge of a High Court ?
   (a) Cannot practice in Supreme Court
   (b) Cannot practice in High Court
   (c) Cannot practice in High Court from where he has retired.
   (d) None of the above

7. Who is empowered to transfer a judge from one High Court to another High Court ?
   (a) President of India
   (b) Chief justice of India
   (c) Law Minister of India
   (d) Union Cabinet

8. The main function of judiciary is :
   (a) Law execution   (b) Law adjudication
   (c) Law application   (d) Law formulation

9. The salaries and emoluments of the judges of the supreme court are changed on :
   (a) The Finance Commission
   (b) The Consolidated Fund of India
   (c) The Contingency Fund of India
   (d) The Reserve Bank of India

10. What does the judicial review function of the supreme court do ?
    (a) Review of its own judgement
    (b) Review the functioning of judiciary in the country
    (c) Undertake periodic function of the constitution
    (d) Examine the constitutional validity of law.

Short Answer Questions

1. What is Common Law ? How it is different from the codified laws ?
2. Explain in brief the Adversial system of law.
3. Differentiate between the procedure established by law and the due process of law.
4. Differentiate between independence of judiciary and impartiality of judges.
5. Define the concept of Judicial Review.
6. What are the different kinds of writs Supreme Court can issue under Article 32 of the Indian Constitution ?
7. Discuss how judicial review is used for the enforcement of fundamental rights.
8. Define division of powers in the context of the Indian Constitution.
9. Short notes on the following :
   (a) Judicial Review
   (b) Judicial Activism
   (c) Basic Structure

Long Answer Questions

1. What is your understanding about judiciary ?
2. India has an organic law as a consequence of the common law system. Elaborate.
3. Explain in detail on the independence of Judiciary and its status in India.
4. Explain the role of courts and its function.

Board Questions

1. A constitutional amendment was passed by Indian Parliament which curtailed the concept of 'Federalism' enshrined in the Indian Constitution. This amendment was held to be invalid by the Supreme Court of India. Here, by virtue of which theory/doctrine, the Supreme Court of India has invalidated the said constitutional amendment ?
   (a) Principle of Natural Justice
   (b) Theory of Separation of Powers
   (c) Doctrine of Basic Structure
   (d) Principle of Legitimate Expectation

2. The residents of P.V. Colony have been paying for civic facilities to Municipal Department for last three years. During monsoons the roads developed cracks and pit holes. The residents requested for repair of the roads. However Municipal Department, which has the responsibility to provide for this, ignored all requests of the residents inspite of continuous reminders. What immediate remedy is available to the residents of P.V. Colony under Article 32/226 of Indian Constitution ?
   (a) Writ of Habeas Corpus
   (b) Writ of Quo-Warranto

    (c) Writ of Mandamus

    (d) Writ of Certiorari

3. Which of the following statements does not hold good for 'Conflict of Laws' ?

    (a) It is a set of rules and principles that govern interstate interactions.

    (b) Its primary objective is to provide for a framework of rules and regulations which help in fostering international relations.

    (c) It is a body constituted of conventions, model laws and domestic laws of state.

    (d) It involves issues like application of Jurisdiction in a particular case.

4. Prakhar, is a citizen of India and a qualified Advocate. In the year 2000, he was appointed as a Second Class Judicial Magistrate in Rajasthan. But in the year 2003, he resigned from the post of Second Class Judicial Magistrate. He started practising as an Advocate in Delhi High Court in the year 2009. In the year 2011, he shifted to Panchkula located in Haryana and since then he is practising as an advocate in Punjab and Haryana High Court. In 2015 he is eligible to be appointed as :

    (a) High Court Judge only

    (b) Both Supreme Court and High Court Judge

    (c) District Judge only

    (d) Supreme Court Judge only

5. Anurag is a qualified Lawyer practicing since 2002 in various District Courts of Delhi. He is having special knowledge and expertise in the field of Criminal Law. Mr. Ankit (appellant) appointed Mr. Anurag as his advocate to file a Special Leave to Appeal (Criminal) before the Supreme Court of India. Mr. Anuraag was not allowed by to do so by the filing authorities of the Supreme Court. Why was Mr. Anurag not allowed to file the Special Leave to Appeal (Criminal), even though he is a qualified lawyer having expertise and experience in the field of Criminal Law ?

6. How power of Judicial Review helps judiciary to safeguard and to ensure the separation of powers of the other two branches of the government in India ?

7. "42nd Amendment Act, 1976 ushered the era of tribunalisation in Indian Judiciary." Explain.

8. Once Lakshmi Kant Pandey filed a petition in the Apex Court against a social organisation named 'Nanhi Khushiyaan'. The organisation was engaged in offering Indian children in adoption to foreign parents. It was alleged that in the guise of adoption Indian children of tender age were not only exposed to the long dreadful journey to distant foreign countries at great risk to their lives but in case they survive they were not provided any shelter and relief homes and in course of time they become beggars or prostitutes for want of proper care. It was also alleged that this social organisation is indulged in these malpractices with few other voluntary agencies.

    (a) Can any person/organisation approach the Apex Court on behalf of a group of persons who are unable to approach the court for relief ?

       If yes, identify and explain this kind of Judicial Activism.

    (b) How can this kind of judicial activism be invoked ?

    (c) State any two characteristics of this kind of judicial activism.

NCERT Questions

True/False

1. The Supreme Court of India came into being in 1947.

2. The law declared by the Supreme Court of India is binding on all courts.

3. India has an integrated system of judiciary.

4. The judges of the Supreme Court of India have life tenure.

5. Subordinate Courts are superior to District Courts in the order of their hierarchy.

6. India is a civil law jurisdiction.

7. The office of Solicitor General and Additional Solicitor General is governed by the Indian Constitution.

Short Answer Questions

1. How is the concept of independence of judiciary linked to the doctrine of separation of powers ?

2. How does independence of judiciary relate to due process of law ?

3. What are the benefits of independence of judiciary ?

4. What are the main roles of the Supreme Court of India ?

5. Comment on the types of jurisdictions that are vested with Courts in India ?

6. What are the common elements in public interest litigation cases ?

7. Differentiate between independence of judiciary and impartiality of judges.

8. What are the existing Constitutional mandates for the appointment of Judges in India ?

9. Provide examples of how judges are trained once appointed.What are the benefits of such trainings ?

10. Discuss the retirement age of judges in India. In the light of global comparison, provide your views regarding extending the retirement age.

11. Discuss in detail the procedure for impeachment. How many times has this process been successful in the history of Indian judiciary ?

12. Define the concept of judicial review ?

13. What are the ways in which the scope of judicial review has evolved in courts in India ?

14. Give few examples to show that judicial review ensures fairness in executive actions.

15. What is doctrine of basic structure of the Constitution ?

Essay Type Questions

1. Write a long essay based on your understanding of the following concept and issues :

   (a) Appointment of judges

   (b) Independence of judiciary

   (c) The role of independence of judiciary in Indian democracy

   (d) Impartiality of judges and procedure to safeguard and remove them from their office.

2. Draw possible linkages amongst the concepts discussed above.

Sample Questions

1. The landmark 1973 Supreme Court case of Keshavanda Bharathi *v.s.* State of Kerala discussed the question about ....

   (a) collegium model of appointment of judges in India

   (b) scope of separation of powers in India

   (c) the basic structure or feature of the constitution

   (d) Power of judicial review

2. A public authority was given the duty to construct a community centre for public in Uddeshya Nagar and land was also allotted for this purpose. But instead of constructing community centre, the public authorities started constructing shops on that allotted land. What remedy is available to the citizens of Uddeshya Nagar under Indian Constitution ?

3. A frustrated judge in an English court finally asked a barrister after witnesses had produced conflicting accounts,' Am I never to hear the truth? 'No, my lord, merely the evidence', replied counsel. To which judicial system does this judge belong ? What is his role in such a system ? Give two disadvantages of this system.

4. 'The Indian Constitution contains several provisions to serve the twin functions of Independence and Impartiality of Indian Judiciary.' Explain the features of the constitution for the independence and impartiality of the judiciary.

❑❑

INTRODUCTION

Matters identifying with property are represented by the Transfer of Property Act, 1882 in India. The object of the *Transfer of Property* Act (called the 'TPA' under the unit of Property Law) is to direct the exchange of property between living persons (inter vivos). It should likewise serve as the code of agreement law representing steady property.

The Transfer of Property Act, 1882 gives clarity on the subject. It is an orderly and uniform law on the exchange of steadfast property in India. In any case it is to be comprehended that Transfer of Property Act does not cover whole measurement of exchange of property. The Act does not cover the circles where property might be exchanged by operation of law, e.g. Execution, Insolvency, Succession, Testamentary aura and so on.

The term *'Property'* or the term transfer of Property is not defined in the Act. Every interest or right that has an economic value denotes property. The term property is used for the objects for which the right of ownership extends. In other words property may be described as any object, which is owned.

TYPES OF PROPERTY

Property is of two kinds : Movable and Immovable.

(i) **Movable Property**–Movable property is one which can be transferred from one place to another and is governed by the Sale of Goods Act.

(ii) **Immovable Property**–Immovable property is governed by the Transfer of Property Act and is not defined in the Act. However, under Section 3, immovable property does not include standing timber, growing crops or grass. Immovable property includes lands, buildings and benefits arising out of land and things attached to the earth. In simple words, any property that is attached to the earth and cannot be transferred from one place to another is called immovable property.

Property is not a term of art, thus is used a synonymous with the right of ownership and sometimes it denotes the thing over which ownership may be exercised. Right of way, Right to collect rent, Right to ferry, Right to fishery, Right to collect lac from trees etc have been recognised to be immovable property by courts.

In *Shanta Bai v. State of Bombay* (1958 SC 532), the distinction between movable and immovable property was observed. If the intention is to reap fruits from the trees, then it is regarded as an immovable property. But if the intention is to cut down the tree and use it as timber, it would be regarded as movable property.

In *Marshall v. Reen* (33 LT 404), there was sale of trees wherein the trees were cut and taken away. The Court held that the sale was not that of immovable property.

TRANSFER

What is Transfer ?

The term *'transfer'* means a process or an act by which something is made over to another. It does not however, mean that the making over of the thing should always be absolute. I may transfer my book to you for a day. I may also transfer it to you absolutely either by sale, gift or in exchange of your book. In either case, what is primarily essential is that I have to hand over the book to you and that act of handing over the book to you is the transfer of the book. Transfer of Property is characterised under Section 5 of the Act. It implies a demonstration by which a living individual passes on property in present or in future to one or all the more living persons or himself (e.g. At the point when a man vests property in most genuine and makes himself sole trustee or when a man moves property in one ability to himself in another limit) or himself and one or all the more living persons.

The word persons incorporate individuals, organisation or an affiliation or collection of persons whether joined or not, association firms. The term transfer does not mean transfer of all the interest of the transferor in the property. E.g. On the off chance that I rent a property for a long time. This lease will be termed as transfer under the transfer of property, despite the fact that it doesn't debilitate the entire of the interest which the transferor is equipped for passing.

Who can Transfer Property?

Any individual who is equipped to contract (individual above 18 years old, having sound mind and not excluded by any law in power) and approved to discard property *viz.*, proprietor of the property or any individual approved to offer the property, can make an exchange. The individual who transfers the property is known as the Transferor and the individual to whom the exchange is made is known as the Transferee.

How can Property be Transferred?

The mode of transfer of property varies according to the value of the property. If the value of the property is more than ₹ 100, then transfer has to be made only by a registered instrument. If the property is tangible and the value of the property is less than ₹ 100, irrespective of the value of the property, then transfer has to be made only by delivery; whereas for intangible property, irrespective of the value of the property, transfer has to be made only by registered instrument. (A registered instrument contains the records of the owner of the property for example: shares, bonds, etc.) A registered instrument has to be attested at least by two persons. To attest means to sign and witness any fact. Attestation means affixing the signature in the registered instrument. The witnesses should mark their signature on the instrument with an intention to attest. Attesting witness need not be aware of the contents of the document. If attestation is invalid, the document cannot be enforced in court of law. Registration of the instrument is an essential legal formality. During registration, the parties to the transfer must be present to affix their signatures in the document and complete the transaction with regard to immovable property. While doing so, the document containing the rights, obligations and liabilities of the parties should be clearly mentioned in the document which is registered. Registration shall take place by affixing a seal of the Registrar office which shall be subsequently included in the official records.

Essentials of a Valid Transfer

The following are the eight essentials of a valid transfer of property :

(i) The transfer must be between two or more living persons. So the transferor and transferee cannot be exactly identical.

(ii) The property which is to be transferred must be transferable in nature.

(iii) According to Section 6 of the Act, the transfer must not be :

- *Opposed to the nature of the interest affected thereby.*
- *For an unlawful object or consideration.*
- *To a person legally disqualified to be a transferee or a transperor.*

(iv) According to Section 7 of the Act, the transfer must be made by person who is :

- *Competent to transfer.*
- *Entitled to the transferable property and*
- *Authorised to dispose of transferable property which does not belong to him.*

(v) Under Section 9, the transfer must be made in the mode prescribed by the Act. All necessary formalities like attestation, registration etc. must be complied with.

(vi) According to Section 13, if, on a transfer, an interest is created in favour of an unborn person, subject to a prior interest created by the same transfer, it must exhaust the whole of the remaining interest of the transferor.

(vii) The transfer must not offend the rule against perpetuity. (Sec.14)

(viii) According to Section 25, when the transfer is conditional, the condition must not be illegal, impossible, immoral or opposed to the public policy.

DOCTRINE OF ELECTION (SECTION 35)

Conditions precedent for Doctrine of Election :

(i) A transfer of property by a person who has no right to transfer;

(ii) As a part of the same transaction, he must confer some benefit on the owner of the property and

(iii) Such owner must elect either to confirm such transfer or to dissent from it.

A person utilising the benefits of an instrument also has to carry the burden attached. This doctrine is based upon a model wherein a person persuades another to act in a manner to his prejudice and derives any advantage from that, then he cannot turn around and claim that he was not liable to perform his part as it was void. This doctrine is universal and is applicable to Hindus, Muslims as well as Christians.

So, this doctrine contains the principle that the exercise of a choice by a person left to himself of his own free will to do one thing or another binds him to the choice which he has voluntarily made, and is founded on the equitable doctrine that he who accepts benefit under an instrument or transaction of his choice must adopt the whole of it or renounce everything inconsistent with it. Thus, it is a general rule that a person cannot approbate and reprobate. Also, the election is confined to the case of a gift or Will and does not apply in case of a legal remedy.

Illustration : A sells his garden as well as his house through one instrument to B. Whereas, B wants to retain only the house and wants to cancel the transfer regarding the garden. According to the Doctrine of election, B has to retain the garden if he wants to retain the house, or cancel the whole transaction. B cannot retain the house and cancel the transfer regarding the garden.

In Cooper *v.* Cooper 1874, LR 7 HL53, the court held that the doctrine of election applied on every instrument and all types of property.

DOCTRINE OF LIS PENDENS

Section 52 of the Transfer of Property Act, provides doctrine of Lis pendens. It is a Latin term which means transfer during pending litigation. It is based on latin maxim *Ut lite pendent nihil innoveteur*. It means that nothing new should be introduced in a pending litigation. This doctrine puts restriction on the Transfer of Property during the pendency of the suit in a court competent to try it.

Objectives :

(i)   Avoid endless litigation.
(ii) To protect one of the parties to the litigation against the act of the order.
(iii) To avoid abuse of legal process.

It is to be remembered that the effect of the rule of lis pendens is not to invalidate or avoid the transfer but to make it subject to the result of the litigation.

This provision operates even if the transferee pendente lite had no notice of the pending suit or proceeding at the time of the transfer.

Essential to Constitute Lis Pendens

(i)   There should be a suit or proceeding.
(ii) Such suit or proceeding is pending before competent court having jurisdiction to try it.
(iii) Such suit or proceeding is not collusive.

(iv) The suit or proceeding must be such which the question of immovable property is directly or substantially in issue.
(v)   The suit or proceeding involving the immovable property must be pending.
(vi) Then neither party to the suit or proceeding shall transfer or otherwise deal with immovable property, which is the subject matter of such a suit.
(vii) So as to defeat the right of party.

Provided (exception) with the leave or permission of the court even during dependency of the suit property can be transferred. But while granting such permission the court may impose certain conditions, which are to be obeyed by the parties. Generally in such case the Court can claim the security from such parties to whom such permission is granted. The Court has discretionary powers. The Court may give permission or not. If any transfer is made in violation of this provision then such transfer are not recognised by law as proceeding *de novo* (fresh) not necessary.

Illustration : A has litigation in determining the title of the property with X. During the period of litigation, A initiates a sale of the property in favour of B. According to the Doctrine of Lis Pendens, the property cannot be sold because the property is involved in litigation.

SALE (Section 54)

According to Section 54 of the TPA Sale means a transfer of ownership (right to possess something) of the property in exchange for a price (money). Seller is the person who transfers the property and buyer is the person to whom the property is transferred. The consideration in a sale is usually money.

Illustration : A sells his house for 2 lakhs to B. This is called sale. Here, A is the seller and B is the buyer. 2 lakhs is the consideration which is money.

Essentials of a Valid Sale

(i)   The seller must be a competent person to transfer.
(ii) The transferee must be a competent person and must not be a person disqualified to be a transferee.
(iii) The subject matter should be transferable immovable property.
(iv) The ownership must be transferred.
(v)   The transfer of ownership must be in exchange for price.
(vi) The price must be paid or promised to pay or partly paid and partly promised to pay.

(vii) The deed of conveyance must be registered in case of transfer of a tangible immovable property of the value of ₹ 100 and upwards.

(viii) In case of tangible immovable property of a value less than ₹ 100, there must be either a registered deed of conveyance, or delivery of property.

RIGHTS AND LIABILITIES OF BUYER AND SELLER

Liabilities of Seller

(i) Disclose defects of the property which is known to the seller and is not known to the buyer;

(ii) Produce to the buyer all documents of title (documents regarding ownership) relating to the property;

(iii) Answer all the questions put to him by the buyer in relation to the property;

(iv) Take care and preserve the property and the documents of title between the date of the contract of sale and the delivery of the property;

(v) Bear all public charges and rent with regard to the property up to the date of sale;

(vi) To give the buyer possession of the property.

Rights of Seller

(i) Collects the rents and profits of the property till the ownership passes to the buyer;

(ii) When ownership has passed on to the buyer from the seller before payment of money in full, the seller can claim the amount from the buyer that is due to him.

Liabilities of Buyer

(i) Disclose to the seller any fact with regard to the property that will increase the value of the property that is known to him;

(ii) Pay to the seller purchase money at the time of completing the sale;

(iii) To bear any loss that arises from the destruction, injury or decrease in value of the property after the ownership has passed to the buyer;

(iv) To pay all public charges and rent that becomes payable after the ownership passed to the buyer.

Rights of Buyer Sec. 55(6)

(i) Before completion of sale, a buyer has a charge on the property for the purchase money paid by him in anticipation of delivery.

(ii) If he has obtained possession of the property agreed to be sold, his possession will operate as a notice to all subsequent transferres of the property, who will be bound by it.

(iii) In case of breach of contract, he can bring a suit for specific performance against the seller. If he succeeds in showing that by resale of the property he would have made profit then he will be entitle to such profits.

(iv) After the ownership has passed to the buyer, perform any lawful action to increase the value of property and the rents and profits with regard to the property;

(v) Where the buyer has paid the purchase money, he can compel the seller for registration of sale.

In *Madam Pillai vs. Badar Kali* [45 Mad 612 (FB)], the plaintiff being the first wife made a claim for maintenance to her husband. The husband orally transferred his lands of the value of ₹ 100 to the plaintiff. Later, he executed an instrument of sale in favour of the defendant for the same property. The plaintiff initiated a suit stating that the transfer was initially made in her favour and the subsequent sale to the defendant was not valid. The defendant stated that the transfer in favour of the plaintiff failed for want of a registered instrument. The Court held that the plaintiff acquired a title by way of oral transfer and she is entitled to the property though the instrument of sale was not registered.

LEASE (Section 105-117)

A lease is a transfer of a right to use the property, made for a certain time, expressed or implied, or in perpetuity. Such transfer of right should be in consideration of a price paid or promised to the transferor by the transferee, who accepts the transfer on such terms. Lease of property from year to year or for any term exceeding one year can be made only by a registered instrument.

In other words, a lease is a transfer of a right to enjoy the property of lessor is put in possession of the property. The rights of ownership are not passed on the transferee. There is only transfer of right of enjoyment in lease.

For a period of three years, A lets out his property for use to B for a sum of ₹ 50,000. This is called lease. A is the lessor and B is the Lessee. If B sub-lets the property to C , Then B will be the lessee and C will be the sub-lessee. The relation between B and C will be of that relation that is between A and B.

Essentials of Lease

(i) The lessor must be competent to contract and have title or authority.

(ii) The lessee must be competent to contract at the date of execution of the lease. A lease to minor is void as it is executed by both lessor and lessee.

(iii) The subject matter of lease must be immovable property.

(iv) There must be a transfer to enjoy the property.

(v) A lease may be made for a certain duration, expressed or implied or in perpetuity.

(vi) In Lease, the consideration is premium plus rent or rent alone or premium alone.

(vii) The lessee must accept transfer. The transfer must be as per the mode indicated in section 107.

(viii) The rights and liabilities of parties of lease determined by.

    (a) Contract.

    (b) Local usage.

Duties of Lessor

Duty to disclose material defect : It is the duty of the lessor to lessee (*Lessee spelling mistake*) to disclose material defect which can cause any injury to any person or property.

Duty to give possession : The lessor is bound to give possession to the lessee otherwise he cannot enforce the obligation of lease.

Duty to secure possession : If lessee is performing his part of contract than it is duty of lessee to secure possession so that lesee can take the possession during any time of lease.

Duty to pay repair money : Duty to pay repair money and not to interrupt the enjoyment.

Duty to give other expenses : If lessee has spent any other money for the maintenance of lease property then lessor is duty bound to give maintenance to the lessee.

Rights of Lessor

Following are the rights of lessor :

(i) Right of information of increasing rent :

Lessor has right of information of any material change which could enhance the value of property of lessor.

(ii) Right to receive rent.

(iii) Right of restoration of property : It is the duty of lessee to restore property in the same position during lease and on the termination return it to lessor in the same form as was at the time of possession.

(iv) Right to re-enter.

(v) Right to eject trespasser.

(vi) Right to terminate the lease.

Duties of Lessee

Following are the duties of lessee :

(i) Duty to disclose the martial fact.

(ii) Duty to pay rent.

(iii) Duty not to commit waste.

(iv) Duty not to erect permanent structure: It is the duty of lessee not to erect permanent structure except for the purpose of lease.

(v) Duty to protect the property.

(vi) Duty to use lease property for same purpose.

Rights of Lessee

Following are the rights of lessee:

(i) Right of accession.

(ii) Right to avoid lease.

(iii) Right to charge for repair.

(iv) Right to change for other payment : Lessee has a right if he made any reasonable payment in respect of lease property he is entitled for the payment.

(v) Right to transfer interest : The lessee may transfer absolutely or by way of mortgage or sublease the whole or any part of his interest in the property.

(vi) Right to take crops : If in lease of uncertain duration the lessee or his legal heirs are entitled to all crops.

(vii) Right to take possession of such property

(viii) Right to remove : Lessee has right to remove while he is in possession of property leased out, the things which he had attached to earth.

(ix) Right to terminate the lease, if the subject matter has been destroyed.

In Gajadhar *vs.* Rombhaee 1938 Nag. 439, a theatre was sub-leased and the sub-lessee was prevented from using the theatre by the original lessor on the ground that a notice was served to the lessee for determining the lease. The sub-lessee had to pay an additional amount to the proprietor (the original lessor) and then take the lease. It was held that there is violation on the part of the original lessor and the sub-lessee can sue the original lessor for damages for violation of quiet enjoyment of the property.

Termination of Lease

(i) By completion of time mentioned in agreement.

(ii) Where termination is conditional then in case of happening of the such event.

(iii) Where the interest of the lessor in the property terminates on or his power to dispose of the same extends only to happening of any event or on happening of such event :

- Merger
- By express surrender
- By implied surrender
- By forfeiture

GIFT (Ss.122-129)

Gift is the transfer of certain existing moveable or immoveable property made voluntarily and without consideration, by one person, called the donor, to another, called the donee, and accepted by or on behalf of the donee. Such acceptance must be made for the lifetime of the donor while he is still capable of giving. If the donee dies before acceptance, the gift is void.

A gift of immovable property must be done by registered instrument signed by the donor and attested by two witnesses and gift of movable property can be done by registered instrument signed and attested or by simply delivery of the property.

Example: A gives his car to B. B accepts the car. But B does not pay anything in return for the car. This is known as Gift. In this case, A is the donor and B is the donee.

If the gift is one single transfer and a part of it is burdened with an obligation, the donee gets nothing unless he accepts it fully. But if the gift is in the form of two or more separate and independent transfers, he may accept one and refuse another.

If a donee who is not competent (*e.g.,* Minor) to accept an onerous gift, he is not bound by his acceptance. However on becoming competent to contract, he retains the property and being aware of the obligation, he is bound by the obligation.

Universal Donee

A Universal Donee is a person to whom the donors whole property is given and who consequently becomes liable for all the debts due by and liabilities of the donor at the time of the gift to the extend of the property comprised in the gift. A donee is a universal donee even if a gift interest in a part of the property is retained by the donor as held in Shahzad Singh *vs.* Madan Gopal, A.I.R 1963 All.146

Revocation of Gift

A gift once made is irrevocable unless :

- If the donor and the donee have agreed that on the happening of a specified event (independent of the will of the donor) the gift should be suspended or revoked. A gift made revocable at the will of the donor is void wholly or in part.

- A gift made under a coercion, fraud, undue influence, misrepresentation.

These rules do not affect the rights of the transferee for consideration without notice. A donation mortis causa (in contemplation of death) of movable property is revocable at the will of the donor or affect any rule of Muhammadan law as per section 129 of the Act. Such gifts are governed by Indian Succession Act, 1925.

EXCHANGE

When two persons mutually transfer the ownership of one thing for the ownership of another, neither thing nor both things being money only, the transaction is called an 'exchange'. A transfer of property in completion of an exchange can be made only in manner provided for the transfer of such property by sale.

Example : A offers to sell his cottage to B. B in consideration of the cottage sells his farm to A. Instead of getting money for his cottage, A has received a farm from B. This is an example for exchange. The rights and liabilities of A will be that of seller towards the sale of the cottage and will be that of buyer towards the sale of the farm. Similarly, the rights and liabilities of B will be that of buyer towards the sale of the cottage and that of seller towards the sale of the farm.

Basis	Sale	Lease	Exchange	Gift
Transfer	Transfer of ownership for price.	Transfer of limited ownership.	Transfer of ownership for some other property.	Transfer of ownership without consideration.
Consideration	Price.	Premium and/or Rent.	Another property.	No consideration.
Mode	Sale deed should be registered.	Lease deed should be registered.	Sale deed should be registered.	Gift of immovable property should be registered.

INTELLECTUAL PROPERTY LAW

Intellectual Property (IP) refers to creations of the mind, such as inventions; literary and artistic works; designs; and symbols, names and images used in commerce.

IP is protected in law by, for example, patents, copyright and trademarks, which enable people to earn recognition or financial benefit from what they invent or create. By striking the right balance between the interests of innovators and the wider public interest, the IP system aims to foster an environment in which creativity and innovation can flourish.

Types of Intellectual Property

Copyright–Copyright is a legal term used to describe the rights that creators have over their literary and artistic works. Works covered by copyright range from books, music, paintings, sculpture and films, to computer programs, data-bases, advertisements, maps and technical drawings.

Patents–A patent is an exclusive right granted for an invention. Generally speaking, a patent provides the patent owner with the right to decide how - or whether - the invention can be used by others. In exchange for this right, the patent owner makes technical information about the invention publicly available in the published patent document.

Trademarks–A trademark is a sign capable of distinguishing the goods or services of one enterprise from those of other enterprises. Trademarks date back to ancient times when craftsmen used to put their signature or "mark" on their products.

Industrial designs–An industrial design consti-tutes the ornamental or aesthetic aspect of an article. A design may consist of three-dimensional features, such as the shape or surface of an article, or of two-dimensional features, such as patterns, lines or colour.

Geographical indications–Geographical indica-tions and appellations of origin are signs used on goods that have a specific geographical origin and possess qualities, a reputation or characteristics that are essentially attributable to that place of origin. Most commonly, a geographical indication includes the name of the place of origin of the goods.

Summary

Introduction–By its very existence, society mandates interaction, exchange or transfer. A property, movable or immovable, is transferred from one person to another under various different situations and circumstances and for different values. The transfer may be a gift, an inheritance or an asset acquired by paying full value.

Transfer–Transfer of property means an act by which a person conveys property to one or more persons, or himself and one or more other persons. The act of transfer may be done in the present or for the future. The person may include an individual, company or association or body of individuals, and any kind of property may be transferred, including the transfer of immovable property. It covers how it is made and its essentials.

Doctrine of election– "Election" means choosing of one right between two rights, when there is clear intention that both the rights cannot be enjoyed but only one. Section 35 of the Transfer of the Property Act defines the "Doctrine of Election". If a person transfers some property which he has no right to transfer, and the same transaction confers any benefit on the owner of the property, such owner must elect either to confirm such transfer or reject it. If he rejects the transfer, he shall relinquish the benefit conferred upon him and the property will revert back to him self or his representative as if it had not been disposed off.

Doctrine of lis pendence– 'Lis' means an action or a suit. 'Pendens' is the present principle of Pendo, meaning continuing or pending, and the doctrine of lis pendens may be defined as the jurisdiction, power,or control that courts have, during the pendency of an action over the property involved therein.

Sale– Sale is a transfer of ownership in exchange for a price paid or promised or part-paid and partpromised. It further covers the Essentials of a valid sale and The Rights and Liabilities of Buyer and Seller.

Lease–A lease is transfer of an interest in an immovable property which is the subject of the lease and that interest is the right to occupy and use the property for which the lease is given for period and on such terms and conditions as agreed between the parties. The transferor of property is called the lessor and the person to whom it is transferred is referred as a lessee, and the consideration so rendered is called rent. It further cover the Essentials of a Valid Lease and The Rights and Duties of Lessor and Leasee and Termination of Lease.

Gift–Gift is a Transfer of Property and is defined in Section 122 of the Transfer of Property Act, 1882. It is a unique transfer of property in the sense that it involves no consideration. The basic essence of a gift is the complete absence of consideration. The law of gifts in India is governed by Sections 122 to 129 of the Transfer of Property Act, 1882.

Exchange– When two persons mutually transfer the ownership of one thing for the ownership of another, neither thing or both things being money only, the transaction is called an 'exchange'. A transfer of property in completion of an exchange can be made only in manner provided for the transfer of such property by sale.

Intellectual Property Law–Intellectual Property (IP) refers to creations of the intellect for which a monopoly is assigned to designated owners by law. Intellectual Property Rights (IPRs) are the protections granted to the creators of IP, and include trademarks, copyright, patents, industrial design rights, and in some jurisdictions trade secrets. Artistic works including music and literature, as well as discoveries, inventions, words, phrases, symbols, and designs can all be protected as intellectual property. It cover Patents, Trademarks, Copyright, Industrial Design and Geographical Indication.

Multiple Choice of Questions

1. The Transfer of Property Act was enacted in the year :
   (a) 1880   (b) 1881
   (c) 1882   (d) 1883.
2. What can be transferred under the Transfer of Property Act, 1882 ?
   (a) An easement along with the dominant heritage
   (b) Political pension
   (c) Spes Successionis
   (d) Stipends allowed to the civil pensioners of the government
3. Concept of 'onerous gift' is embodied in which section of TP Act ?
   (a) Section-125   (b) Section-127
   (c) Section-128   (d) Section-129
4. The term 'transfer' under the Transfer of Property Act, 1882, refers to
   (a) partly or whole transfer
   (b) absolute or conditional transfer
   (c) contingent transfer
   (d) both (a) and (b) are correct.
5. The principle of lispendens embodied in section 52 of the Transfer of Property Act, 1882 pertains to :

   (a) bonafide purchase   (b) public policy
   (c) auction sale   (d) none of these

Short Answer Questions

1. What is Property ?
2. Who can transfer the Property and how can it be transferred ?
3. Doctrine of Election. Explain.
4. What is the difference between Exchange and Gift? Give examples.

Long Answer Questions

1. What is Transfer and what are the essentials of a valid Transfer ?
2. Explain the doctrine of Lis pendence and its objects with examples.
3. What is sale ? Explain the rights and duties of Seller and Buyer.
4. What is Lease ? Explain the rights of Lessor and Leasee.
5. Short note on the following:
   (a) Sales   (b) Lease
   (c) Exchange   (d) Gift
6. Differentiate with examples the above topics.

NCERT Questions

1. Write a short note on property and kinds of property.
2. What are the essential elements of a transfer ? Who can transfer an immovable property ? How can an immovable property be transferred ?
3. What is intellectual property ? Explain the types of intellectual property.

Sample Questions

1. A sells his garden as well as his house through one instrument to B. Whereas B wants to retain only the house and wants to cancel the transfer regarding the garden. Can B have the right to partial selection ?
   (a) Yes, B has the right to selection.
   (b) Yes, B can have partial selection only if ratified by A.
   (c) No, B has to accept or reject the transfer in totality.
   (d) No, because House and garden are inseparable.

❏❏

INTRODUCTION

In An Economic Analysis of Law, Judge Richard A. Posner (a former law professor of University of Chicago) suggests that contract law performs three significant economic functions :

1. It helps maintaining incentives for individuals to exchange goods and services efficiently.

2. It reduces the costs of economic transactions because its very existence means that the parties need not go to the trouble of negotiating a variety of rules and terms is already spelled out.

3. The law of contracts alerts the parties to the troubles that have arisen in the past, thus making it easier to plan the transactions more intelligently and avoid potential pitfalls. Richard A. Posner, Economic Analysis of Law (New York: Aspen, 1973).

The most common way of making a contract is through an agreement. The two parties may agree to something through mutual negotiations and when one party makes an offer and the other party accepts the same then arises an agreement which can be enforceable by law.

Indian Contract Act, 1872 is the main source of law regulating the contracts in India. It determines the circumstances in which promises are made to the parties to a contract that shall be legally binding on them. All of us enter into a contract on daily basis. Indian Contract Act deals with the enforcement of these rights and duties.

AGREEMENT

According to Section 2(e) "every promise and every set of promises forming the consideration for each other is an agreement." In an agreement there is a promise from both the parties. An agreement consists of an offer by one party and its acceptance by the other.

AGREEMENT = OFFER + ACCEPTANCE.

A person cannot enter into an agreement with himself. There has to be a proposal or offer from one party to other and the other party has to accept that proposal or offer. Then the agreement would be formed. It is said that an acceptance is to offer is what a lighted matchstick to a train of gunpowder. If there is no offer, there cannot be an acceptance. The parties to an agreement must have *consensus ad idem* while entering into the contract. It means that they must agree upon same thing in same manner. They must have understood the terms and conditions of the agreement before giving consent.

Example : A promises to deliver his watch to B and in return B promises to pay a sum of 2000 to A. This is said to be an agreement between A and B.

CONTRACT

According to section 2(h) of the Indian Contract Act, 1872, an agreement enforceable by law is a contract.

All agreements are not enforceable by law hence, all agreements are not contracts.

Some agreements are enforced by law and some are not. For example, an agreement to sell a radio set may be a contract but an agreement to go to watch a movie may be a mere agreement not enforceable by law. The agreements which are enforceable in the court of law are only regarded as contracts. Thus, all agreements are not contracts.

AGREEMENT + ENFORCEABLE IN A COURT OF LAW = CONTRACTS

In a main case Balfour vs. Balfour (1919, 5 KB 571), the legitimacy of a contract entered between a couple was being referred to. The couple went on leave to England and the wife fell sick in England. The specialists who treated the wife exhorted her to take complete bed rest and stay in England keeping in mind the end goal to proceed with the treatment. She stayed in England. At the point when the leave was over, the husband went to Ceylone where he was utilised and guaranteed to send a total of $ 30 to the wife consistently for her stay in England. He sent the amount for quite a while and later on because of misunderstandings between them, he quit sending the sum. The wife filed the case to recoup the payments. The Court dismissed it on the ground that the understanding went into between the couple was not a contract. It was just an ethical commitment and the gatherings never proposed to make any lawful relationship. The decision clearly demonstrates that understandings that make a legitimate commitment are just contracts and those that don't mean to make lawful relationship are not contracts.

Agreement	Contract
Agreement = offer + acceptance.	Contract = Agreement + enforceability.
All agreements are not contracts.	All contracts are agreements.
An agreement may not create legal obligation.	All contracts create legal obligation.
Agreement is not a concluded or a binding contract in all cases.	Contract is concluded and binding on the concerned parties.

TYPES OF CONTRACTS

(i) On the basis of formation : Express, Implied, Quasi Contracts.

(ii) On the basis of Nature of Consideration - Bilateral contracts and unilateral contracts.

(iii) On the basis of Execution : Executed and executory contracts

(iv) On the basis of validity. Valid, void, voidable, illegal and unenforceable contracts.

On the basis of Formation

On this base Contracts can be classified into three groups, namely Express, Implied and Quasi Contracts.

(i) Express Contracts : The Contracts where there is expression or conversation are called Express Contracts.

Example: A has offered to sell his house and B has given acceptance. It is an Express Contract.

(ii) Implied Contract : The Contracts where there is no expression are called implied contracts.

Example: Sitting in a bus can be taken as example to implied contract between passenger and owner of the bus.

(iii) Quasi Contract : In case of Quasi Contract there will be no offer and acceptance so, there will be no Contractual relations between the partners. Such a Contract which is created by Virtue of law is called Quasi Contract. Sections 68 to 72 of Contract Act read about the situations where court can create Quasi Contract.

Example: A case on this occasion is Chowal *vs.* Cooper. In this case A`s husband is no more. She is very poor and therefore not capable of meeting even cost of cremation. B, one of her relatives, understands her position and spends his own money for cremation. It is done without A`s request. Afterwards B claims his amount from A where A refuses to pay. Here court creates a Quasi Contract between them under section 68 *i.e.,* when necessaries are supplied.

On the basis of Nature of Consideration

On this base, Contracts are of two types. Namely Bilateral Contracts and Unilateral Contracts.

(i) Bilateral Contracts : If considerations in both directions are to be moved after the contract, it is called Bilateral Contract.

Example : A Contract has got formed between X and Y on 1st January. According to which X has to deliver goods to Y on 3rd January and Y has to pay amount on the same day. It is a bilateral contract.

(ii) Unilateral Contract : If considerations are to be moved in one direction only after the Contract, it is called Unilateral Contract.

Example : A has lost his purse and B is its finder. Thereafter B searches for A and hands it over to A. Then A offers to pay ₹1000 to B to which B gives his acceptance. Here, after the Contract consideration moves from A to B only. It is a Unilateral Contract.

On the basis of Execution

On this base Contracts can be classified into two groups, namely, Executed and Executory Contracts. If performance is completed, it is called executed contract. In case where contractual obligations are to be performed in future, it is called executory contract.

On the basis of Validity

On this base Contracts can be classified into five groups. namely Valid, Void, Voidable, Illegal and Unenforceable Contracts.

(i) Valid : The Contracts which are enforceable in a court of law are called Valid Contracts. To attain Validity the Contract should have certain features like consensus ad idem, Certainty, free consent, two directional consideration, fulfillment of legal formalities, legal obligations, lawful object, capacity of parties, possibility of performance, etc.

Example : There is a Contract between X and Y and let us assume that their contract has all those above said features. It is a Valid Contract.

(ii) Void : A Contract which is not enforceable in a court of law is called Void Contract. If a Contract is deficient in any one or more of the above features (Except free consent and legal formalities). It is called a Void Contract.

A void contract cannot be made valid by parties to the contract by their consent.

Example : there is a Contract between X and Y where Y is a minor who has no capacity to make a contract. It is a Void Contract.

(iii) Voidable : A Contract which is deficient in only free consent, is called Voidable Contract. That means it is a Contract which is made under a certain pressure either physical or mental. At the option of suffering party, a voidable contract may become either Valid or Void in future.

Example : There is a Contract between A and B where B has forcibly made A involved in the Contract. It is voidable at the option of A.

(iv) Illegal : If the contract has an unlawful object it is called an Illegal Contract.

Example : There is a contract between X and Z according to which Z has to murder Y for a consideration of ₹ 10000 from X. It is an illegal contract.

(v) Unenforceable : A contract which has not properly fulfilled legal formalities is called an unenforceable contract. That means unenforceable contract suffers from some technical defects like insufficient stamp etc. After rectification of that technical defect, it becomes enforceable or valid contract.

Example : A and B have drafted their agreement on ₹ 10 stamp where it is to be written actually on ₹ 100 stamp. It is an unforceable contract.

ESSENTIAL ELEMENTS OF A VALID CONTRACT

Section 10 of the Indian Contract Act talks about the essentials of a valid contract. "All agreements are contracts if they are made by the free consent of parties competent to contract, for a lawful consideration and with a lawful object and are not hereby expressly declared to be void.

Nothing herein contained shall affect any law in force in India, and not hereby expressly repealed, by which any contract is required to be made in writing or in the presence of witnesses, or any law relating to the registration of documents."

The essentials needed for a valid contract are as follows :

(i)   Proper offer and its acceptance.

(ii)   Lawful object.

(iii)   Agreement not expressly declared void.

(iv)   Intention to create legal relationship.

(v)   Free Consent.

(vi)   Capacity of parties to contract.

(vii) Certainty of meaning.

(viii) Possibility of performance.

(ix)   Lawful consideration.

(x)   Legal formalities.

GENERAL PRINCIPLES OF MAKING A CONTRACT

Proposal or Offer and Acceptance

In order to constitute a vaild contract there must be a lawful offer and lawful acceptance of that offer. Proposal and offer both are used in the same sense and there is no difference in their meanings. It is defined under section 2(a) - "When one person signifies to another his willingness to do or to abstain from doing anything with a view to abstaining the ascent of that offer such or such act or abstinence he is said to make a proposal."

The person who makes the proposal is called proposer, offeror or promisor. The person to whom offer is made is called offeree or promisee.

● An offer and acceptance must be definite and certain.

● The promisor and promisee must communicate properly to each other. A communication in electronic form or over emails also amount to communication of offer and acceptance.

● A contract to be valid, there must exist consensus-ad-idem. It means identity of minds between the parties to a contract.

● There will be no agreement, if the proposal is made without the intention of creating legal rights and obligations.

● An offer lapses by revocation or withdrawal.

● Any offer can be revoked before acceptance.

Example : A has two houses namely X and Y. A offers to sell X to B and accepts thinking that it is Y. Here is no identity of minds and hence not enforceable.

In Cooke vs. Oxley (1790)3 T R 65, A offered to sell 266 hogshed at a certain price and promised to keep it open for acceptance by B till 4 PM of that day. Before that time A sold them to C, B accepted before 4PM but after the revocation by A. It was held that the offer was already revoked.

In Lalman Shukla vs Gauri Dutt (1913) 11 ALJ 489 the court held that an action without the knowledge of the proposal is no acceptance.

In Carlill vs. Carbolic smoke ball company (1983) IQB256 advertised in the newspaper that who so ever would take smoke balls, manufactured by it, according to the printed instructions would not contract influenza. The company offered a reward of $100 to anyone who contracted influenza after taking its smoke balls according to the printed instructions. It was added that $1000 was deposited with alliance bank to show the sincerity of the company. Mrs. Carlill used the smoke balls according to the directions given but contracted influenza. It was held that the offer was general one and Mrs. Carlill had accepted it by acting according to the advertisement and therefore the company could not get away from the responsibility by saying that it was a mere puff. She was entitled to get reward.

Consideration

Section 2(d) of The Indian Contract Act, 1872 defines consideration as given under : "When, at the desire of the promisor, the promisee or any other person has done or abstained from doing, or does or abstains from doing or promises to do or abstain from doing something, such act or abstinence or promise is called a consideration for the promise."

Consideration is an important element in a contract. A contract without consideration is not valid. Consideration means quid pro quo *i.e.*, 'something in return' for the offer. It can be in the nature of an act or forbearance, may be past, present or future. It should be real, competent and having some value in the eyes of law.

Essential Ingredients of Consideration

(i)   Consideration must be given at the desire of the promisor.

(ii) Consideration must be given by the promisee or any other person.

(iii) Consideration may be present, in past or future.

(iv) There must be some act of abstinence or promise by the promisee, which constitute consideration.

Example : A promises to put life to B's dead wife, if B pays him ₹ 1000. A's promise is physically impossible of performance hence there is no real consideration.

Example : A offers to sell his car for ₹ 50,000 to B. B accepts the offer. In this case, the consideration of A is his car and the consideration of B is ₹ 50,000.

In Durga Prasad vs. Baldeo (1880, 3All 221), The offended party, on the request of the Collector of the town, worked at his own expense, certain shops in a bazaar. The shops came to be involved by the litigants who, in thought of the offended party having used cash in the development, guaranteed to pay him a commission on his articles sold through their agency in the bazaar. The offended party's activity to recover the commission was rejected. It was held in light of the fact that as the development had not been done according to the yearning of the litigants, but at the request of the collector. Henceforth, the thought was not legitimate and the defendants not at risk for the same.

It is essential that consideration must move at the desire of the promisor. If consideration is given voluntarily or at the instance of any third party, it will not be a valid consideration.

Capacity to Contract

Section 11 of The Indian Contract Act specifies that every person is competent to contract :

(i)   He should not be a minor *i.e.*, an individual who has not attained the age of majority *i.e.*, 18 years in normal case and 21 years if guardian is appointed by the Court.

(ii) He should be of sound mind while making a contract. A person who is usually of unsound mind, but occasionally of sound mind, can make a contract when he is of sound mind. Similarly if a person is usually of sound mind, but occasionally of unsound mind, may not make a valid contract when he is of unsound mind.

(iii) He is not disqualified from contracting by any other law to which he is subject.

Example : A minor falsely exaggerates his age and takes conveyance of an engine auto in the wake of executing a promissory note for the dealer at its cost. The minor can't be constrained to pay the sum to the promissory note, yet the Court on fair grounds may arrange the minor to give back the auto to the broker, in the event that it is still with the minor.

Mohori Bibee *vs* Dharmodas Ghoshe (1903) 30 IA. 114 (P.C) is a leading case on nature of minors agreement. In this case Plaintiff Dharmodas Ghoshe while he was minor mortgaged his property in favour of defendant, a money lender. It was held that the minors contract is void ab intio (since beginning).

Free Consent

It is one of the essential elements of a valid contract as it is evidenced by section 10 which provides that all agreements are contracts if they are made by the free consent of the parties. According to Section 14, consent is said to be free when it is not caused by :

● Coercion, or

● Undue influence, or

● Fraud, or

● Misrepresentation, or

● Mistake.

According to Section 13, "Two or more persons are said to consent when they agree upon the same thing in the same sense." Thus, consent involves identity of minds in respect of the subject matter of the contract. In English Law, this is called 'consensus ad-idem'.

When there is no consent at all, the agreement is void ab-initio, *i.e.*, it is not enforceable at the option of either party. When there is consent but it is not free (*i.e.*, when it is caused by coercion or undue influence or fraud or misrepresentation), the contract is usually voidable at the option of the party whose consent was so caused.

Example : X has one Maruti car and one fiat car. He wants to sell fiat car. Y does not know that X has two cars. Y offers to buy X's Maruti car ₹ 50,000. X accepts the offer thinking it to be an offer for his Fiat car. Here, there is no identity of mind in respect of the subject of the subject matter. Hence there is no consent at all and the agreement is void ab-initio.

UNLAWFUL AGREEMENT

In the event that the object of the understanding is to play out an unlawful demonstration, then the agreement is unenforceable. The object of the assent is ought not to be unlawful, improper or contradicted to society.

As for example, A promises to obtain for B an employment in the public service, and B promises to pay ₹ 1,000 to A. The agreement is void, as the consideration for it is unlawful.

Again, A, B and C enter into an agreement for the division among them of gains acquired or to be acquired by fraud. The agreement is void as its object is unlawful.

Let us suppose that A, who is B's mukhtar, promises to exercise his influence, as such, with B in favour of C and C promises to pay ₹ 1,000 to A. The agreement is void because it is immoral.

Any agreement for restraint of trade, marriage and legal proceeding is void as the object of the agreement is unlawful.

WAGERING AGREEMENT

The word 'wager' means 'a bet' something stated to be lost or won on the result of a doubtful issue, and, therefore, wagering agreements are nothing but ordinary betting agreements. Section 30 of the Indian Contract Act talks about wagering agreements, which reads as 'agreements by way of wager are void'. The section does not define 'wager.'

Section 30 states that, "Agreements by way of wager are void; and no suit shall be brought for recovering anything alleged to be won on any wager, or entrusted to any person to abide by the result of any game or other uncertain event on which any wager is made".

Essentials of Wagering Agreements:

(i)   Promise to pay money or moneys worth

(ii)   Uncertain event

(iii)   One to lose, other to win

(iv)   No control over the event

(v)   Past, present or future events

(vi)   No other interest in the event

(vii)   Unlawful event/lawful event

A Wagering Agreement is void and unenforceable in the court of law.

CONTINGENT CONTRACT

A 'contingent contract' is a contract to do or not to do something, if some event, collateral to such contract, does or does not happen. Generally, insurance contracts are contingent contract. Life Insurance is not a contingent contract as the death of a man is certain event.

Example : A contracts to pay to B ₹ 10,000 if B's house is burnt. This is a contingent contract.

Basis of Distinction	Wagering Agreement	Contingent Contract
Reciprocal promises	Consists of reciprocal promises.	It may or may not consist of reciprocal promises.
Main/collateral future event	Future event is essential to the contract.	Future event is collateral to the contract.
Interest of parties	If parties have no other interest in the subject matter of the agreement except winning or losing of the wagering amount.	Parties may have other interest as well.
Nature	It is always of contingent nature.	It is not always of wagering nature.
Validity	Void.	Valid.

DISCHARGE OF A CONTRACT

Discharge of a contract means termination of the contractual relations between the parties to a contract. A contract is said to be discharged when the rights and obligations of the parties under the contract come to an end.

Modes of discharge of contract :

(i)   By performance
(ii) By mutual agreement
(iii) By operation of law
(iv) By impossibility of performance
(v)   By lapse of time
(vi) By breach

(i) Discharge by Performance

Each of the party to the contract is bound to perform its part of the obligation. When the parties have made their due performance of the contract, their liability under the contract comes to an end, in such a case, the contract is said to be discharged by performance.

Example : A offer to sell his dining set to B for ₹ 10,000. B pays ₹ 10,000 to A and A delivers his dining set to B. Here the contract gets discharged by performance as both the parties fulfilled their promises.

(ii) Discharge by Mutual Agreement

Since a contract is created by mutual agreement, it can also be discharged by mutual agreement. A contract can be discharged by mutual agreement in any of the following ways :

Novation [Section 62] : Novation implies the substitution of another agreement for the first contract.

Examples : A owes B ₹ 10,000. A enters into an agreement with B and gives him a mortgage of A's estate for ₹ 5,000 in place of the debt of ₹ 10,000. This is a new contract and extinguishes the old.

Rescission [Section 62] : Rescission means cancellation of the contract by any party or all the parties to a contract.

Alteration [Section 62] : Alteration implies an adjustment in the terms of an agreement with common assent of the gatherings. Adjustment releases the first contract and makes another agreement. In any case, gatherings to the new contract must not change.

Remission [Section 63] : Remission implies acknowledgment by the promisee of a' lesser satisfaction of the guarantee made. As per Section 63,

"Every promisee may dispense with or remit, wholly or in part, the performance of the promise made to him, or may extend the time for such performance, or may accept instead of it any satisfaction which he thinks fit".

Examples : A owes B under a contract a sum of money the amount of which has not be ascertained. A without ascertaining the amount gives B a random sum. B in satisfaction thereof accepts the sum given by A. This is a discharge of the whole debt, whatever may be the amount.

Waiver : It implies deliberate surrender of a right under the contract. Thus, it amounts to releasing a person of certain legal obligation under a contract.

Example: Y employs Z to paint a picture for him. Later on, Y forbids him from doing so. Z is no longer bound to perform the promise.

Merger : When inferior rights of a person under a contract merge with superior rights under a new contract, the contract with the inferior rights will come to an end.

Example : X was a tenant of Y's house. X purchased this house. X's tenancy right is merged with his ownership rights i.e., tenancy agreement will come to end when X becomes the owner of the house. Tenancy right is an inferior right as compared to the ownership right which is a superior right.

(iii) Discharge by Operation of Law

A contract may be discharged by operation of law in the following cases :

By Death of the Promisor : A contract including the individual aptitude or capacity of the promisor is released on the demise of the promisor.

By Insolvency : When a man is pronounced indebted, he is released from his risk up to the date of his bankruptcy.

By Unauthorised Material Alteration : If any gathering makes any material modification in the terms of the contract without the approval of the other party, the contract arrives at an end.

By the Identity of Promisor and Promisee : When the promisor turns into the promisee, alternate gatherings are released.

(iv) Discharge by Impossibility of Performance

The effects of impossibility of the performance of a contract under section 56 may be discussed under the following heads :

Effects of Initial Impossibility : "An agreement to do an act impossible in itself is void". This section is based on the maxim 'les non cogit ad impossibilia' impliying that the law does not compel a man to do what he can possibly perform.

Example : A contracts to marry B being already married to C, and being forbidden by the law to which he is subject to practice polygamy. The arrangement by A to marry B is void.

Effects of Supervening Impossibility : The performance of the contract may be possible when the contract is entered into but because of some event, the performance may be subsequently become impossible or unlawful. For example, A contracts to take in cargo for B at a foreign port. A's government afterwards declares war against the country in which the port is situated. The contracts becomes void when war is declared.

Supervening impossibility takes place by the following :

● Destruction of the subject matter

● Death or incapacity

● Non-existence of state of things having an effect directly or indirectly on the contract

● Outbreak of war

● Change or amendments in law.

(v) Discharge by Lapse of Time

An agreement is released in the event if it is not performed or upheld inside a predefined period, called the period of limitation. The Limitation Act, 1963 has endorsed the distinctive periods for various contracts, *e.g.*, time of constraint for practicing right to recoup an obligation is 3 years, and to recuperate a steady property is 12 years. The legally binding gatherings can't practice their rights after the expiry of time of restriction.

(vi) Discharge by Breach of Contract

A contract is said to be discharged by breach of contract if any party to the contract refuses or fails to perform his part of the contract or his act makes it impossible to perform his obligation under the contract. A breach of contract may occur in the following two ways :

Anticipatory Breach of Contract : Anticipatory breach of contract occurs when party declares his intention of not performing the contract before the performance is due. For example, A is to supply certain goods to B, on 1st December and he informs B by 1st November that we will not be able to deliver it by said date decided by them. In this case, A has committed an anticipatory breach of contract.

Actual Breach of Contract : Actual breach of contract occurs when any party to a contract refuses or fails to perform his part of the contract at the time fixed for performance, it is called an actual breach of contract on due date of performance . For example: A is to supply certain goods to B on 1st December but fails to do so. Then in that case he has made an actual breach.

REMEDY FOR BREACH OF CONTRACT

When one of the party fails to carry out its mutually agreed obligation then the aggrieved party may have legal recourse in any of the following manner :

1. **Specific performance of the Contract :** The distressed party can file a suit for specific performance of the contract in place of suing the guilty party to make compensation of the breach or make him specifically perform the obligation mentioned in the contract.

2. **Injunction :** The aggrieved party may bring a permanent or temporary injunction to restrain the guilty party from making breach of contract.

3. **Damages :** Section 73 of the Contract Act is lays down the provision relating to damages. It provides that the party, who breaches a contract, is liable to compensate the injured party for any loss or damage caused, due to the breach of contract.

For compensation to be payable, Two things should be taken into consideration

(i) The loss or damage should have arisen as a natural consequence of the breach, or

(ii) It should have been something the parties could have reasonably expected to arise from a breach of the contract.

Under this section, the burden of proof lies on the injured party. This section, however, provides that compensation shall not be awarded for any remote or indirect loss sustained by the parties.

Section 73 also provides that the same principles will apply for breach of a quasi-contractual obligation, *i.e.*, in the event that an obligation resembling that created by contract has not been discharged, the injured party is entitled to receive compensation as if a contractual obligation has been breached. Damages under Section 73 of the Act are compensatory and not penal in nature.

The explanation to this section further provides that in estimating the loss or damage arising from a breach of contract, the existing cost of remedying the inconvenience caused may be taken into account.

Example: A agrees to deliver 40 bags of rice to B for ₹ 20,000 on 5th July 2014. On 5th July 2014, A delivers only 20 bags of rice to B. B is entitled for damages from A for the loss that he suffered because of A (non-delivery of 20 bags of rice).

Summary

Introduction to Contracts–Contracts are an important part of commercial law because all commercial law transactions usually begin with an agreement or a contract.

Agreements–The act of two or more persons, who unite in expressing a mutual and common purpose, with the view of altering their rights and obligations.

Contracts–Law of contract was enacted which lays down the legal rules relating to promises: their formation, their performance, and their enforceability.

Types of Contracts– On the basis of Formation, On the basis of Nature of Consideration, On the basis of Execution and On the basis of Validity.

- **On the basis of formation :** Contracts can be classified into three groups, namely Express, Implied, Quasi Contracts.
- **Contracts on the basis of Nature of Consideration**, are namely bilateral contracts and unilateral contracts.
- **Contracts on the basis of Execution :** It can be classified into two groups namely, executed and executory contracts

Types of Contracts : On the basis of validity. It can be classified into 5 groups namely valid, void, voidable, illegal and unenforceable contracts.

Essentials of a Valid Contract–Proper offer and its acceptance, Lawful object, Agreement not expressly declared void, Intention to create legal relationship, Free Consent, Capacity of parties to contract, Certainty of meaning, Possibility of performance, Lawful consideration and Legal formalities.

Offer and Acceptance–The expression of an offer to contract on certain terms by one person (the 'offeror') to another person (the "offeree"), and an indication by the offeree of its acceptance of those terms.

Consideration–It is anything of value promised to another when making a contract.

Capacity to Contract– Contractual party must be a 'competent person' having legal capacity.

Free Consent– Free consent is one of the most important essential elements of a valid contract. The term free consent refers to meeting of free and fresh minds of two parties of an agreement when two parties take and understand, purpose, subject matter and terms and conditions of the agreement in the same sense it is free consent.

Unlawful Agreement–An agreement whose object is opposed to the law of the land may be either unlawful or simply void, depending upon the provisions of the law to which it is opposed.

Wager Contracts–The meaning of 'wagering' is staking something of value upon the result of some future uncertain event, such as a horse race, or upon the ascertainment of the truth concerning some past or present event, shall be null and void, and no suit shall be brought or maintained in any court of law or equity for recovering any sum of money or valuable thing alleged to be won upon any wager.

Contingent Contracts–Contingent contracts usually occur when both negotiating parties fail to reach an agreement. The contract is characterised as 'contingent' because the terms are not final and are based on certain events or conditions occurring.

Discharge of Contract–Contract creates relation between the parties and binds them over. Termination of such contractual relations is called discharge of contract. The following are different modes of discharge or termination of contract.

Discharge by Performance–If both parties perform their contractual obligations promptly, the contract is said to be discharged by performance. It is the ideal method that number of contracts gets terminated in this way.

Discharge by Mutual understanding or by Agreement–This can be as following :

- **By Alterations :** Whenever material alterations in contract are made, then it is said that old contract has got discharged and a new contract has come into force.
- **By Renewal :** At times parties to the contracts may substitute completely new contract in the place of old contract. Now the old contract has got discharged.
- **By Recession :** In case of recession old contract gets discharged and there will be no formation of new contract.

Discharge by Operation of Law–This can be as following :

- **By Death :** Whenever one of the parties comes across death, contractual relations will come to an end.

- **By Insolvency :** When one of the parties to the contract becomes insolvent, he forgoes capacity to contract and those contracts which were made by that person will get discharge.

- **By Lunacy :** When one of the parties gets attached by lunacy discharge of contract takes place.

Right and Liability going into the hands of same party–Contract creates right to one party and liability to the other when right and liability reach the same person, the result is discharge of contract.

Discharge by Impossibility–If impossibility has already come into force before the contract itself, it is called pre-contractual impossibility. Here discharge of contract takes place soon after formation of contract. The impossibility which comes into force after the contract is called post-contractual impossibility. Here contractual relations will exists only up to occurrence of impossibility.

Discharge by Lapse of Time–Limitation act has specified duration to perform different contracts. The duration thus specified is called limitation period. Soon after expiry of limitation period, the contract gets discharged.

Discharge by Breach of Contract–Failure in performance of contractual obligation is called breach of contract. Discharge of contract takes place by breach of contract also. Breach of contract is of two types, namely; Actual breach and Anticipatory breach. In case where contract is breached by party on the date of performance, it is called actual breach. If breach of contract takes place before data of performance, it is called anticipatory breach.

Damages–The term damages is to be understood as compensation. Whenever one of the party in the contract comes across breach of contract, the other party has some rights. Out of those rights, they has the right to sue for damages *i.e.,* damages for breach of contract. The objective of court in arranging for compensation is to bring the situation as if there is no contract between the parties.

Multiple Choice of Questions

1. An agreement enforceable at law is a :
   (a) Enforceable acceptance
   (b) Accepted offer
   (c) Approved promise
   (d) Contract

2. Every promise and every set of promises, forming the consideration for each other is an :
   (a) Agreement   (b) Contract
   (c) Offer   (d) Acceptance

3. Offer as defined under section 2(a) is :
   (a) Communication from one person to another
   (b) Suggestion by one person to another
   (c) Willingness to do or abstain from doing an act in order to obtain the assent of other thereto
   (d) None of the above

4. An agreement in connection with horse racing is :
   (a) Unlawful   (b) Void
   (c) Voidable   (d) Valid

5. A contingent contract :
   (a) Is void
   (b) Never becomes void
   (c) Becomes void when the event becomes impossible
   (d) Is voidable

6. Communication of a proposal is complete :
   (a) When it is put in the course of transaction
   (b) When it comes to the knowledge of a person to whom it is made
   (c) When the proposal is communicated to the person to whom it is made
   (d) All the above

7. In a valid contract what comes first :
   (a) Enforceability   (b) Acceptance
   (c) Promise   (d) Proposal

8. A propoasal can be accepted :
   (a) By notice of acceptance
   (b) By performance of a condition of proposal
   (c) By acceptance of consideration for a reciprocal promise
   (d) All the above

9. Consideration should be something in return of promise which :
   (a) Both the law and the parties regard having some value
   (b) Only law regards having some value
   (c) Only parties regrds having some value
   (d) Only adequate value necessary

10. Contract without consideration made in writing and registered and made on account of natural love and affection is :
    (a) Void   (b) Voidable
    (c) Valid   (d) Unenforceable

11. Arrange the following concepts in which they appear in the chapter. Use the codes :
    A. Invitation to offer B. Damage
    C. Offer   D. Damages

Codes :

    (a) A, C, B and D   (b) A, C, D and B

    (c) C, A, B and D   (d) A, D, C and B

Short Answer Questions

1. Contract law serves some important economic functions. What are they ?
2. What is agreement ?
3. Explain contract with the help of Balfour *v.* Balfour.
4. Differentiate wagering agreement with contingent contract.
5. What are damages in contract ?
6. Define Void agreement.
7. What are remedies available in case of breach of contract ?

Long Answer Questions

1. On the basis of formation, nature of consideration, basis of execution and the basis of validity classify the contract ?
2. What are the essentials of a valid contract ?
3. What is discharge of contract ? Explain with cases wherever required.

Board Questions

1. There was a dispute between Perry & Jenny Co., an Indian body corporate and Reed Bros. & Co., a United Kingdom body corporate regarding a contractual obligation. The parties to the dispute, by way of an agreement, appointed Mr. Clark to resolve their dispute. While the legal proceedings were going on, Mr. Clark granted some interim relief to Reed Bros. & Co., also, while taking final decision, Mr. Clark did not followed the laws or reasoning laid down in earlier decisions, rather decided the disputes according to his conception of what is fair and just.

    (a) Identify and explain the role of Mr. Clark, in the given situation.

    (b) Is the decision given by Mr. Clark binding on the parties, as he did not strictly follow the law or the reasoning of earlier case decisions? Give reason for your response.

NCERT Questions

1. What is a contract and what are the components that a contract should have ?
2. Elaborate the statement 'All contracts are agreements but all agreements are not contracts'.
3. Write a short note on the following :

    (a) Consideration

    (b) Capacity to contract

    (c) Wager

    (d) Contingent contract

    (e) Discharge by Agreement or Consent

    (f) Discharge by Impossibility

4. What is Consent ? What are the elements that consent should be free from ?
5. Give a brief note on Unlawful Agreements.
6. What are the differences between Wager and Contingent contract ?

Essay Type Questions

1. Write an essay on Offer and Acceptance along with case law.

Sample Questions

1. Shine Soap Co. advertised that it would give a reward of ₹ 1,000 who developed skin disease after using, 'Aroma' soap of the company for a certain period according to the printed directions. Ms. Supriya purchased the advertised 'Aroma' and developed skin disease in spite of using this soap according to the printed instructions. She claimed reward of ₹ 1,000. The company refused the reward on the ground that offer was not made to her and that in any case she had not communicated her acceptance of the offer. Decide whether Ms. Supriya can claim the reward or not. Refer the relevant case law, if any.

❑❑

INTRODUCTION

The word tort has been derived from the Latin word 'tortum' which means to twist. In general, it means conduct that adversely affects the legal right of others and is thus, 'wrong'. If there is a violation of any right, there must be a way to compensate or to restore the right. This is essentially what the maxim, 'Ubi jusl ibi remedium' implies. Where ever there is a wrong, there is a remedy. Indeed, a right has no value if there is no way to enforce it. Such rights of individuals primarily originate from two sources–contractual obligations and inherent rights. While the violation of contractual right has clear remedy that arises from the contract itself, the violation of inherent rights that are available to all the persons in general does not have a clear remedy because there is no explicit contract between the two parties. Such violations are called wrongs and it is for such wrongs that the law of torts has been developed.

For example, one has a right against all other persons to be free of noise in the night. If somebody starts playing music loudly, then he violates one's right to be noise free. He is, thus, doing a wrong deed and even though there is no contract between the two, one can sue him for damages.

There can be innumerable types of acts that can transgress the rights of others but it is not possible to come up with a definition that can accommodate all the cases. However, the following are some definitions from the experts :

According to **Salmond**, "A tort is a civil wrong for which the remedy is action in common law for unliquidated damages and which is not exclusively a breach of contract or breach of trust or other equitable obligation."

Winfield defined tort as "Tortious liability arises from the breach of duty primarily affixed by law." The duty is towards persons in general and its breach is redressable by an action for unliquidated damages.

In the words of **Lord Denning**, "The province of tort is to allocate responsibility for injurious conduct."

Thus, it can be said that tort is an act while the law of tort is the branch of law that provides relief to the person who has been injured due to a tortious act. The nature of tort can be understood by distinguishing it from crime and contractual civil liabilities. It can be said that tort is the residual of wrongful acts that are not crime and that do not fall under contractual liabilities. Thus, if a wrongful act is neither crime nor a violation of a contract, it may fall under tort. The damages are unliquidated and are decided only by the common sense of the courts.

SOURCES OF LAW OF TORTS IN INDIA

(i) Common Law (for example, Judicial Decisions)

(ii) Statutory Law (for example, Motor Vehicle Act of 1988 and Consumer Protection Act of 1986).

Tort differentiated with Crime and Breach of Contract

S.No.	Torts	Breach of Contract
1.	Tort occurs when the right available to all the persons in general (right in rem) is violated without the existence of any contract.	A breach of contract occurs due to a breach of a duty (right in personam) agreed upon by the parties themselves.
2.	Victim is compensated for unliquidated damages as per the judgment of the judges. Thus, damages are always unliquidated.	Victim is compensated as per the terms of the contract and damages are usually liquidated.
3.	Duty is fixed by the law of the land and is towards all the persons.	Duty towards each other is affixed by the contract agreed to by the parties.
4.	Doctrine of privity of contract does not apply because there is no contract between the parties.	Only the parties within the private of contract can initiate the suit.

5.	Tort applies even in cases where a contract is void. For example, a minor may be liable in Tort.	When a contract is void, there is no question of compensation. For example, a contract with a minor is *void ab initio* and so a minor cannot be held liable for anything.
6.	Justice is met by compensating the victim for his injury and exemplary damages may also be awarded to the victim.	Justice is met only by compensating the victim for actual loss.

Tort distinguished from Crime

S.No.	Tort	Crime
1.	Tort occurs when the right available to all the persons in general (right in rem) is violated without the existence of any contract.	Crime occurs when the right available to all the persons in general (right in rem) is violated and it also seriously affects the society.
2.	Act is comparatively less serious and affects only the person.	Act is comparatively more serious and affects the person as well as the society.
3.	Intention is usually irrelevant.	Intention is the most important element in establishing criminal liability.
4.	It is a private wrong.	It is a public wrong.
5.	Since it is a private wrong the wronged individual must file a suit himself for damages.	Since it is a public wrong, the suit is filed by the govt.
6.	The suit is for damages.	The suit is for punishment.
7.	Compromise is possible between the parties. For example, a person who has been defamed, can compromise with the defamer for a certain sum of money.	There is no compromise for the punishment. For example, if a person is guilty of murder, he cannot pay money and reduce his sentence.
8.	Justice is met by compensating the victim for his injury and exemplary damages may also be awarded to the victim.	Justice is met by punishing the aggressor by prison or fine. In some specific cases as given in IPC compensation may be given to the victim.
9.	Tortious acts are usually not criminal acts.	Several criminal acts such as assault and battery are also grounds for tortious suit.

PURPOSE OF LAW OF TORT

1. **Deterrence–** Tort law ensures that the defendant compensates the victim for a wrongful act. This deters one from injuring others as it encourages defendants to be mindful and careful.

2. **Fair and just response–** Tort law ensures that the victim is compensated by the response of defendant to satisfy the demands of justice. The defendants are made liable for their wrongful act.

3. **Loss-spreading–** Tort law can be used as a tool to spread loss to a wider community. For example, where the manufacturer of a product has to pay compensation, the manufacturer may recover the costs by transferring this to the consumers by increasing the price of the product. In another example of automobile insurance, all drivers are required to pay auto insurance premiums, which are then used by the insurance companies to compensate the victims.

Kinds of Wrongful Acts

There are basically three types of torts:

- intentional torts;
- negligence; and
- strict liability.

Intentional Tort

Occurs when a person intends to perform an action that causes harm to another. For intentional tort to be proven, it is not required for the person causing the harm to intentionally cause an actual injury, they must only intend to perform the act. For instance, if a person intentionally frightens a person with a bad heart, who then has a heart attack as a result of the action, it would be an intentional tort even though the person did not have the intention of causing the heart attack.

1. Battery and Assault– While assault and battery were traditionally classified as two very distinct crimes, modern laws pair them. On the other hand, an assault can take place without battery and battery can take place without assault.

Assault is referred to any intentional act that causes another person to be fearful of immediate harm. This required the perpetrator to have the means or ability to carry out his threat, making the victim's fear valid, and no actual physical contact was required.

For example, Mr. A targeted a gun to Mr. B but didn't shot. Though Mr. A didn't shot, it would amount to Assault as it caused Mr. B to be fearful of immediate harm.

Battery, on the other hand, referred to an intentional and offensive physical contact with a victim who had not given his consent to be touched. Merely touching someone without his consent could potentially be considered battery, even if force wasn't applied. Battery is the actual application of force to the person of another done without justification in a rude, angry, insolent or revengeful manner.

2. False Imprisonment– It is the act of restraining a person against his/her will in a bounded area without any justification. False imprisonment generally refers to the confinement of a person without the consent of such person or without legal authority. For example, if a person wrongly prevents another from leaving a room or vehicle when that person wants to leave, it amounts to false imprisonment.

The elements of false imprisonment are :
(i) The defendant intended to restrict the plaintiff's freedom of movement;
(ii) The defendant, directly or indirectly, restricted the plaintiff's freedom of movement; and
(iii) The plaintiff was aware that his or her movement was restricted. False imprisonment is viable tort in a number of circumstances.

3. Trespass to Land– Trespass to land occurs where a person directly enters upon another's land without permission, or remains upon the land, or places or projects any object upon the land. This tort is actionable per se without the need to prove damage.

4. Trespass to Chattels– When the defendant has the intent to use or inter meddle with a chattel (moveable personal property), which was in the possession of the claimant and when this actually happens and causes significant or perpetual dispossession, deprivation of use, or damage as to condition, quality, or value of the chattel, or causes some other harm to claimant's legally secured interest, it amounts to the trespass to chattels.

For example, if the defendant paints the car of claimant that was parked on the side of the street, without the consent of the claimant while the claimant was away, this amounts to trespass to chattels.

5. Conversion–Conversion (or trover) is the action that is taken in cases where there is total destruction of the goods. Essentially the action for conversion is an allegation that a person is dealing with a chattel in a way that is inconsistent with the immediate possession of a person who has a proprietary right in the chattel.

For example, you lend a stereo to a friend. The friend, without your consent, pledges the stereo to a pawnbroker to raise some money for his needs. The friend has committed conversion of the goods.

The tort of conversion is committed when the property is wrongfully taken, parted with, sold, detained, destroyed or denial of the lawful owners right.

The remedies available are recapturing, obtaining order for restoration of property or suit for damages.

Negligence

The word 'negligence' denotes mere carelessness. In legal sense it signifies failure to exercise standard of care which the doer as a reasonable man should have exercised in the circumstances. In general, there is a legal duty to take care when it was reasonably foreseeable that failure to do so was likely to cause injury.

For Example : If a man walks across a crowd of people carrying sharp edged tools in his hand, he is under the duty to ensure that he does no injury to those around him. He has to be more careful than a person carries umbrella. A man with umbrella has to be more careful than a person carrying nothing at all.

Essentials of Negligence

(i) **The defendant owes a duty of care to the plaintiff;**
(ii) **The defendant made a breach of that duty; and**
(iii) **The plaintiff suffered damage as a consequence thereof.**

Donoghue vs. Stevenson (1932) (*snail in a bottle case*)– 'A' purchased a bottle of ginger beer from a retailer for the appellant. She consumed that and seriously suffered in her health. She found some snail at the bottom of the bottle. She sued for compensation. The defendant pleaded that he did not owe any duty of care towards the plaintiff. The House of Lords held that the manufacturer owed her a duty to take care that the bottle did not contain any noxious matter, and that he would be liable on the breach of the duty.

On analyzing Donoghue vs. Stevenson, it can be seen that the defendant had a duty and that duty was breached. Because of the defendant's breach of duty, the plaintiff had suffered the damage. Thus, negligence was occurred on part of defendant.

Strict Liability

Strict liability is the legal responsibility for damages or injury, even if the person found strictly liable was not at fault. In order to prove strict liability in tort, plaintiff needs to prove only that the tort happened and the defendant was responsible for the act or omission. In the case of strict liability, neither good faith nor the fact that the defendant took all possible precautions are valid defenses. Strict liability often applies when people engaged in inherently dangerous activities.

Ryland vs. Fletcher (1868)

This case establishes the principle of **Rule of Strict Liability** as follows :

- The person who for his own purposes brings on his land and collects and keeps there anything likely to do mischief

- If it escapes

- He is prima facie answerable for all the damage which is the natural consequence of its escape.

There are five exceptions to the rule of Strict liability.

(i) Act of God

(ii) Wrong act of stranger

(iii) Plaintiff's own fault

(iv) Common benefit

(v) Statutory authority

In India, a principle stricter than strict liablity has been evolved after two disasters. First one is Bhopal gas leak disaster of 1984 in Bhopal where a factory of the Union Carbide Corporation had a major leakage of the gas methyl isocynate that killed 2260 and injured around 600,000 people. In the second incident of oleum gas leakage in 1985 in Delhi where a factory of the Shri Ram Foods and Fertilizer Industries leaked oleum gas that killed one person and few others hospitalized. Because of such magnitude of the disasters, no exceptions of strict liability are available in this liability. This kind of liability is known as Absolute liability.

SUMMARY OF THE KINDS OF HARMS

Here are the summary of the examples of the many ways in which the claimant may suffer injuries that have been discussed in this chapter.

Property Interests in land–The law of tort protects the claimant's interests in her landed property by preventing intentional intrusions or trespass of the property by the defendant or the wrong-doer. The claimant may also suffer harm by the damage caused due to careless or negligence of the defendant. When the defendant interferes with the claimant's right to enjoy his/her land, the defendant commits the tort of nuisance.

Other types of Property–Tort law prohibits taking away of tangible property deliberately, which amounts to the tort of 'conversion'. The damage to the property may also occur due to carelessness or negligence.

Bodily Injury–Tort law protects the claimant against any harm to his/her interests of bodily integrity. Tort of battery and assault applies to any intentional harm caused to the body. Harm may also be caused by negligence as well as any breach of statutory duty like, traffic laws, health laws and so on. Mental distress is an element in bodily injury which raises any compensation to the victim.

Economic Interests–To a lesser extent, the economic interests are also protected by the law of tort. Injury caused by both intentional as well as negligence can cause economic harm to the claimant.

Summary

Intoduction– A tort is simply a civil wrong. There are three general types of torts that may cause injury to another person. In civil law, torts are grounds for lawsuits to compensate a grieving party for any damages or injuries suffered.

Tort– Torts are wrong doings that are done by one party against another. As a result of the wrong doing, the injured person may take civil action against the other party.

Purpose of Tort–Tortfeasor, or defendant, had a duty to act or behave in a certain way. Plaintiff must prove that the behaviour demonstrated by the tortfeasor did not conform to the duty owed to the plaintiff. The plaintiff suffered an injury or loss as a result.

Kinds of Wrongful Act–Intentional torts, Negligence torts and Strict liability torts.

Battery and Assualt–Battery is the intentional offensive or harmful touching of another person without their consent. Assault is often defined as an attempt to injure to someone else and in some circumstances can include threats or threatening behaviour against others.

False Imprisonment–If someone interferes with a person's right to move about freely. Then that person has committed false imprisonment.

Trespass to Land–Interfering with somebody's real property. Real property is land. It also includes things built on the land, things that are attached to the land permanently and whatever might be under the property.

Trespass to chattles–It is a tort whereby the infringing party has intentionally interfered with another person's lawful possession of a chattel (movable personal property). The interference can be any physical contact with the chattel in a quantifiable way, or any dispossession of the chattel (whether by taking it, destroying it, or barring the owner's access to it).

Conversion–Interfering with a person's right to personal property. If a friend borrows something and never returns it, your friend has converted your property to his/her own and interfered with your right of ownership.

Unlawful harassment–Defendant may be held liable for any act of deliberate physical harm to the victim even where no battery or assault is involved. For example, if the defendant lies to the claimant that the latter's son met with a road accident, which causes nervous shock to the claimant resulting in illness, this constitutes tort of unlawful harassment. Sexual harassment may also amount to tort of unlawful harassment.

Invasion of Privacy– A person's right to be left alone includes the right to be free from unwanted publicity. People must stay out of others private matters.

Negligence–'Negligence' is not the same as 'carelessness', because someone might be exercising as much care as they are capable of, yet still fall below the level of competence expected of them. It can be generally defined as conduct that is culpable because it falls short of what a reasonable person would do to protect another individual from foreseeable risks of harm.

Strict Liability– It is the imposition of liability on a party without a finding of fault (such as negligence or tortious intent). The claimant need only prove that the tort occurred and that the defendant was responsible. The law imputes strict liability to situations it considers to be inherently dangerous. It discourages reckless behaviour and needless loss by forcing potential defendants to take every possible precaution.

Kinds of Harms– Includes property interests in land, other types of property, bodily injury and economic interests.

Multiple Choice of Questions

1. The word tort has been derived from the latin word :
   (a) Tortum   (b) Tortus
   (c) Tort   (d) None of the above

2. There are two parties to a civil tort action. They are :
   (a) Plaintiff and tortfeasor
   (b) Plaintiff and injured party
   (c) Tort feasor and defendant
   (d) Plaintiff and reasonable person
   (e) Plaintiff and attorney

3. Tort means :
   (a) A wrong
   (b) A legal civil wrong (however, every civil wrong is not a tort)
   (c) A legal wrong
   (d) All of the above

4. Brenda was using a curling iron on Amanda's hair. As Brenda swiveled the chair around to get to Amanda's bangs, she accidentally burned Amanda's neck. Amanda was so upset with the burn mark she decided to sue Brenda for assault and battery. What will most likely happen in this case?
   (a) Brenda did not commit assault and battery upon Amanda because it was not intentional.
   (b) Brenda should have been more careful and her actions caused injury. It is assault and battery.
   (c) Amanda has no way of knowing Brenda's motives so the assumption is that the act was intentional and assault occurred.
   (d) Amanda has no way of knowing Brenda's motives so the assumption is that the act was intentional and battery occurred.
   (e) In this case, Brenda should not be doing hair with a license and will probably be fined for doing so.

5. Samara and Jim were practicing their salsa routine for the upcoming talent show. Jim was a bit overjealous on his dip, causing Samara to hit

her head on the floor. Upset that her big debut would be ruined as a result, she sued Jim. She wasn't concerned about money, she wanted revenge. She wanted Jim to spend a few nights in jail. What will likely happen?

(a) One cannot be jailed or imprisoned as punishment for a tort claim.

(b) Jim assaulted Samara and should spend a few days in jail.

(c) Samara assumed the risk of dancing with a non-professional. The dance studio is liable for all injuries.

(d) Samara stands a good chance of having Jim placed under arrest because he should not have dipped her so low.

(e) Jim will have to go to criminal court to sort this out.

6. The Great Flying Carmelo has a high wire act in a local casino. He suspends himself over the casino floor and does very dangerous tricks. On the weekends, he practices in the yard of his rented house. This particular weekend, he fell and injured his back and neck. What is the scope of liability for Carmelo's landlord?

(a) Nothing, a dangerous act must injure another person, not the person performing the act.

(b) Product liability because the high wire is in the back yard.

(c) Abnormally dangerous acts because walking on a high wire is dangerous.

(d) Tortous misconduct because Carmelo should know better.

(e) Negligence for not telling Carmelo not to install a hire wire in the yard.

7. Marlo's pet baboon, Boo Boo, broke free from her cage. She ran all over town looking for food and mischief. She nipped a neighbour's finger as he tried to lure Boo Boo back home. Marlo claims no liability because he never intended for Boo Boo to bite anyone. What will likely happen?

(a) Marlo will be liable because strict liability does not require intent.

(b) Marlo is free of liability because Boo Boo released herself.

(c) The neighbour is liable because he placed his finger in harms way.

(d) Boo Boo is liable because she is over 18 years of age.

(e) The court will use criteria listed under Abnormally Dangerous Acts to sort the mess out.

8. Which of the following is an essential constituent of negligence ?

(i) Defendant was under a legal duty to exercise due care

(ii) This duty was owed to plaintiff

(iii) Defendant committed breach of such duty.

(iv) That the breach of such duty was the direct and proximate cause of the damage alleged.

(a) (i), (ii) and (iii) are correct

(b) (i), (ii), (iii) and (iv) are correct

(c) (ii), (iii) and (iv) are correct

(d) (i), (ii) and (iv) are correct.

Short Answer Questions

1. A tort is a civil injury but all civil injuries are not Tort. Explain.

2. What are the objectives behind having tort law ?

3. What is intentional tort ? Explain at least three different kinds of intentional tort.

4. Bumbo has a snake juggling act in the local circus. He often brings home his Pythons after work. One day, the snakes get loose and find their way to Millie's back yard. Milly walks over to the snakes to shoo them away and is bitten on the hand. What tort is Bumbo liable for ? Will bumbo be penalized for his negligent act ?

Long Answer Questions

1. What is the difference between :

(a) Tort law and Criminal law

(b) Tort law and Breach of contract

2. What is tort of negligence and how do duty of care relate with negligence ?

3. What is strict liability principle ? Give one example.

Board Questions

1. Consider the given situations and answer the questions that follows :

(a) Chirag intending to harm Harshit throws an iron ball at Harshit and misses his head as Harshit moves his head away from the direction of the iron ball.

(b) Nimit intentionally locks Garima in a store room on 15th floor of their office building and Garima knows that she is trapped.

(c) Sahil sent a friend request to Jhanvi on Facebook and Jhanvi reject his friend request as she was not interested. Later on Sahil started sending her unwanted messages and phone calls.

(d) Group of 10 friends visited a museum. One of the boy named Gagan (of this group) clicked few photographs of a girl named Vaani (of this group) without her consent and later on posted those photographs on his Facebook timeline without her permission.

(i) Identify the type of intentional tort in situations given above.

(ii) Explain any two types of intentional tort identified above in part (i) of the question.

NCERT Questions

1. What are the sources of tort law ?

2. What is intentional tort ? Explain at least three different kinds of intentional tort.

Sample Questions

1. Diya and a friend Priya were at a cafe in GK Market. Priya ordered and paid for a bottle of Mango Mania for Diya. The Mango Mania was in an opaque bottle. Diya drank some of the contents and her friend lifted the bottle to pour the remainder of the Mango Mania into the tumbler. The remains of a snail in a state of decomposition dropped out of the bottle into the tumbler. Diya later complained of stomach pain and her doctor diagnosed her as having gastro-enteritis and being in a state of severe shock. Diya sued Sip Drinks, the manufacturer of the drink, for negligence. Explain the tort of negligence in the light of the above situation.

❑❑

Criminal Laws in India

INTRODUCTION

The basis of criminal law is that there are certain standards of behaviour of moral principles which society requires to be observed; and the breach of them is an offence not merely against the person who is injured but against society as a whole. All acts condemned by morality are not crimes. Criminality and morality are co-extensive.

DEFINITION OF CRIME

Crime is defined as "an act punishable by law as forbidden by statute or injuries to the public welfare". A crime can be said to an act of commission or omission, contrary to law tending to the prejudice of a community for which punishment can be inflicted as the result of the judicial proceedings taken in the name of the state.

Blackstone also defines crime as "violation of the public rights and duties due to the whole community, considered as a community, in its social aggregate capacity".

Thus, a crime may be defined as "an act or omission, sinful or non-sinful, which a society or a study has of thought fit to punish or otherwise deal with under its laws for the time being in force." The different acts and omissions so punishable under the law are known as 'Crimes'.

Categories of Crime

Crimes against Persons : Crimes against persons (also called personal crimes) include murder, aggravated assault, rape and robbery.

Crimes against Property : Property crimes involve theft of property without bodily harm, such as burglary, larceny, auto theft and arson.

Crimes against Morality : There are several crimes where there is no bodily harm or any kind of harm to the property as well. Prostitution, illegal gambling and illegal drug use are all examples of such crimes. Also, Crimes against morality are also called victimless crimes because more than often there is no complainant or victim and it is generally the State which takes suo motu cognizance of these offences.

White Collar Crime : White-collar crimes are generally economic offences that are committed by people of high social status. Instance of corruption, bribery and large-scale scams fall in the category of white collar crimes.

Organised Crime : Organised crime is crime committed by structured groups typically involving the distribution of illegal goods and services to others. Organised crime is just not restricted to Mafias, but the term can refer to any group that exercises control over large illegal enterprises (such as the drug trade, illegal gambling, prostitution, weapons smuggling, or money laundering). Betting on sports, illegal sale of firearms and hawala transactions are all examples of organised crime.

Stages of Crime

There are four stages in commission of a Crime.

They are as follows:

1. Intention
2. Preparation
3. Attempt
4. Accomplishment

1. Intention to Commit a Crime : This is the first stage in commission of a crime. Intention to commit a crime is not punishable unless it is made known to others either by words or conduct. E.g. Waging a War against the Government is punishable. In this case, mere intention to commit is punishable. Similarly, mere assembly of persons to commit a dacoity is punishable even though there is no preparation for it.

2. Preparation : Preparation consists in devising means for the commission of a crime. It is difficult for the prosecution to prove that necessary preparation has been made for the commission of the offence. Indian Penal Code does not punish acts done in the stage of preparation. Example : In case a person purchases a pistol and loads it with bullets, it is not possible to prove that the person is carrying the pistol to kill some other person.

In the Indian Law, mere preparation to commit an offence is punishable in the following offences.

- Waging War
- Preparation to commit a dacoity
- Preparation for counterfeiting coins and Government stamps
- Possessing counterfeit coins, false weight or measurement and forged documents

3. Attempt : It is also known as the 'Preliminary Crime'. Section XXIII of the IPC, 1860 deals with 'of Attempt to Commit Offences' and provides the punishment for attempt. Attempt is the direct movements towards the commission after preparations are made. An attempt is complete when a person intending to pick another's pocket thrusts his hand into the pocket, but finds it empty.

Essentials of Attempt

(i)   Guilty's intention to commit an offence.

(ii)   Some act done towards committing the offence.

(iii) The act must fall short of the completed offence.

4. Accomplishment/Commission : This is the last stage in the commission of a crime. The accused is guilty of the offence only if he succeeds in his act. Otherwise, he is guilty of attempt only.

ELEMENTS OF A CRIME

Crimes have two basic elements : the 'guilty mind' and the 'guilty act'. The technical terms for these elements are their Latin names : 'mens rea' meaning 'guilty mind' and 'actus reus' meaning the "thing done." Generally, a crime is committed when a person commits a guilty act accompanied by a guilty mind.

"Actus non facit reum nisi mens sit rea" : This is the famous Latin maxim of criminal law. This maxim means "The act itself does not constitute guilt unless done with a guilty mind." This maxim is popularly known as 'Mens Rea'.

Mens Rea is a well settled principle of common law in England. In every statutory offence, mens rea is an essential ingredient. It is presumed that the wrong-doer did the offence with an ill intention. The words 'mens rea' are not used anywhere in the Indian Penal Code. However the framers of the Code used the equivalent words to those of mens rea in the Code very frequently. Such expressions are – Fraudulently (Section 25); Dishonestly (Section 24); Reason to believe (Section 26); Voluntarily (Section 39); intentionally; etc. Moreover in the Indian Penal Code, a separate Chapter (Chapter-IV) on General Exceptions is provided. Chapter-IV (Section 76 to 106)

explains the circumstances, where options of criminal intent may be presumed. Comparing with English Law, mens rea has been applied by the Indian Courts, and it is now firmly settled law that mens rea is an essential ingredient of offence.

Actus reus

The word "actus" connotes a 'deed' which is a physical result of human conduct. The word "reus" means 'forbidden by law, actus reus in common parlance means a 'guilty act'. It is made up of three constituent parts, namely :

- An action or a conduct
- The result of that action or conduct
- Such act/conduct being prohibited by law

Therefore, one can say that actus reus is an act which is bad or prohibited, blameworthy or culpable.

Now, there are certain unique situations when the act in itself may appear to be a criminal act, yet it cannot be termed as actus reus.

Illustrations :

- An executioner's job is to hang (no actus reus)
- An army man kills as a part of his duty (no actus reus)

STRICT LIABILITY

An exception to the requirement of a criminal intent element is strict liability. Strict liability offences have no intent element. This is a modern statutory trend, which abrogates the common law approach that behavior is only criminal when the defendant commits acts with a guilty mind. Sometimes the rationale for strict liability crimes is the protection of public's health, safety and welfare. Thus strict liability offences are often vehicle code or tax code violations, mandating a less severe punishment. With a strict liability crime, the prosecution has to prove only the criminal act and possibly causation and harm or attendant circumstances, depending on the elements of the offence.

Example of a Strict Liability Offence

A vehicle code provision makes it a crime to "travel in a vehicle over the posted speed limit." This is a strict liability offence. So if a law enforcement officer captures radar information which indicates that a person was traveling in a vehicle five miles per hour over the posted speed limit, she/he can probably be convicted of speeding under the statute.

Motive and Intention

'Motive' refers to the reason or 'why' the crime was committed. It is often the background of the suspect in committing the alleged crime. As a background, motive comes before intent. Unlike intent, motive can be determined, but its existence doesn't exactly prove guilt. It can be refuted by evidence or an alibi on a suspected person's part (often referred to as 'a person of interest' in criminal jargon). A motive is often based on the probability that the person has reason to commit the crime but no supporting evidence that the motive was carried out in the action. Motive is an initial factor but not a conclusive action to link a person to the crime. Motive is also based in the realm of psychology. Motive, as a psychological term, is also known as the drive and is often classified into two main types :

1. The physiological motives and
2. The psychological or social motives.

'Intent', on the other hand, is the supposed action or purpose of the crime. It is the result of the motive and has a higher level of culpability since a harmful action was committed. Intent is characterised as a deliberate action and conscious effort to break the law and commit the offence. Intent resides in the field of law where it is defined as the planning and longing to perform an act. It is present in both criminal law and tort law. To be specific, a scenario of intent in criminal law often involves the prosecutor in a court of law filing a charge of a crime against a suspect with veritable motive and intent. Since the intent is the final goal of the motive, it needs to be proven in order to prove that the suspect did to commit the crime. Intent has more legal standing and weight compared to motive in a court of law and is a requirement to make a case along with the means and opportunity.

CRIMINAL LAW IN INDIA

Objectives of Criminal Law

Five objectives are widely accepted for enforcement of the criminal law by punishments: retribution, deterrence, incapacitation, rehabilitation and restoration. These objective vary across jurisdictions.

1. Retribution–Retribution means wrong doer pays for his wrong doing, since a person who is wronged would like to avenge himself. The state considers it necessary to inflict some pain or injury on the wrong doer in order to prevent private vengeance. An eye for an eye and tooth for tooth is deemed to be the rule of natural justice. This theory basically deals with 'righting of balance'. If a criminal has done wrong towards a person or property he needs to be given a penalty in a manner which balances out the wrong done. For example, if a person has committed murder, he can be delivered capital punishment to balance out the suffering caused to the victim and his or her family.

Expiation–It considers punishment which as a form as expiation means to suffer punishment is to pay a debt due to the law that has been violated. According to this theory : Guilt + Punishment = Innocence.

2. Deterrence– The object of the punishment is to show that crime never pays. Crime is ill bargain for the offender. Deterrence serves as a major tool in maintaining the general law and order in the society, especially from the perspective of Crime. Criminal acts are penalised so as to deter individuals from repeating it or even entering into it in the first place. The rigor of penal discipline has made a terror and a warning to the offender and others. The advocates of capital punishment rely on deterrent theory as capital punishment cannot have any retributive or reformative value. Its only value is by deterrence.

3. Incapacitation–The objective of this theory is to segregate the criminals from the rest of the society. For the crimes committed, they suffer a kind of banishment by staying in prisons and in some cases they are also subject to capital punishment. This theory works in three ways :

(i) By inspiring all prospective wrong doers with the fear of punishment.
(ii) Disabling the wrong doer with fear of punishment.
(iii) By transforming the offender, by a process of reformation and re-education so that he would not commit crime again.

4. Rehabilitation–Aims at transforming an offender into a valuable member of society. Its primary goal is to prevent further offence by convincing the offenders that their conduct was wrong.

5. Restoration– This is a victim-oriented theory of punishment. The goal is to repair, through state authority, if any injury inflicted upon the victim by the offender. For example, one who embezzles will be required to repay the amount improperly acquired. Restoration is commonly combined with other main goals of criminal justice and is closely related to concepts in the civil law, i.e., returning the victim to his or her original position before the injury.

Sources of Criminal Law

There are several legislations dealing with Criminal Law. However, two important sources are:

1. **The Indian Penal Code, 1860,** which defines various crimes such as murder, theft, etc.

2. **Code of Criminal Procedure, 1973,** which lays down the procedure for both the police to investigate crimes and for trial of offences.

In addition the following legislations are also important :

(i) The Indian Evidence Act, 1872, which stipulates the kind of evidence admissible in court.

(ii) Special Criminal Laws passed by the Parliament or State Legislatures such as the Prevention of Corruption Act, Food Adulteration Act, Dowry Prevention Act, Commission of Sati Act etc. Each of these laws defines crimes that are in addition to those defined under the IPC.

INDIAN PENAL CODE, 1860

The Indian Penal Code has its roots since the time of the British rule in India, formulating in year 1860 and came into force in 1862. While drafting, other criminal laws in the World like the French Penal Code and the Code of Louisiana in the USA were consulted. Amendments have been made to it in order to incorporate a lot of changes and jurisdiction clauses.

Objective of the Indian Penal Code

The objective of this Act is to provide a general Penal Code for India. Though this Code consolidates the whole of the law on the subject and is exhaustive on the matters in respect of which it declares the law, many more penal statutes governing various offences have been created in addition to this code.

The Code is amended several times. One such amendment is the inclusions of section 498(A). The Act is last amended in 2019. There are twenty three chapters. The total numbers of sections contained in the Indian Penal Code are five hundred eleven. All these sections pertain to a particular category of crimes committed by civilians of Indian origin.

The Indian Penal Code is thus the most fundamental document of all the law enforcer as well as the entire judiciary in India. The Indian Penal Code does not include any special favours for any special person at some position. Thus, the Indian Penal Code stands alike for government employees, as for a common man, and even for a judicial officer. This builds up the faith of the common citizens in the law making and enforcing bodies in the country and prevents any sort of corruption or misuse of power on the part of the people in power.

Broad classification of crimes under the Indian Penal Code (IPC)

Crimes Against Body–Murder, Culpable Homicide not amounting to Murder, Kidnapping and Abduction, Assault, wrongful confinement, wrongful restraint etc.

Crimes Against Property–Dacoity, Robbery, Burglary, Theft, Extortion, Criminal trespass, mischief, etc.

Crimes Against Public Order–Riots, Arson, Affray, unlawful assembly.

Economic Crimes– Cheating, Counterfeiting.

Crimes Against Women–Rape, Dowry Death, Cruelty by Husband and Relatives, Molestation, Sexual harassment and Importation of Girls.

Crimes Against Children Child– Rape, Kidnapping and Abduction of Children, Selling/Buying of girls for Prostitution, Abetment to Suicide, Infanticide and Foeticide.

Other crimes in IPC– Defamation (crime against reputation), giving false evidence in court, offence done in elections, offence against religion.

CRIMINAL PROCEDURE CODE 1973 (CrPC)

The object of Criminal Procedure Code is to provide machinery for the punishment of offenders against the substantive Criminal law. In layman's language, the Criminal Procedure Code (CrPC) lays the rules for conduct of proceedings against any person who has committed an offence under any Criminal law, whether it is I.P.C or other Criminal law.

Classification of Offences

Depending on the nature and gravity of an offence's if they can be classified under any of the following heads :

1. Bailable and non-bailable offence.

2. Cognizable and non-cognizable offence.

3. Compoundable and non-compoundable offence.

1. Bailable and Non-Bailable Offence

Under the Law, there are two kinds of offences, namely Bailable and Non-Bailable Offences. Specifically,

Section 2(a) defines Bailable Offence as well as Non-Bailable Offence.

Section 2(a) 'Bailable offence' means an offence which is shown as bailable in the First Schedule, or which is made bailable by any other law for the time being in force : and 'non-bailable offence' means any other offence for which the accused do not have a right to obtain bail.

The following are a few points to differentiate between the two.

(i) In the case of bailable offences, it is binding upon the investigating officer to grant bail. However, in case of a non-bailable offence the police do not grant bail. The decision is taken by a Judicial Magistrate/Judge only.

(ii) In the case of a bailable offence, if the accused produces proper surety after his arrest and fulfils other conditions, it is binding upon the investigating officer to release him.

(iii) In the case of a non-bailable offence, the investigating officer must produce the accused before the Judicial Magistrate/Judge concerned within 24 hours of the arrest. At that time, the accused has a right to apply for bail himself or through his representative/lawyer.

(iv) Similarly, if the accused has been subjected to any misbehaviour by police after arrest, he has an opportunity to complain against the same before the Judicial Magistrate/Judge. However following are some offences which are classified as 'Bailable offence' by the code itself :

- Being a member of an unlawful Assembly.
- Rioting, armed with deadly weapon.
- Public servant disobeying a direction of the law with intent to cause injury to any person.
- Wearing Garb or carrying token used by public servant with fraudulent intents.
- Bribery in relation to elections.
- False statement in connection with elections.
- Refusing oath when duly required to take oath by a public servant.

However following are some offences which are classified as 'Non- Bailable offence' by the code itself.

- Murder (S.302) IPC
- Dowry Death (S.304-B) IPC
- Attempt to murder (S.307) IPC
- Voluntary causing grievous hurt. (S.326) IPC
- Kidnapping (S. 363) IPC
- Rape (S. 376) etc.

2. **Cognizable and Non-cognizable Offence Cognizable Offences**

(i) **Section 2(c)** of The Criminal Procedure Code, 1973 says that cognizable offences or cognizable cases are those under which a police officer can arrest without an arrest warrant.

(ii) Cognizable offences are those offences which are serious in nature. Example- murder, rape, dowry death, kidnapping, theft, criminal breach of trust and unnatural offences.

(iii) **Section 154** of CrPC provides, that under a cognizable offence or case, The Police Officer has to receive the First Information Report (FIR) relating to the cognizable offence, which can be without the Magistrate's permission and enter it in the General Diary and immediately start the investigation.

(iv) If a Cognizable offence has been committed, a Police Officer can investigate without the Magistrate's permission.

Non-Cognizable Offences

(i) **Section 2 (l)** of CrPC says, that non-cognizable offences or cases are those under which a police officer cannot arrest without a warrant.

(ii) Non-Cognizable offences are those which are not much serious in nature. Example-assault, cheating, forgery and fefamation.

(iii) **Section 155** of CrPC provides that in a non-cognizable offence or case, the police officer cannot receive or record the FIR unless he obtains prior permission from the Magistrate.

(iv) Under a Non-Cognizable offence/case, in order to start the investigation, it is important for the police officer to obtain the permission from the Magistrate.

3. **Compoundable and Non-Compoundable**

Compoundable Offences

(i) Compoundable Offences are classified under section 320 of Criminal Procedure Code.

(ii) Compoundable Offences are those offences which are less serious in nature.

(iii) Compoundable offences mostly affect private persons.

(iv) Compoundable offences are mainly of two types namely – (i) Compoundable with the permission of the Court (ii) Compoundable without the permission of the Court.

(v) Compoundable offences can be compromised by the victim and the offender, with or without the permission of the court.

(vi) Under a Compoundable offence, upon a compromise, the offender is acquitted without any trial.

Non-Compoundable Offences

(i) Non-Compoundable offences are classified under CrPC.

(ii) Non-Compoundable offences are those offences which are serious in nature.

(iii) Under a non-compoundable offence, a private party as well as the society, both are affected.

(iv) Under a non-compoundable offence, no compromise is allowed. Even the court does not have the authority and power to compound such offence.

(v) Under a non-compoundable offence, full trail is held which ends with the acquittal or conviction of the offender based on the evidence given.

HOW IS A CRIMINAL PROCEEDING INITIATED

For every different type of criminal proceeding a separate procedure is involved. However in general, a brief procedure, as to how a criminal case commences, is as follows :

- The first step for initiation of any criminal case is the complaint.The victim is called a complainant, and complainant should lodge his complaint to the police station of that area, where the offence has been committed, or where he resides. A complaint can be on behalf of the victim also. Generally, the complaint should be lodged within 24 hour of the commission of offence. However, the limitation time is different for some offences.

- This complaint can be treated as F.I.R. by the police officer *i.e.*, First Information Report on receipt of information (155).

- On receipt of such information, the concerned police officer shall record the information in writing and the person giving information shall sign it.

CRIMINAL TRIAL IN INDIAN LAW

From charge to conviction or acquittal, the criminal procedure in India is governed by the CrPC 1973. It divides the procedure to be followed for administration of criminal justice into three stages namely :

1. **Investigation**–Where evidences are to be collected.

2. **Inquiry**–A judicial proceeding where judge ensures for himself before going on trial, that there are reasonable grounds to believe that the person is guilty.

3. **Trial**–The judicial adjudication of a person's guilt or innocence.

According to the provisions of CrPC, there are three types of criminal trial.

(i) **Trial of Warrant Cases**

- Relates to offences punishable with death, imprisonment for life or imprisonment for a term exceeding two years.

- Employed in most offences such as theft, rape, murder, kidnapping, cheating etc., except in cases of defamation.

- The trial procedure in respect of these offences is contained in sections 238-250.

- The CrPC provides for two types of procedure for the trial of warrant cases by a Magistrate, viz. those instituted upon a police report where lot of record made during investigations by the police is made available to the court and to the accused person and those instituted upon complaint *i.e.*, otherwise than on police report where such record cannot be available.

(ii) **Trial of Summons Cases**

- A summon case means a case relating to an offence, and not being a warrant case. These cases are tried with much less formality than warrant cases, the manner of their trial is less elaborated and the method of preparing the record (of evidence) is less formal.

- An abridged form of warrants trial, where some proceedings are omitted to ensure swift process but at the same time basic postulates of fair trial are retained.

- Cases relating to an offence punishable with imprisonment not exceeding 2 years.

- If a magistrate, after examining the case, does not find it fit to be called as a summons case, he may convert it into a warrant case.

- The trial procedure prescribed for these cases are contained in sections 251-259.

- In respect to these cases, there is no need to frame a charge. The session court gives substance of the accusation (notice) to the accused when the person appears in pursuance to the summons.

- The court has the power to convert a summons case into a warrant case, if the magistrate thinks that it is in the interest of justice.

Summary Trial

- The trial procedure for these cases is contained in sections 260-265.
- An abridged form of regular trial and is resorted to in order to save time in trying petty cases.

Section 260(2) of the code lists certain offences which may be tried summarily by any Chief Judicial Magistrate, any Metropolitan Magistrate or any Judicial Magistrate First Class. A First Class Magistrate must first be authorised by the respective High Court to that effect before he may try cases summarily under this section.

Offences triable in a summary way :

(i) Offences not punishable with death, life imprisonment, or imprisonment for a term exceeding 2 years.

(ii) Theft under section 379, 380, and 381 of the IPC provided that the value of the stolen property is below ₹ 2000.

(iii) Receiving or retaining stolen property under section 411 of the IPC where the value of the stolen property is below ₹ 2000.

(iv) Assisting in the concealment or disposal of stolen property, under section 414 of the IPC, the value of the stolen property being below ₹ 2000.

(v) Lurking house-trespass (section 454 of the IPC) and house-breaking (section 456 of the IPC) by night.

(vi) Abetment of any of the above mentioned offences.

(vii) Attempt to commit any of the above mentioned offences.

(viii) Offences with respect to which complaints may be made under section 20 of the Cattle Trespass Act, 1871.

Stages of Criminal Trial in India

1. Registration of F.I.R

(i) Lodged under section 154 Cr.P.C of the code which provides for the manner in which such information is to be recorded.

(ii) Statement of the informant as recorded under section 154 is said to be the First Information Report. Its main object is to set the criminal law in motion.

(iii) FIR means the information, by whomsoever given, to the officer in charge of a police station in relation to the commission of a cognizable offence and which is first in point of time and on the strength of which the investigation into that offence is commenced.

(iv) Its evidentiary value: It is not substantive evidence *i.e.,* not the evidence of the facts which it mentions. Its importance as conveying the earliest information regarding the occurrence cannot be doubted. It can be used to corroborate the informant under section 157 of the Indian Evidence Act, 1872, or to contradict him under section 145 of the act, if the informant is called as a witness at the time of trial.

2. Commencement of investigation

(i) It includes all the efforts of a police officer for collection of evidence: Proceeding to the spot; ascertaining facts and circumstances; discovery and arrest of the suspected offender; collection of evidence relating to the commission of offence, which may consist of the examination of various persons including the accused and taking of their statements in writing and the search of places or seizure of things considered necessary for their investigation and to be produced at the trial; formation of opinion as to whether on the basis of the material collected there is a case to place the accused before a magistrate for trial and if so, taking the necessary steps for the chargesheet.

(ii) Investigation ends in a police report to the magistrate.

(iii) It leads an investigating officer to reach a conclusion whether a chargesheet has to be filed or a closure report has to be filed.

3. Conviction on plea of guilty

After framing of charges the judge proceeds to take the 'plea of guilt' which is an opportunity to the accused to acknowledge that he pleads guilty and does not wish to contest the case. Here the judge responsibility is onerous :

(i) To ensure that the plea of guilt is free and voluntary,

(ii) He has to ensure that if there had been no plead of guilt was the prosecution version if unrebutted would have led to conviction. If both the requirements are met-then judge can record and accept plea of guilt and convict the accused after listening to him on sentence.

4. Recording of the prosecution evidence

Examination of prosecution witness by the police prosecutor, marking of exhibits and cross examination by defense counsel.

5. Statement of the Accused

Section 313 of the criminal procedure empowers the court to ask for explanation from the accused if any. The basic idea is to give an opportunity of being heard to an accused and explain the facts and circumstances appearing in the evidence against him. Under this section, an accused shall not be administered an oath and the accused may refuse to answer the questions so asked. The answers given by the accused may be taken into consideration in such inquiry or trial and put in evidence for or against him.

6. Evidence of Defense

In cases of accused not being acquitted by the court, the defense is given an opportunity to present any defense evidence in support of the accused. The defense can also produce its witnesses and the said witnesses are cross-examined by the prosecution. However, in India the defense does not provide defense evidence as the criminal justice system puts burden of proof on the prosecution to prove that a person is guilty of an offence beyond the reasonable doubt.

7. Final arguments on both the sides

Once the public prosecutor and the defense counsel present their arguments, the court generally reserve its judgment.

8. Judgment

Judgment is the final reasoned decision of the court as to the guilt or innocence of the accused. After application of judicial mind, the judge delivers a final judgment holding an accused guilty of an offence or acquitting him of the particular offence. If a person is acquitted, the prosecution is given time to file an appeal and if a person is convicted of a particular offence, then date is fixed for arguments on sentence. Once a person is convicted of an offence, both the sides present their arguments on what punishment should be awarded to an accused. This is done in cases which are punished with death or life imprisonment. After the arguments on sentence, the court finally decides what should be the punishment for the accused.

THE INDIAN EVIDENCE ACT, 1872

The word 'evidence' is derived from the Latin term 'evidens' or 'evidere' which means 'to show clearly' or 'to discover clearly', 'to ascertain' or 'to prove'. The objective of the Evidence Act is to prevent laxity and negligence in the admissibility of evidence and to introduce a full-proof and uniform rule of practice than what was previously used. The Indian Evidence Act, 1872 is largely based on the English law of Evidence. The Act does not claim to be exhaustive. Courts may look at the relevant English Common Law for interpretation as long as it is not inconsistent with the Act. The Act consolidates, defines and amends the laws of evidence. It is a special law and hence, will not be affected by any other enactment containing provisions on matter of evidence unless and until it is expressly stated in such enactment or it has been repealed or annulled by another statute.

Parties cannot contract to exclude the provisions of the Act. Courts cannot exclude relevant evidence made relevant under the Act. Similarly, evidence excluded by the Act will be inadmissible even if essential to ascertain the truth. The Act deals with Relevancy of Facts, Mode of Proof and Production and Effect of Evidence. The following principles are called the basic principles and the exceptions to the above principles.

(i) Evidence must be confined to the matters in issue.

(ii) Hearsay evidence may not be admitted.

(iii) The best evidence must be given in all cases.

(iv) All facts having rational probative value are admissible in evidence, unless excluded by a positive rule of paramount importance.

The Act is divided into three parts :

Part I – Relevancy of facts or what facts may or may not be proved. These are dealt with in detail in **(Sections 5 to 55).**

Part II – How the relevant facts are to be proved? This part deals with matters, which need not be proved under law and also how facts-in-issue or relevant facts are proved through oral and documentary evidence (Sections 56 to 100).

Part III – By whom and in what manner must the evidence be produced. It deals with the procedure for production of evidence and the effects of evidence (Sections 101 to 167).

Confession

The word 'confession' appears for the first time in Section 24 of the Indian evidence Act. This section comes under the heading of Admission so it is clear that the confessions are merely one species of admission. Confession is not defined in the Act. Justice Stephen in his digest of the law of evidence states, "Confession is an admission made at any time by a person charged with a crime stating or suggesting the inference that he committed that crime."

Forms of Confession

1. Judicial Confession–When a confession is made to the court itself then it will be called judicial confession. Judicial confessions are made before a magistrate or in court in the due course of legal proceedings. A judicial confession has been defined to mean 'plea of guilty on arrangement (made before a court) if made freely by a person in a state of mind'.

2. Extra Judicial Confessions–Extra-judicial confessions are made by the accused elsewhere than before a magistrate or in court. It is not necessary that the statements should have been addressed to any definite individual. It may have taken place in the form of a prayer.It may be a confession to a private person. An extra-judicial confession has been defined to mean "a free and voluntary confession of guilt by a person accused of a crime in the course of conversation with persons other than judge or magistrate seized of the charge against himself".

Admission and Confession : Sections 17 to 31 deals with admission generally and include Sections 24 to 30 which deal with confession as distinguished from admission.

Difference between a Confession and an Admission under Evidence Act :

There are certain key points that keep confession distinct from admission. They are numbered as follows :

(i) The term confession is used in criminal proceeding, statement by which the accused admits his guilt is confession. It consists of all the statements made by an accused which must either admit in terms, the offence or all facts constituting offence. A confession must be true and voluntary. While, the term admission is used in civil proceeding. Statement made by the accused is admission.

(ii) Confession can be retracted but admission cannot be retracted.

(iii) Confession may be of both kinds *i.e.,* oral or documentary whereas an admission is always exculpatory.

(iv) All confessions may be recognised as an admission but all admissions are not confession.

(v) A confession must be made before the Judicial Magistrate or in front of the court whereas admission may be made to any person outside of the court.

(vi) Confession is a species but admission is a genus.

(vii) A confession is admissible only when it fulfills the conditions mentioned under section 24-26 of the Evidence Act 1872, while an admission is admissible under section 21-23 of the Evidence Act 1872.

(viii) Confession given freely can be treated as a conclusive proof of guilt but admission related with the fact in issue or relevant fact, is not a conclusive proof of evidence.

(ix) Confession of guilt by an accused person to a police officer cannot be proved in criminal proceeding where admission of guilt by a person to a police officer may be proved in civil proceeding.

Crimes under the Special and Local Laws

Certain acts are to be considered criminal acts even when they are not to be found in IPC. This is because they have been identified as crimes in Special and Local Laws. An Illustrative list of such statues is given below.

- Arms Act, 1959;
- Narcotic Drugs and Psychotropic Substances Act, 1985;
- Gambling Act, 1867;
- Excise Act, 1944;
- Prohibition Act;
- Explosives and Explosive substances Act, 1884 &1908.
- Immoral Traffic (Prevention) Act, 1956;
- Railways Act, 1989;
- Registration of Foreigners Act, 1930;
- Protection of Civil Rights Act, 1955;
- Indian Passport Act, 1967;
- Essential Commodities Act, 1955;
- Terrorist and Disruptive Activities Act;
- Antiquities and Art Treasures Act, 1972
- Dowry Prohibition Act, 1961;
- Child Marriage Restraint Act, 1929;
- Indecent Representation of Women (Prohibition Act, 1986;
- Copyright Act, 1957;
- Sati Prevention Act,1987;

- SC/ST (Prevention of Atrocities) Act,1989;
- Forest Act, 1927;
- Juvenile Justice (Care and Protection of Children) Act 2000, as amended in 2006 latest amended in 2015
- Other crimes (not specified above) under Special and Local Laws including Cyber Laws

Summary

Introduction–Criminal law governs crimes, including felonies and misdemeanors. Crimes are generally referred to as offenses against the state. The standard of proof for crimes is 'beyond a reasonable doubt'.

Types of Crimes–It can be categorised in many ways. One of the simple way to remember it is crimes against persons, crimes against property, crimes against morality, white-collar crime and organised crimes.

Stages of Crimes – There are 4 stages. They are Intention, Preparation, Attempt and Accomplishment.

Elements of Crime–There are two elements of crime. They are **actus reus** and **mens reus. Actus rea** represents the physical aspects of crime. It has been defined as such result of human conduct as the law seeks to prevent. In other words some overt act or illegal omission must take place in pursuance of the guilty intension.

Whereas, **mens rea** represents the mental aspects there can be no crime of any nature without mens era or an evil mind. Every crime requires a mental element and that is considered as the fundamental principle of criminal liability. The basic requirement of the principle mens rea is that the accused must have been aware of those elements in the act which make the crime with which he is charged.

Strict Liability–Strict Liability doctrine can be define as the acts or omissions which are held liable without the mens rea (mental intent). It is a standard for liability which may exist in either a criminal or civil context. A rule specifying strict liability makes a person legally responsible for the damage and loss caused by his or her acts and omissions regardless of culpability including the fault in criminal law.

Criminal Law–Indian Criminal Laws are divided into three major acts *i.e.,* Indian Penal Code, 1860, Code of Criminal Procedure, 1973 and Indian Evidence Act, 1872. Besides these major acts, special Criminal Laws are also passed by Indian Parliament

i.e., NDPS, Prevention of Corruption Act, Food Adulteration Act, Dowry Prevention Act,the Defence of India Act,etc. thousands of minor laws are made in India.

Indian Penal Code– The Indian Penal Code (IPC) is the main criminal code of India. It is a comprehensive code intended to cover all substantive aspects of criminal law. The objective of this Act is to provide a general penal code for India. Though it is not an initial objective, but the Act does not repeal the penal laws which were in force at the time of coming into force in India. This was so because the Code does not contain all the offences and it was possible that some offences might have still been left out of the Code, which were not intended to be exempted from penal consequences. Though this Code consolidates the whole of the law on the subject and is exhaustive on the matters in respect of which it declares the law, many more penal statutes governing various offences have been created in addition to the code.

Criminal Proceure Code–It is the main legislation on procedure for administration of substantive criminal law in India. It was enacted in 1973 and came into force on 1 April, 1974. It provides the machinery for the investigation of crime, apprehension of suspected criminals, collection of evidence, determination of guilt or innocence of the accused person and the determination of punishment of the guilty. Additionally, it also deals with public nuisance, prevention of offences and maintenance of wife, child and parents.

Classification of Crimes–The crimes are classified in three ways; bailable and non-bailable offence, cognizable and non-cognizable and compondable and non-compoundable offences.

How is criminal proceedings initiated—

1. Pre-trial stages- (i) registration of an FIR (ii) investigation.

2. Trial stages :

   - filing of the chargesheet
   - framing of charges/ serving of notice
   - recording of the prosecution evidence
   - statement of the accused
   - evidence of defence
   - final arguments of both the sides
   - delivery of sentence
   - agruments of sentence
   - judgement with punishment

This procedure is a general procedure for how a criminal trial is initiated. There are different trials in our criminal procedure code :

- summons case
- warrant case
- summary trial

Indian Evidence Act, 1872– Evidence is the raw material which a judge or adjudicator uses to reach 'findings of fact'. The findings of fact that the evidence generates are - for all their flaws - 'what happened' for all intents and purposes of the legal proceeding. If you do not agree with the fact-finding that has been made (or even if you know it to be wrong), recognise that the rules of evidence are the best rules that law know of to reach the necessary goal of fact finding In its original sense the word 'evidence' signifies, the state of being evident *i.e.*, plain, apparent or notorious. But, it is applied to that which tends to render evidence or generate proof. The fact sought to be proved is called the principal fact; the fact which tends to establish it, the evidentiary fact.

Admission–Admission is a voluntary acknowledgment of a fact. Importance is given to those admissions that goes against the interests of the person making the admission.

Confession–The term confession is not defined anywhere in Indian Evidence Act. But it is thought that an Admission in case of a criminal matter is Confession.

Forms of Confession–There are two kinds of confession.

- **Judicial Confession–**Are those which are made before a magistrate or in court in the due course of legal proceedings. A judicial confession has been defined to mean 'plea of guilty on arrangement (made before a court) if made freely by a person in a fit state of mind'.

- **Extra-Judicial Confessions–** Are those which are made by the accused elsewhere than before a magistrate or in court. It is not necessary that the statements should have been addressed to any definite individual. It may have taken place in the form of a prayer. It may be a confession to a private person. An extra-judicial confession has been defined to mean 'a free and voluntary confession of guilt by a person accused of a crime in the course of conversation with persons other than judge or magistrate seized of the charge against himself.

Multiple Choice of Questions

1. An act is crime (in the content of Indian law) as :
    - (a) It is so declared by public
    - (b) It is so dictated by morality
    - (c) Statute makes it
    - (d) Commom law has declared it

2. Mark the correct answer :
    - (a) Crime is essentially an immoral act
    - (b) Crime is an illegal act
    - (c) Crime is essentially a socially reprehensible act
    - (d) Crime is essentially an anti-religious act

3. Criminal law consists of :
    - (a) Definition of offences and punishment for them (IPC)
    - (b) Procedure for investigation, prosecution, trial (CrPc) etc.
    - (c) It includes prevention of offences as well
    - (d) All are correct

4. The IPC came into effect from :
    - (a) 6 October, 1860   (b) 1 September, 1872
    - (c) 1 July, 1882   (d) 6 December, 1890

5. If a person who is a citizen of India commits any offence out of India, he :
    - (a) cannot be prosecuted in India, as the act was not committed in India
    - (b) cannot be prosecuted in the country where the act was committed
    - (c) can be prosecuted in India in any place in which he may be found
    - (d) cannot be prosecuted neither in India, not in the country where the crime was committed

6. The essential ingredients of crime are:
    - (a) Motive, mens rea and actus reus
    - (b) Motive, intention and knowledge
    - (c) Mens rea and actus reus
    - (d) Knowledge, intention and action

7. *Actus reus* is defined as "such result of human conduct as the law seeks to prevent". In the light of this observation, which of the following statements is incorrect :
    - (a) *Actus reus* means act of omission or commission, which is called conduct
    - (b) *Actus reus* means conduct prohibited by law
    - (c) *Actus reus* means voluntary as well as involuntary human actions
    - (d) *Actus reus* includes results of an act *i.e.*, injury

8. The maxim *'actus non facit reum, nisi mens sit rea'* means :
   (a) Guilty minds gives birth to crime
   (b) There can be no crime without a guilty mind
   (c) Crime is a child of guilty mind
   (d) Criminal mind leads to crime

9. Which one of the following statements correctly describes the concept of *mens rea* ?
   (a) *Mens rea* need to be present at the stage of planinf, but not a the stage of commission of the offence
   (b) *Mens rea* should be excluded unless the statute specifically requires it to be proved
   (c) Absolute prohibition is not required to negate *mens rea*
   (d) If the statute is silent about *mens rea*, as a general rule it should be read into the statute

10. Illegal signifies :
   (a) Everything which is an offence
   (b) Everything which is prohibited by law
   (c) Everything which furnishes ground for civil action
   (d) All of the above

Short Answer Questions

1. Define crime. Explain how does the criminal law of India works ?
2. Explain the types and stages of crime.
3. Explain the maxim 'actus non facit reum nisi mens sit rea.
4. Explain strict liability with the help of examples.
5. How many objectives are there for the enforcement of criminal law by punishments ?
6. What is the importance of the penal code ?
7. Explain the principles of the evidence act.

Long Answer Questions

1. How is a criminal proceeding initiated in India ?
2. Differentiate between the following :
   (a) Bailable and non-bailable offence
   (b) Compoundable and non-compoundable
   (c) Cognizable and non- cognizable
   (d) Warrant case and summons case
   (e) Admission and confession

Board Questions

1. "A common misconception is that motive and intention are same concepts when it comes to crime."

   Consider the statement given above and explain the concept of 'Intention' and a 'Motive' in terms of criminal law. Also give one difference between these two.

2. Consider the following situations and explain by giving reasons, whether any fundamental rights has been violated or not under Article 20 of the Indian Constitution.
   (a) Arpit was charged and convicted of theft of property from Sachin. Arpit was subsequently charged and tried for robbery on the same facts.
   (b) Nandini was charged with the offence of murder of a Member of Parliament (M.P.). During the police investigation, a list of questions was provided to Nandini. She refused to answer those questions. Is she bound to answer, against her wishes ?

3. Ratan Singh committed an offence u/s 304 B (Dowry Death) of Indian Penal Code for which the prescribed punishment is imprisonment for a term, which shall not be less than seven years but may extend to imprisonment for life.
   (a) Identify the type of criminal trial in the above mentioned situation.
   (b) Explain the various stages of criminal trial identified above.

NCERT Questions

1. What are the various kinds of crime under the IPC ?
2. Is defamation a crime ? If so, under which body of law ?
3. How is a summons case different from a warrant case ?
4. What is the concept of plea bargaining ?
5. What does compounding stand for ?

Sample Questions

1. A boy is sinking in the swimming pool of a resort. A man who is beside the pool does not make any attempt to save this boy. Will the man be criminally liable ? If yes why, if no why not?

❏❏

6 | Administrative Law

INTRODUCTION

Administrative law is the body of law that governs the activities of administrative agencies of the government which comprise of rule making or legislation (when delegated to them by the Legislature as and when the need be), adjudication (to pronounce decisions while giving judgments on certain matters) and implementation/enforcement of public policy.

Administrative law is recognised as the most outstanding legal development of the 20th century. The 19th century was characterised by the welfare state wherein there was minimum government control, free enterprise, contractual freedom, etc. Individualistic theories flourished in this period. The state played a negative role. It was primarily a police state which helped in maintenance of law and order, protecting the nation from external aggression, dispensing justice to its citizens and collecting taxes for financing such activities. However, in the 20th century, the evils of this system were realised. Due to contractual freedom and freedom of enterprise, there was unequal distribution of wealth. This led to several socialist movements specially ones in which the grievances of laborers was voiced. Thus, a need was felt that the state shall be more than a police state. It shall help in alleviating the poor, regulating individual enterprise and most importantly bringing about social justice.

The functions of the state today may be put into five broad categories, namely :

(i)   as a protector,

(ii) provider,

(iii) entrepreneur,

(iv) economic controller and

(v)   arbiter.

Administrative law helps in balancing public power and personal rights. If exercised properly, vast administrative powers could lead to a well-functioning welfare state and if not exercised properly it would lead to administrative despotism.

Administrative law provides several limitations on executive power in the form of :

- rule of law,
- separation of powers,
- principles of natural justice,
- judicial and parliamentary controls,
- administrative appeals, ombudsman, etc.

Scope of Administrative Law

Administrative law determines the organisation, powers and duties of administrative authorities. The emphasis of Administrative Law is on procedures for formal adjudication based on the principles of Natural Justice and for rule making. The concept of Administrative Law is founded on the following principles :

- Power is conferred on the administration by law.
- No power is absolute or uncontrolled howsoever broad the nature of the same might be.
- There should be reasonable restrictions on exercise of such powers depending on the situation.

Significance of Administrative Law

It is very significant because if it did not exist then the very concept of having a democracy and a government to work for the people would be self-defeating because in this case there would be no responsibility or accountability of the public officials to anybody and the administration would run arbitrarily thus creating a huge monster that would eat up the very system. There would be disturbance in the balance in areas such as police law, international trade, manufacturing, environmental, taxation, broadcasting immigration and transportation.

Reasons for its Growth

(i) Rise in complexity warranted handling of variable by the state authorities in order to provide functioning in that area with necessary certainty and prescriptions.

(ii) Industrial revolution that resulted in the coming up of cities and new types of economic transactions necessitated handling of affairs by government in order to facilitate production, supply and exchange of products and services.

(iii) Technological inventions and the increasing specialisation have called for the increased need of specialised handling of affairs by government officials.

(iv) To allow necessary flexibility in the administrative system so that the challenges arising due to social and economic factors could be addressed more adequately and efficiently.

(v) To allow experimentation in order to ensure the application of best fit model in a given circumstance.

(vi) To allow participation of people in the administrative functioning to provide the necessary authority to the administrative officials so that they can address the challenges arising due to extraordinary circumstances or emergency situations.

Objectives to the Growth of Administrative Law

To keep within the limits the public powers of the government through :

● **Ultra vires**– keeping powers within a certain ambit.

● **The separation of powers**– ensuring the role of judiciary to keep the legislative and executive arms accountable.

● **Rule of Law**– courts overseeing decisions made by the executive and providing access to justice.

Quasi Judicial Action

The word 'quasi' means 'not exactly.' Generally, an authority is described as 'quasi- judicial' when it has some of the attributes or trappings of judicial functions, but not all. A quasi-judicial function stands midway between a judicial function and an administrative function. A quasi-judicial decision is nearer the administrative decision in terms of its discretionary element and nearer the judicial decision in terms of procedure and objectivity of its end-product.

Simply Administrative Action

Simply administrative functions are those functions which are neither legislative nor judicial in character. An administrative order is generally based on governmental policy or expediency. Execution of governmental policy is known as simply administrative action.

Ministerial Action

In ministerial action there is no discretion available to administrative authority on execution of governmental policy. The administrative authority needs to execute in the manner in the way they have been directed. This is known as ministerial action.

Administrative action and Non-administrative action

Government Officer's decision to compulsorily acquire land and Government Officer's decision to declare a person not fit and proper to hold a financial services license are few examples of administrative actions.

Administrative Law and Constitutional Law : Key Difference

ADMINISTRATIVE LAW	CONSTITUTIONAL LAW
It deals with the organs and functions in motion.	It deals with the organs and such functions at the state of rest.
It deals with various organs of the state and controls the exercise of powers by the executive.	It deals with the structure of the various organs of the state and regulates their relations with each other and with individuals.
It fills in details of those fundamentals and basic structure laid down by the constitution.	It lays down fundamentals and basic structure.
It is based on written statutes, precedents., etc.	It is based on a written constitution.

TYPES OF ADMINISTRATIVE ACTION

Legislative Administrative Action

Legislative functions of the executive consist of making rules, regulations, bye-laws, etc. It includes delegated functions also.

Legislative decisions (*e.g.,* the making of laws; however, delegated legislation may be reviewable on a similar basis to administrative decisions), Broad policy decisions (*e.g.,* deciding to reduce a grants program) and Government Officer's decision not to grant a visa Employment decisions (*e.g.,* decisions to hire an employee; however, administrative law may apply to public service misconduct decisions) are few examples of Non-Administrative Action.

BASIC FUNDAMENTAL PRINCIPLES OF ADMINISTRATIVE LAW

Rule of Law

The origin of concept of the rule of law can be traced to Sir Edward Coke who was the then chief justice when James I was the king of England. Sir Edward coke maintained that even king was subject of the law thus establishing the supremacy of the law over the executive.

Prof A.V. Dicey evolved the concept of Rule of Law while he was delivering lectures to the law students in Oxford University, England. The concept of Rule of Law can be traced from the time of the Romans, who called it 'Just Law', to the Medieval period where it was called the 'Law of God.' The social contractualists, such as Hobbes, Locke and Rousseau, called the Rule of Law as the Natural Law. The entire basis of administrative law is the principle of the rule of law.

According to Dicey, the Rule of Law is one of the fundamental principles of the English Legal System. In 1885 his book monumental treatise, 'The Law of the Constitution', he attributed the following three meanings to the said doctrine:

(i) Supremacy of law.

(ii) Equality before law and

(iii) Predominance of legal spirit.

Supremacy of Law

Explaining the first principle, Dicey stated that rule of law means the absolute supremacy or predominance of regular law as opposed to the influence of arbitrary power or wide discretionary power. It excludes the existence of arbitrariness, of prerogative or even wide discretionary power on the part of the government. According to this doctrine, no man can be arrested, punished or be lawfully made to suffer in body or goods except by due process of law and for a breach of law established in the ordinary legal manner before the ordinary courts of the land. Dicey described this principle as 'the central and most characteristic feature' of Common Law.

Equality before Law

Explaining the second principle of the rule of law, Dicey stated that there must be equality before the law or the equal subjection of all classes to the ordinary law of the land administered by the ordinary law courts. According to Dicey, any encroachment on the jurisdiction of the courts and any restrictions on the subject's unimpeded access to them are bound to jeopardize his rights.

Predominance of Legal Spirit (*Judge – made Constitution*)

Explaining the third principle, Dicey stated that in many countries rights such as the right to personal liberty, freedom from arrest, freedom to hold public meetings, etc., are guaranteed by a written Constitution. Dicey emphasised the role of the courts of law as guarantors of liberty and suggested that the rights would be secured more adequately if they were enforceable in the courts of law than by mere declaration of those rights in a document, as in the latter case, they can be ignored, curtailed or trampled upon.

Rule of Law and Indian Constitution

Dicey's rule of law has been adopted and incorporated in the Constitution of India. The Preamble itself enunciates the ideals of Justice, Liberty and Equality.

- In Part III of the Constitution these concepts are enshrined as Fundamental Rights and are made enforceable.

- The Constitution is supreme and all the three organs of the government, viz. Legislature, Executive and Judiciary are subordinate to and have to act in consonance with the Constitution.

- The doctrine of judicial review is embodied in the Constitution and the subjects can approach the High Courts and the Supreme Court for the enforcement of Fundamental Rights guaranteed under the Constitution. If the executive or the government abuses the power vested in it or if the action is malafide (in bad faith), the same can be quashed by the ordinary courts of law.

- All rules, regulations, ordinances, bye-laws, notifications, customs and usages are 'laws' within the meaning of Article 13 of the Constitution and if they are inconsistent with or contrary to any of the provisions thereof, they can be declared ultra vires by the Supreme Court and by High Courts.

- The President and the Judges of the Supreme Court and High Courts are required to take an oath to preserve, protect and defend the Constitution.

- As per Article 21 of the Constitution, no person shall be deprived of his life or personal liberty except according to procedure established by law or of his property saves by authority of law.

● Executive and legislative powers of States and the Union have to be exercised in accordance with the provisions of the Constitution. Government and public officials are not above law. The maxim *'The King can do no wrong'* does not apply in India.

● There is *equality before the law and equal protection of laws*. Government and public authorities are also subject to the jurisdiction of ordinary courts of law and for similar wrongs are to be tried and punished similarly. They are not immune from ordinary legal process nor are any provision made regarding separate administrative courts and tribunals.

● In public service also the doctrine of equality is accepted. Suits for breach of contract and torts committed by pubic authorities can be filed in ordinary law courts and damages can be recovered from State Government or Union Government for the acts of their employees.

Thus, it appears that the doctrine of rule of law is embodied in the Constitution of India, and is treated as the basic structure of the Constitution.

DOCTRINE OF SEPARATION OF POWERS

It is generally accepted that there are three main categories of governmental functions – Legislative, Executive, and Judicial. Likewise, there are three main organs of the government in a State-Legislature, Executive and Judiciary. According to the theory of separation of powers, these three powers and functions of the government must, in a free democracy, always be kept separate and be exercised by three separate organs of the government. Thus, the Legislature cannot exercise executive or judicial power; the Executive cannot exercise legislative or judicial power and the Judiciary cannot exercise legislative or executive power of the government.

The object of the doctrine is to have "a Government of Law rather than of official will or whim." Historically, during the reign of Louis XIV promoted Montesquieu to pursue the theory with force and vigor, Louis XIV was full-fledged monarch, he excercised all possible powers legislative, executive and judicial. This autocratic monarch in France promoted Monstesquieu to formulate this doctrine in a systematic and scientific form in his book Espirt de lois (The spirit of laws) in 1748.

Montesquieu's great point was that if the total power of the government is divided among autonomous organs, one will act as a check upon the other and in the check liberty can survive. Again, almost all the jurists accept one feature of this doctrine that the judiciary must be independent of and separate from the remaining two organs of the government, viz., Legislature and Executive. According to Prof. Friedmann strict separation of powers is a theoretical absurdity and a practical impossibility.

Separation of Powers in India

On a casual glance at the provisions of the Constitution of India, one may be inclined to say that the doctrine of Separation of Powers is accepted in India. Under the Indian Constitution, executive powers are with the President, legislative powers with the Parliament and judicial powers with the Judiciary (Supreme Court, High Courts and sub-ordinate courts). Some jurists are of the opinion that the doctrine of Separation of Powers has been accepted in the Constitution of India and is a part of the basic structure of the Constitution.

But if we study the constitutional provisions carefully, it is clear that the doctrine of Separation of Powers has not been accepted in India in its strict sense. There is no provision in the Constitution itself regarding the division of functions of the government and the exercise thereof. Though, under Articles 53(1) and 154(1), the executive power of the Union and States is vested in the President and the Governors respectively, there is no corresponding provision vesting the legislative and judicial power in any particular organ. The President has wide legislative powers. He can issue Ordinances, make laws for a state after the State Legislature is dissolved, adopt the laws or make necessary modifications and the exercise of this legislative power is immune from judicial review. He performs judicial functions also. He decides disputes regarding the age of a judge of a High Court or the Supreme Court for the purpose of retiring him and cases of disqualification of members of any House of Parliament.

Likewise, Parliament exercises legislative functions and is competent to make any law not inconsistent with the provisions of the Constitution, but many legislative functions are delegated to the executive. In certain matters, Parliament exercises judicial functions also. Thus, it can decide the question of breach of its privilege and, if proved, can punish the person concerned. In case of impeachment of the President, one House acts as a prosecutor and the other House investigates the charges and decides whether they were proved or not. The latter is a purely judicial function.

On the other hand, many powers which are strictly judicial have been excluded from the purview of courts. Though judiciary exercises all judicial powers, at the same time, it exercises certain executive or administrative functions also. The High Court has supervisory powers over all subordinate courts and tribunals and also power to transfer cases. The High Courts and the Supreme Court have legislative powers; they also frame rules regulating their own procedure for the conduct and disposal of cases.

Thus, the doctrine of separation of powers is not accepted fully in the Constitution of India, and one may agree with the observations of Mukherjea, J. in Ram Jawaya *vs.* State of Punjab, "The Indian Constitution has not indeed recognised the doctrine of separation of powers in its absolute rigidity but the functions of the different parts or branches of the government have been sufficiently differentiated and consequently it can very well be said that our Constitution does not contemplate assumption, by one organ or part of the State, of functions that essentially belong to another."

PRINCIPLES OF NATURAL JUSTICE

"The Principles of Natural Justice are easy to proclaim, but their precise extent is far less easy to define". No precise definition is possible for Natural Justice. The word 'Natural Justice' is derived from the Roman word 'Jus Naturale', which means principles of natural law, justice, equity and good conscience. Natural Justice is not something derived from Laws of nature. Laws of nature promote the survival rather than justice. Therefore, 'natural' justice, is not justice found in nature; it is a compendium (collection) of concepts which must be naturally associated with justice, whether these concepts are incorporated in law or not. Natural Justice is also known as substantial justice, fundamental justice and universal justice or fair play in action. Rules of natural justice are the minimum standards of fair decision-making imposed on persons or bodies acting in a judicial capacity. Rules of natural justice are not rules embodied in any statute.

Features

(i)   An important concept in administrative law.

(ii)   Fundamental rules of justice, breach of which will prevent justice being seen or done.

(iii) It's a great humanising principle intended to invest law with fairness, to secure justice and prevent miscarriage of justice.

(iv)   Implied mandatory requirement, non-observance of which invalidates the exercise of power.

(v)   It will always apply, however silent a statue may be.

Essential Ingredients of Natural Justice

The essential ingredients of Natural Justice are the following :

Rules Against Bias: This rule originates from the Latin Maxim 'nemo judex in causa sua' which means that a person will not judge a case in which he is himself interested. The fundamental principle of justice is that justice should not only be done but undoubtedly be seen to be done. To serve this purpose it is necessary that a person who decides on matter should not have any substantial interest either in the subject matter to the parties in dispute. In short this rule states the first requirement of Natural Justice that the judge must be impartial and neutral and must be free from bias.

Right to be Heard (Fair Hearing): The rule has its origin in the Latin Maxim 'Audi alteram partem' which means 'Hear the other party'. According to this rule any person whose rights or interest is being affected should be given reasonable opportunity to defend him. Natural Justice requires that the person who is likely to be affected by the decision must be heard before a decision is given. The hearing may be oral or it can be through a written representation. This, in turn entails that such a person must be informed about the nature of the enquiry and if any charges have been framed against him, of the charges.

Reasoned Decisions: The doctrine of reasoned decisions was not considered a part of Natural Justice and adjudicatory bodies were not obliged to give reasons for their decisions. In UK legal provisions made to this effect in Tribunals and Inquiries Act 1971 and in USA Administrative Procedure Act under Sec 8B it is stipulated that administrative decisions must be accompanied by findings and conclusions as well as reasons upon all material issues of law, facts or discretion. In India there is no such statutory requirement of giving reasons. In Maneka Gandhi vs. Union of India (AIR 1978) SC held that giving reasons is a healthy check against abuse or misuse of power. An order passed by an enquiry officer or administrative agency must be a speaking order. If the order is not supported by reasons, it will amount to violation of the rules of natural justice. When a higher authority reverses the order of lower authority, reasons must be clearly stated but when appellate authority affirms and order, need to state reasons.

Duty to Act Fairly : The Decision in Kraipak vs. Union of India (AIR 1970) by Supreme Court of India established the principle that duty to act fairly lies on any authority whether administrative or Quasi-Judicial. The duty to act fairly may not cover all principles of natural justice but it imposes an obligation on the authority to be fair. The question whether an authority had acted fairly or not will depend on the circumstances of the case. **Validity of an order on failure to observe natural justice :** Failure to observe the principles of natural justice will make a decision null and void ab initio. A quasi-Judicial or Administrative decision made in violation of the principles of natural justice wherever it can be read as an implied requirement of law is null and void. (Swedeshi Cotton Mills vs. Union of India (1981) 1 SCC).

Delegated legislation (also referred to as secondary legislation or subordinate legislation or subsidiary legislation) is law made by an executive authority under powers given to them by primary legislation in order to implement and administer the requirements of that primary legislation. It is law made by a person or body other than the legislature but with the legislature's authority. Often, a legislature passes statutes that set out broad outlines and principles and delegates authority to an executive branch official to issue delegated legislation that flesh out the details (substantive regulations) and provide procedures for implementing the substantive provisions of the statute and substantive regulations (procedural regulations).

Most of the enactments provide for the powers for making rules, regulations, by-laws or other statutory instruments which are exercised by specified subordinate authorities. Such legislation is to be made within the framework of the powers so delegated by the legislature and is, therefore, known as delegated legislation. Thus all law making which take place outside the legislature expressed as rules, regulations, bye laws, orders, schemes, directions or notifications etc. is termed as delegated legislation.

Delegated Legislation : Position under Constitution of India

The Legislature is quite competent to delegate to other authorities. To frame the rules to carry out the law made by it. In D. S. Gerewal *vs.* The State of Punjab, the justice of the Hon'ble Supreme Court dealt in detail the powers of delegated legislation under the Article 312 of Indian Constitution. He observed: "There is nothing in the words of Article 312 which takes away the usual power of delegation, which ordinarily resides in the legislature.

Mechanisms of Control against Illegitimate Administrative Processes

In the United States of America, the procedural control is effective within the prescribed guidelines. In the United Kingdom, Parliamentary control is extremely strong and effective given that theirs is an unwritten constitution with the supremacy of Parliament. In India, it is neither the procedural control nor the Parliament which has an absolute power. Hence, Indians turn to the judiciary to frame the scope of administrative anomalies and privileges of the Parliament. In such cases, the Court starts with a presumption of constitutionality. If for a law/rule/regulation, two interpretations are possible, the court will follow the one which makes the law constitutional. Hence, a balanced and holistic approach is adopted while assessing and adjudicating upon administrative matters since the court has to always aim at delivering justice and at the same time ensure that it does not transcend its own domain and pose a part of the legislature.

Grounds of Challenge of Rules and Regulations

Rules and regulations framed by administrative authorities can always be challenged on the grounds of uncertainty and vagueness. Arbitrariness is in the presence of no causality between the rule and the object sought to be achieved by the said rule. It is also clear that when there is a patent denial of equality, arbitrariness will be in force. Furthermore, reasons form an essential aspect of administrative action as dearth of reasons reflects the non-application of mind. The value of 'reasonableness' in Administrative Law has increased manifold times especially in the post-Renaissance period. To decipher the reasonableness one needs to pay attention to the prevalent customs, traditions and practices while acting under the ambit of Administrative law.

Control Over Administrative Discretion and Rule-making

Under the Constitution of India, the general Parliamentary control in the form of debates, notices, adjournments etc., operate as a potent weapon. Special controls such as the 'lay in' provisions and consideration for special committees are also of prime significance. Lay in provisions refers to delegated administrative rules that are laid on the table of the house and only on the approval of the Parliament or the respective legislature will those rules said to have the power of law. 'Lay in' in turn, can be of two kinds- recommendatory or mandatory. While in the former, affirmative Parliamentary approval may not be required, in the latter, such approval is non-negotiable and vital.

Remedies under Administrative Law

The government machinery cannot be excused under the statutory immunities against any wrongs on the people. Administrative Law provides various remedies which a citizen can seek against a wrongful administrative commission or omission. For example, the government grants a construction contract to A. After A has begun operations, the contract is revoked on the grounds that the government changed its policy. A, in this case, has a remedy against the government's high handedness.

There are different kinds of remedies available against wrongful actions. Different statutes provide for guidelines and benchmarks which are to be adhered to by the administration. Apart from consti-tutional and statutory remedies; control over the administration can also be exercised by non-consti-tutional and non-statutory means, wherein the media and the social media assume an important role.

Droit Administrative Law

Under the French Legal system, known as *droit administratif*, there are two types of laws and two sets of courts independent of each other. Where ordinary courts administer ordinary civil law between individuals, administrative courts administer the law between the subject and the State. An administrative authority or official is not subject to the jurisdiction of ordinary civil courts exercising powers under the civil law in disputes between private individuals. All claims and disputes in which these authorities or officials are parties which fall outside the scope of the jurisdiction of ordinary courts then they are dealt with and decided by special tribunals. Though the system of droit administrative if is very old, it was regularly put into practice by Napoleon in the 18th century.

In France, administration was under the control of 'real Judges', who were impartial and objective in true sense. Actual study of droit administrative has proved that no single institution has done so much for the protection of private citizens against the excesses of administration as has been done by *Counseil de'Etat* which was considered to be a model for other countries. The Conseil de'Etat is composed of eminent civil servants, deals with a variety of matters like claim of damages for wrongful acts of government servants, income-tax, pensions, disputed elections, personal claims of civil servants against the State for wrongful dismissal or suspension and so on. It has interfered with administrative orders on the ground of error of law, lack of jurisdiction, irregu-larity of procedure and detournement depouvior (misapplication of power). It has exercised its jurisdiction liberally.

Criticism of the Droit System

Prof. A.V. Dicey denounced the Droit system of administration as being a system where no justice was possible while in theory Dicey's renunciation appeared reasonable; in practice it is often rightly pointed out that this system of justice was far more efficient than its contemporary common law systems. Moreover, in 1872, the government passed a decree known as the Blanco decree by which this *Counseil de'Etat* was made an independent system of court where direct filing of cases as well as open hearings were allowed. Hence, speedy administration was a characteristic of Droit and an institution was created by the name of Tribunal Desk Conflict which was to decide where different types of cases were to go - whether to the civil law court or to the administrative law court.

Effectiveness of Droit

Notwithstanding the legitimate theoretical objections to the Droit system, it cannot be denied that this system gave some of the most revered doctrines of Administrative Law.

Doctrine of legitimate expectation: Wherein, the Court recognised due Governmental liability in case the promises to the citizens were not honored.

Doctrine of proportionality : The classical definition of proportionality has been given by Lord Diplock in *R V. goldsmith* (1983) 1 WLR 151 when his Lordship rather ponderously stated "you must not use a steam hammer to crack a nut if a nut cracker would do". Hence, proportionality broadly requires that government action must be no more intrusive than is necessary to meet an important public purpose.

Doctrine of governmental liability : This basi-cally determines that on what basis the government will be held responsible for the violation of another's right. Such liability is based on the twin assessment of fault and risk.

Summary

Introduction–Administrative law deals with the powers and functions of the administrative authorities, the manner in which the powers are to be exercised and remedies which are available to the aggrieved persons when those powers are abused by these authorities.

Types of Administrative Action–There are three types of administrative action. They are as follows :

(i) **Rulemaking**–Administrative agencies use rulemaking process to create, or proclaim regulations.

(ii) **Adjudication**–Administrative adjudication is exercise of judicial powers by an administrative agency.

(iii) **Investigation**–Administrative agencies have power to conduct investigations.

Rule of Law– The rule of law is the legal principle that law should govern a nation, as opposed to being governed by arbitrary decisions of individual government officials. According to Dicey, the Rule of Law attributed three meanings to the this doctrine. They are – Supremacy of law, Equality before Law and Predominance of legal spirit.

Separation of Powers–The three organs of the government which we know as the executive, the judiciary and legislature represent the people and their will in our country and are responsible for the smooth running of a democratic government in our society. The legislature is the law-making body, the executive is responsible for the enforcement of all such laws and the judiciary deals with the cases that arise from a breach of law. Thus they are all interlinked organs of the government and their roles and functions tend to overlap with each other, as it isn't possible to separate the three from each other completely.

Principle of natural justice–The principles of natural justice have their roots in two Latin maxims : 'Audi alteram partem' and 'nemo judex in causa sua'. The first one means that a person who has charged, must be heard before any decision is taken and the second maxim means that a person will not judge a matter in which he is interested. The 3rd principle has come into existence and followed by the judiciary is that a judgement should be a speaking one which means it should state the reasons behind arriving at a particular decision.

Delegated Legislation–When the function of legislation is entrusted to organs other than the legislature by the legislature itself, the legislation made by such organs is called delegated legislation. Under this it has further explained the growth and the critisism of delegated legislation.

Droit Administrative–Under the French Legal system, known as droit administratif, there are two types of laws and two sets of courts independent of each other. Where ordinary courts administer ordinary civil law between people, administrative courts administer the law between the subject and the State. An administrative authority or official is not subject to the jurisdiction of ordinary civil courts exercising powers under the civil law in disputes between private individuals. All claims and disputes in which these authorities or officials are parties fall outside the scope of the jurisdiction of ordinary courts and they are dealt with and decided by special tribunals. Further it has explained its critisim and effectiveness of Droit Administrative.

Doctrine of Legitimate Expectation–It is a ground of judicial review in administrative law to protect a procedural or substantive interest when a public authority rescinds from a representation made to a person. It is based on the principles of natural justice and fairness, and seeks to prevent authorities from abusing power.

Doctrine of Propotionality–The principle of proportionality envisages that a public authority ought to maintain a sense of proportion between his particular goals and the means he employs to achieve those goals, so that his action impinges on the individual rights to the minimum extent to preserve the public interest. This means that administrative action ought to bear a reasonable relationship to the general purpose for which the power has been conferred.

Doctrine of Government Liability– It determines that on what basis the government will be held responsible for the violation of another's right. Such liability is based on the twin assessment of fault and risk.

Multiple Choice of Questions

1. Using the codes below, find the correct answers : Administrative law deals with

   i. The powers of constitutional authorities

   ii. The powers of judicial review

   iii. The powers of the administartive authorities

   iv. The powers of the legislative authorities

   Codes :

   (a) Only (i) and (ii) are correct

(b) Only (ii) is correct

(c) Only (iii) is correct

(d) (i),(ii),(iii) and (iv) are correct.

2. Find the correct answer from the following statement :

(a) A quasi-judicial body may never review its own decisions unless authorised by the statute

(b) A quasi-judicial body may review its own decisions if there is grave error of law in it

(c) A quasi-judicial body may review its own decisions if there is violation of natural justice.

(d) All tribunals may review their decisions.

3. The rule of 'Audi alteram partem' requires reasonable opportunity of hearing. Hearing may be :

(a) Only in writing

(b) Only orally

(c) Written or oral

(d) Written and oral both.

4. Administrative law is the law relating to the powers and procedure of :

(a) The Parliament

(b) The legislature

(c) The administrative authorities

(d) Judiciary

5. Find the correct answer :

The principles of natural justice are :

i. No person can be judged in his own case

ii. No person shall be condemned unheard.

Codes :

(a) Only (i) is correct

(b) Only (ii) is correct

(c) (i) and (ii) are correct

(d) None of the above is correct.

6. What is the effect of violation of the rule: 'Audi alteram Partem' on an administrative action ?

(a) Mere irregularity (b) Null and void

(c) An illegality   (d) Voidable

7. The judicial control over administrative acts emanate from doctrine of :

(a) Separation of powers

(b) Judicial review

(c) Rule of law

(d) Delegated legislation

Short Answer Questions

1. Distinguish the discipline of Administrative Law from Constitutional Law.

2. What is the scope or purpose of Administrative Law ?

3. List the different types of administrative actions and give examples.

4. Explain the need of having the doctrine of separation of powers in the scheme of most constitutions across the globe.

5. Explain some of the remedies available in the gambit of administrative law against the State.

Long Answer Questions

1. Can a system like the Droit system of administration be successful in a country like India ?

2. Separation of powers, as illustrated by Montesquieu is impossible to be achieved. Give reasons.

3. Do you think that delegated legislation as a phenomenon should be discouraged due to lack of accountability ? Give reasons.

4. How can the policy of any given law be assessed from its bare text ?

5. Discuss the role of principles of natural justice in Administrative Law ?

NCERT Questions

1. What has the Kesavananda Bharati v. State of Kerala case stated about the Basic Structure Doctrine ?

2. Outline the positive and the negative features of the Droit system of Administration.

True/False

1. The study of administrative law must always limit to the domain of Constitution.

2. The Droit administrative system is a classic example of how even theoretically bad systems can become practically sound, if operated with sincerity.

3. Delegated legislations are permissible in the Indian judicial system but only with checks and balances.

4. Principles of natural justice are applicable only when incorporated in a statute.

5. The rule of law is only a philosophical concept with no statutory basis.

6. No country in the world operates on the classical idea of separation of power as visualized by Montesquieu.

7. Administrative law continues to hold its relevance even as the State's role as an entrepreneur is receding.

Sample Questions

1. What does the Latin phrase audialterampartem mean ?

    (a) 'listen to the other side'

    (b) 'one cannot be forced to be a witness against himself'

    (c) 'justice delayed is justice denied'

    (d) 'ignorance of law is no excuse'

2. "You must not use a steam hammer to crack a nut if a nut cracker would do." This statement refers to which doctrine of Administrative Law.

    (a) Doctrine of Legitimate expectation

    (b) Doctrine of proportionality

    (c) Doctrine of Governmental liability

    (d) Doctrine of Separation of powers.

❏❏

Arbitration, Tribunal Adjudication and Alternate Dispute Resolution

Adversarial and Inquisitorial Systems

Adversarial System

In this justice system an accused has the right to remain silent, the right to a lawyer and you are also innocent until proven guilty. The rights of the accused is a crucial aspect. In most common law countries *e.g.,* Wales, England and the United States of America, a system of justice called the adversarial system is used.

The adversarial system implies that two parties assume opposite positions in debating the guilt or innocence of an individual. In this scenario, the judge is required to be neutral at the contest unfolding before him or her. The role of the judge in this arrangement is to ensure the trial proceeds according to the procedural rules of trial or due process of law and that evidence entered is done so according to established rules and guidelines.

The evidence and witnesses that are called are left up to the two arguing parties, the defense counsel and the crown. The judge is not involved in what is presented to the court. If the crown wishes not to call certain evidence or individuals as witnesses even though it may help shed light on the case, the judge cannot intervene. This leaves the two parties in charge of the case and the direction it takes.

Advantages of the adversarial system include :

(i)   The judges reserve comment until all evidence from both parties are heard.

(ii) This makes the judge appear more neutral since judgment must be reserved until all the evidence are heard.

Disadvantages of the adversarial system include :

(i)   The finding of evidence rests on the resources of the two parties which may be unequal.

(ii) Parties only provide evidence favourable to their arguments.

Inquisitorial System

The **inquisitorial system** is the common procedural approach in most civil law jurisdictions. In an inquisitorial system, a judge is involved in the preparation of evidence along with the police and in how the various parties are to present their case at the trial. The judge questions witnesses in depth and can even call witnesses to appear while prosecution and defense parties can ask follow up questions. The judge plays the central role in finding the truth and all the evidence that either proves the innocence or guilt of the accused before the court. The judge takes on the role of prosecutor and judge in the inquisitorial system. Some other major distinctions are that there are no jury trials in an inquisitorial system and a judge can compel an accused to make statements and answer questions.

Advantages of inquisitorial system :

(i)   Decision maker has more active role.

(ii) Witnesses are mostly called by decision maker.

(iii) Less reliance on legal representatives.

(iv) The decision dependence controls the production of evidence.

(v)   Cost of inquisitorial system is mainly born by the state.

(vi) Use of mainly written statements reduces costs.

Disadvantages of inquisitorial system :

(i)   The judge is less impartial.

(ii) The parties may feel at the mercy of the investigating judge.

(iii) Parties not able to call own experts.

(iv) Greater reliance on written evidence.

(v)   Judge is aware of character reports and past records.

Comparisons between the Adversary and Inquistory system

Points of Discrimination	Adversary	Inquistory
Legal Premise	Parlisan advocacy by the two opposing sides will but lead to the determination of truth.	Truth is best discovered through a disinterested inquiry conducted by a magistrate.
Judge	Referee between the defence and the prosecutor jury, haly secret.	Fact-finder, busy declare verdict : judge, open.
Produce Evidence	The defendant and the prosecutor.	The judge.
Pro-Inquisitorial System	Control lies more in the hands of the judges reduces the disturbance of the attorneys.	Equal opportunity to present opinion, fairness and maintain public confident.

Alternative Dispute Resolution

"It is the spirit and not the form of law that keeps the justice alive." –L. J. Earl Warren

The concept of Conflict Management through Alternative Dispute Resolution (ADR) has introduced a new mechanism of dispute resolution that is non adversarial. A dispute is basically *'lis inter partes'* (which means legal suit between the parties) and the justice dispensation system in India has found an alternative to Adversarial litigation in the form of ADR Mechanism. It is a form of dispute resolution.

New method of dispute resolution such as ADR facilitates parties to deal with the underlying issues in dispute in a more cost-effective manner and with increased efficiency. In addition, these processes have the advantage of providing parties with the opportunity to reduce hostility, regain a sense of control, gain acceptance of the outcome, resolve conflict in a peaceful manner, and achieve a greater sense of justice in each individual case. The resolution of disputes takes place usually in private and is more viable, economic, and efficient.

Need for ADR in India

The system of dispensing justice in India has come under great stress for several reasons mainly because of the huge pendency of cases in courts. In India, the number of cases filed in the courts has shown a tremendous increase in recent years resulting in pendency and delays underlining the need for alternative dispute resolution methods. In a developing country like India with major economic reforms under way within the framework of the rule of law, strategies for swifter resolution of disputes for lessening the burden on the courts and to provide means for expeditious resolution of disputes, there is no better option but to strive to develop alternative modes of dispute resolution (ADR) by establishing facilities for providing settlement of disputes through arbitration, conciliation, mediation and negotiation.

Impacts of ADR

The Supreme Court in several cases repeatedly pointed out the need to change the law. The Public Accounts Committee too deprecated the Arbitration Act of 1940. The Government of India thought it necessary to provide a new forum and procedure for resolving inter-national and domestic disputes quickly. Thus 'The Arbitration and Conciliation Act, 1996' came into being. The law relating to Arbitration and Conciliation is almost the same as in the advanced countries. Conciliation has been given statutory recognition as a means for settlement of the disputes in terms of this Act. In addition to this, the new Act also guarantees independence and impartiality of the arbitrators irrespective of their nationality. The new Act of 1996 brought in several changes to expedite the process of arbitration. This legislation has developed confidence among foreign parties interested to invest in India or to go for joint ventures, foreign investment, transfer of technology and foreign collaborations.

Advantage of Alternate Dispute Resolution :

(i) It is less expensive.

(ii) It is less time consuming.

(iii) It is free from technicalities as in the case of conducting cases in law Courts.

(iv) The parties are free to discuss their difference of opinion without any fear of disclosure of this fact before any law Courts.

(v) The last but not the least is the fact that parties are having the feeling that there is no losing or winning feeling among the parties and at the same time they are having the feeling that their grievance is redressed and the relationship between the parties is restored.

Legislative and Constitutional Recognition of Alternative Dispute Redressal in India

(i) The Legal Services Authorities Act, 1987 brought about the establishment of Lok Adalat System for settlement of disputes cheaply and expeditiously and also in the spirit of compromise by give and take formula.

(ii) Section 30 of the Arbitration and Conciliation Act, 1996 encourages arbitrators, with the agreement of the parties, to use mediation, conciliation or other procedures at any time during the arbitration proceedings to encourage settlement.

(iii) Further still, the Civil Procedure Code (Amendment) Act, 1999 carries Section 89 which is designed to enable the courts to bring about a settlement of dispute outside the Court. As and when the Amendment comes to be enforced, the four methods listed in the section and known as court-ordered or court- annexed ADRs would become statutory alternatives to litigation for settlement of disputes and would be legally enforceable.

(iv) It is now made obligatory for the Court to refer the dispute after issues are framed for settlement with the concurrence of the parties either by way of :

- Arbitration,
- Conciliation,
- Judicial settlement including settlement through Lok Adalat, or
- Mediation

Where the parties fail to get their disputes settled through any of the Alternative Dispute Resolution methods, the suit would come back to proceed further in the Court it was filed.

(v) Alternative Dispute Resolution in India was founded on the Constitutional basis of Articles 14 and 21 which deal with Equality before Law and Right to life and personal liberty respectively.

(vi) ADR also tries to achieve the Directive Principle of State Policy relating to Equal justice and Free Legal Aid as laid down under Article 39-A of the Constitution.

TYPES OF ADR

Arbitration

Arbitration is the private, judicial determination of a dispute, by an independent third party. An arbitration hearing may involve the use of an individual arbitrator or a tribunal. A tribunal may consist of any number of arbitrators though some legal systems insist on an odd number for obvious reasons of wishing to avoid a tie. One and three are the most common numbers of arbitrators. The disputing parties hand over their power to decide the dispute to the arbitrator(s). Arbitration is an alternative to court action (litigation), and generally, just as final and binding (unlike mediation, negotiation and conciliation which are non-binding).

Classifications of Arbitration

There are various arbitrations depending upon the terms, subject matter of the dispute and the law governing the arbitration agreement. Some types of such arbitrations are discussed below :

Domestic Arbitration–Domestic arbitration refers to arbitration, which takes place in India, wherein parties are Indians and disputes are decided in accordance with the substantive law of India. The term 'domestic arbitration' as such has not been defined in the Arbitration and Conciliation Act of 1996. However a co joint reading of Section 2 (2) (7) of the Act 1996, it is apparent that 'domestic arbitration' means an arbitration in which the arbitral proceedings are held in India, and in accordance with Indian substantive and procedural law, and the cause of action for the dispute has wholly arisen in India, or where the parties are subject to Indian jurisdiction.

Foreign Arbitration–When arbitration proceedings are conducted in a place outside india and the award is required to be enforced in india it is called foreign arbitration.

Ad-hoc Arbitration–Without resorting to an Institution, if the parties themselves agree and arrange for arbitration, it is termed as Ad-hoc arbitration. It may be domestic, international or foreign arbitration. Ad-hoc arbitration means that the arbitration is not conducted pursuant to the rules of an arbitral institution. Since, parties are not obliged to submit their arbitration to the rules of an arbitral institution; they may largely stipulate their own rules of procedure. In other words, Ad-hoc arbitration is a do it yourself arbitration.

Institutional Arbitration–When arbitration is conducted by an arbitral institution, it is called institutional arbitration. The parties may specify, in the arbitration agreement, to refer the dispute or differences to be determined in conformity with the rules of a particular arbitral institution. 'Institutional Arbitration' is arbitration conducted under the rules laid down by an established arbitral organisation.

Statutory Arbitration–When arbitration is conducted in accordance with the provisions of a special enactment, which specifically provides for arbitration in respect of disputes arising on matters covered by that enactment, it is called statutory arbitration.

International Commercial Arbitration–When arbitration takes place within India or outside India containing ingredients of foreign origin in relation to the parties or the subject matter of the dispute is called as international arbitration. To satisfy the definition of international arbitration it is suffice if any one of the parties to the dispute is resident or domiciled outside India or if the subject matter of dispute is abroad.

Fast Track Arbitration–Fast Track Arbitration also called as documents only arbitration is time bound arbitration, with stricter rules of a procedure, which do not allow for any laxity or scope for extensions of time and delays. Fast track arbitrations are best suited in those cases, which can be resolved on the foundation of documents and that oral hearings and witnesses are not necessary. The reduced span of time makes it cost effective.

Advantages of Arbitration

(i) **Choice of Decision Maker**–For example, parties can choose a technical person as arbitrator if the dispute is of a technical nature so that the evidence will be more readily understood.

(ii) **Efficiency**–Arbitration can usually be heard sooner than it takes for court proceedings to be heard. As well, the arbitration hearing is shorter in length and the preparation work is less demanding.

(iii) **Privacy**–Arbitration hearings are confidential, because in private meetings, the media and members of the public are not able to attend. As well, final decisions are not published, nor are they directly accessible.

(iv) **Convenience**–Hearings are arranged at times and places to suit the parties, arbitrators and witnesses.

(v) **Flexibility**–The procedures can be segmented, streamlined or simplified, according to the circumstances. There are minimum legal technicalities and formalities.

(vi) **Finality**–There is in general, no right to appeal in arbitration. (Although, the court has limited powers to set aside or remit an award).

(vii) **Expert**–Arbitrator is usually expert in the subject matter and hence, can understand the dispute quickly and thoroughly. A judge in the court may not be able to fully appreciate the problem, if it is of intricate technical nature.

Disadvantages of Arbitration

(i) **Cost**–One or both of the parties will pay for the arbitrator's services, while the court system provides an adjudicator who does not charge a fee. The fees for an arbitrator can be hefty. **If the matter is complicated but the amount of money involved is modest, then the arbitrator's fee may make arbitration uneconomical.**

(ii) **'Splitting the Baby'**–Thomas Crowley states that because of the relaxation of rules of evidence in arbitration, and the power of the arbitrator to 'do arbitrator may render an award that, rather than granting complete relief to one side, splits the baby by giving each side part of what they requested. Thus both parties leave the table feeling that justice was not served.

(iii) **No Appeal**–Unless there is evidence of outright corruption or fraud, the award is binding and usually not appealable.

(iv) **Narcotic/Chilling Effects**–Chilling occurs when neither party is willing to compromise during negotiations in anticipation of an arbitrated settlement. The narcotic effect refers to an increasing dependence of the parties on arbitration, resulting in a loss of ability to negotiate.

(v) **Discovery may be more limited with arbitration**– In litigation, discovery is the process of requiring the opposing party or even a person or business entity who is not a party to the case to provide certain information or documents. As a result, many times arbitration is not agreed to until after the parties are already in litigation and discovery is completed. By that time, the opportunity to avoid costs by using arbitration may be diminished. If certain information from a witness is presented by documents, then there is no opportunity to cross-examine the testimony of that witness.

Steps in an Arbitration

The process of arbitration differs among cases.

The following is a list of the main steps in arbitration; however it should not be viewed as an exhaustive list.

● **Initiating the Arbitration**–A request by one party for a dispute to be referred to arbitration.

● **Appointment of Arbitrator**–Arbitrators may be appointed by one of three ways :

(i) Directly by the disputing parties,

(ii) By existing tribunal members,

(iii) By an external party.

● **Preliminary Meeting**–It is a good idea to have a meeting between the arbitrator and the parties, along with their legal counsel, to discuss an appropriate process and timetable.

- **Statement of Claim and Response**–The claimant sets out a summary of the matters in dispute and the remedy sought in a statement of claim. This is needed to inform the respondent of what needs to be answered. These statements are called the 'pleadings'. Their purpose is to identify the issues and avoid surprises.

- **Discovery and Inspection**–These are legal procedures through which the parties investigate background information. Each party is required to list all relevant documents, which are in their control.

- **Interchange of Evidence**–The written evidence is exchanged and given to the arbitrator for review prior to the hearing.

- **Hearing**–The hearing is a meeting in which the arbitrator listens to any oral statements, questioning of witnesses and can ask for clarification of any information.

- **Legal Submissions**–The lawyers of both parties provide the arbitrator with a summary of their evidence and applicable laws.

- **Award**–The arbitrator considers all the information and makes a decision. An award is written to summarize the proceedings and give the decisions.

Administrative Tribunals

With the acceptance of welfare ideology, there was on increase in growth of public services and public servants. The courts, particularly the High Courts were inundated with cases concerning service matters and could not offer much need remedy to the government servants. Thus occurs the dissatisfaction among the employees, irrespective of the class, category or group to which they belong.

The Swaran Singh Committee therefore, inter-alia recommended the establishment of Administrative Tribunals as a part of Constitutional adjudicative system. Resultantly the Constitution (42nd Amendment) Act, 1976 inserted Part XIV-A to the Constitution of India consisting of Articles 323A and 323B.

Article 323A provides for the establishment of Administrative Tribunals for adjudication or trial of disputes and complaints with respect to recruitment, conditions of service of persons appointed to public services and other allied matters.

Article 323B makes provision for the creation of Tribunals for adjudication or trial of disputes, complaints or offences connected with tax, foreign exchange, industrial and labour disputes, land reforms, ceiling on urban property, election to Parliament and State Legislatures, etc. Parliament has power to enact any law under Article 323A while both Parliament and State Legislatures can make laws on matters of Article 323B, subject to their legislative competence. The Tribunals enjoy the powers of the High Court in respect of service matters of the employees covered by the Act.

The Administrative Tribunal Act, 1985 provides for the establishment of one Central Administrative Tribunal (CAT) and a State Administrative Tribunal (SAT) for each state. The Tribunal consists of a Chairman, Vice-Chairman and Members. These Members are drawn from the judicial as well as the administrative streams. The appeal against the decisions of the CAT lies with the Supreme Court of India.

The main characteristics of Administrative Tribunal are as follows :

(i) Administrative Tribunal is the creation of a statue. Administrative Tribunal is not a court. It is an executive body. It stands somewhere between court and an administrative body.

(ii) Administrative Tribunal is bound to act judicially and follow the principle of natural justice.

(iii) It has some of the trappings of a court and are required to act openly fairly and impartiality.

(iv) An Administrative Tribunal is not bound by the strict rules of procedure and evidence prescribed by the civil procedure court.

Advantages of Administrative Tribunal

The main advantages of the administrative tribunals are :

(i) **Flexibility :** Administrative adjudication has brought about flexibility and adaptability in the judicial as well as administrative tribunals.

(ii) **Adequate Justice :** In the fast changing world of today, administrative tribunals are not only the most appropriate means of administrative action, but also the most effective means of giving fair justice to the individuals.

(iii) **Less Expensive :** Administrative justice ensures cheap and quick justice. As against this, procedure in the law courts is long and cumbersome and litigation is costly.

(iv) **Relief to Courts :** The system also gives the much-needed relief to ordinary courts of law, which are already overburdened with numerous suits.

Disadvantages of Administrative Tribunals

Some of the main drawbacks are mentioned below.

(i) Administrative adjudication is a negation of Rule of Law. Administrative tribunals, with their separate laws and procedures often made by themselves, puts a serious limitation upon the celebrated principles of Rule of Law.

(ii) Administrative tribunals have in most cases, no set procedures and sometimes they violate even the principles of natural justice.

(iii) Administrative tribunals often hold summary trials and they do not follow any precedents. As such it is not possible to predict the course of future decisions.

(iv) The civil and criminal courts have a uniform pattern of administering justice and centuries of experience in the administration of civil and criminal laws have borne testimony to the advantages of uniform procedure. A uniform code of procedure in administrative adjudication is not there.

(v) Administrative tribunals are manned by administrators and technical heads who may not have the background of law or training of judicial work. Some of them may not possess the independent outlook of a Judge.

Mediation

Mediation, as used in law, is a form of Alternative Dispute resolution (ADR), a way of resolving disputes between two or more parties with concrete effects. Typically, a third party or the mediator, assists the parties to negotiate a settlement. Disputants may mediate disputes in a variety of domains, such as commercial, legal, diplomatic, workplace, community and family matters.

Mediation is a flexible process that can be used to settle disputes in a whole range of situations such as :

- consumer disputes.
- contract disputes.
- family disputes.
- neighbourhood disputes.

The role of the mediator is to help parties reach a solution to their problem and to arrive at an outcome that both parties are happy to accept. Mediators avoid taking sides, making judgments or giving guidance. They are simply responsible for developing effective communica-tions and building consensus between the parties. The focus of a mediation meeting is to reach a common sense settlement agreeable to both parties in a case. Mediation is a voluntary process and will only take place if both parties agree. It is a confidential process where the terms of discussion are not disclosed to any party outside the mediation hearing. If parties are unable to reach agreement, they can still go to court. Details about what went on at the mediation will not be disclosed or used at a court hearing. Both parties share the cost of mediation, which depends on the value and complexity of the claim.

Generally mediation can be used for most civil (noncriminal) disputes, including those involving contracts, leases, small business ownership, employment and divorce. Divorcing couples might mediate to work out a mutually agreeable child custody agreement or estranged business partners might choose mediation to work out an agreement to divide their business. Non-violent criminal matters, such as claims of verbal or other personal harassment, can also be successfully mediated.

Mediation Procedure

Stage 1 Mediator's opening statement : After the disputants are seated at a table, the mediator introduces everyone, explains the goals and rules of the mediation, and encourages each side to work cooperatively towards a settlement.

Stage 2 Disputants' Opening Statements : Each party is invited to describe, in his or her own words, what the dispute is about and how he or she has been affected by it, and to present some general ideas about resolving it. While one person is speaking, the other is not allowed to interrupt.

Stage 3 Joint Discussion : The mediator may try to get the parties talking directly about what was said in the opening statements. This is the time to determine what issues need to be addressed.

Stage 4 Private Caucuses : The private caucus is a chance for each party to meet privately with the mediator (usually in a nearby room) to discuss the strengths and weaknesses of his or her position and new ideas for settlement. The mediator may caucus with each side just once, or several times, as needed. These private meetings are considered the guts of mediation.

Stage 5 Joint Negotiation : After caucuses, the mediator may bring the parties back together to negotiate directly.

Stage 6 Closure : This is the end of the mediation. If an agreement has been reached, the mediator may put its main provisions in writing as the parties listen. The mediator may ask each side to sign the written summary of agreement or suggest they can take it to lawyers for review. If the parties want to, they can write up and sign a legally binding contract. If no agreement was reached, the mediator will review whatever progress has been made and advise every one of their options, such as meeting again later, going to arbitration or going to court.

How is mediation different from arbitration ?

A mediator normally has no authority to render a decision. It's up to the parties themselves with the mediator's help to work informally toward their own agreement.

An arbitrator, on the other hand, conducts a contested hearing between the parties and then, acting as a judge, rends a legally binding decision. Arbitration resembles a court proceeding.

Types of Mediation

There are various types of mediation which are explained below :

Evaluative Mediation– It is a process modeled on settlement conferences held by judges. An evaluative mediator assists the parties in reaching resolution by pointing out the weaknesses of their cases and predicting what a judge or jury would be likely to do. The evaluative mediator structures the process, and directly influences the outcome of mediation.

Faciliative Mediation–In this the mediator structures a process to assist the parties in reaching a mutually agreeable resolution. The mediator asks questions, validates and normalises parties' points of view, searches for interests underneath the positions taken by parties and assists the parties in finding and analysing options for resolution. The facilitative mediator does not make recommendations to the parties, give his or her own advice or opinion as to the outcome of the case, or predict what a court would do in the case. The mediator is in charge of the process, while the parties are in charge of the outcome. Facilitative mediators want to ensure that parties come to agreements based on information and understanding.

Transformative Mediation–Transformative med-iation is based on the values of 'empowerment' of each of the parties as much as possible and 'recognition' by each of the parties of the other parties' needs, interests, values and points of view. The potential for transformative mediation is that any or all parties or their relationships may be transformed during the mediation.

Mediation with Arbitration–Mediation with arbitration - Mediation has sometimes been utilised to good effect when coupled with arbitration, particularly binding arbitration, in a process called 'mediation/arbitration'. The process begins as a standard mediation, but if mediation fails, the mediator becomes an arbiter. This process is more appropriate in civil matters where rules of evidence or jurisdiction are not in dispute. It resembles, in some respects, criminal plea bargaining and Confucian judicial procedure, wherein the judge also plays the role of prosecutor.

Online Mediation–Online mediation employs online technology to provide disputants access to mediators and each other despite geographic distance, disability or other barriers to direct meeting.

Conciliation

Conciliation is an alternative out-of-court dispute resolution instrument. Like mediation, conciliation is a voluntary, flexible, confidential, and interest based process. The parties seek to reach an amicable dispute settlement with the assistance of the conciliator, who acts as a neutral third party. The main difference between conciliation and mediation proceedings is that, at some point during the conciliation, the conciliator will be asked by the parties to provide them with a non-binding settlement proposal. Mediators, by contrast, in most cases refrain from making such a proposal.

Main Benefits

Conciliation ensures party autonomy : The parties can choose the timing, language, place, structure and content of the conciliation proceedings.

Conciliation ensures the expertise of the deci-sion maker : The parties are free to select their conciliator. A conciliator does not have to have a specific professional background. A conciliator should be impartial and independent.

Conciliation is time and cost efficient : Due to the informal and flexible nature of conciliation proceedings, they can be conducted in a time and cost-efficient manner.

Conciliation ensures confidentiality : Disputes can be settled discretely and business secrets will remain confidential.

Lok Adalat

The Lok Adalat system constituted under National Legal Services Authority Act, 1987 is a uniquely Indian approach. It roughly means 'People's Court'. India has had a long history of resolving disputes through the mediation of village elders. The system of Lok Adalats is an improvement on that and is based on Gandhian principles. This is a non-adversarial system, where mock courts (called Lok Adalats) are held by the State Authority, District Authority, Supreme Court Legal Services Committee, High Court Legal Services Committee, or Taluk Legal Services Committee, periodically for exercising such jurisdiction as they think to be fit. These are usually presided by retired judges, social activists, or members of legal profession. It does not have jurisdiction on matters related to non-compoundable offences. There is no court fee and no rigid procedural requirement (i.e., no need to follow process given by Civil Procedure Code or Evidence Act), which makes the process very fast. Parties can directly interact with the judge, which is impossible in regular courts. Cases that are pending in regular courts can be transferred to a Lok Adalat if both the parties agree. A case can also be transferred to a Lok Adalat if one party applies to the court and the court sees some chance of settlement after giving an opportunity of being heard to the other party.

The Lok Adalat is presided over by a sitting or retired judicial officer as the chairman, with two other members, usually a lawyer and a social worker. The focus in Lok Adalats is on compromise. When no compromise is reached, the matter goes back to the court. However, if a compromise is reached, an award is made and is binding on the parties. It is enforced as a decree of a civil court. An important aspect of Lok Adalat is that the award is final and cannot be appealed, not even under Article 226 because it is a judgement by consent. All proceedings of a Lok Adalat are deemed to be judicial proceedings and every Lok Adalat is deemed to be a Civil Court. Lok Adalat, established by the government, settles dispute through conciliation and compromise. The First Lok Adalat was held in Chennai in 1986.

Advantages of Lok Adalat

Conciliated settlement : Lok Adalats are meant for conciliated settlement of disputes outside court which is what most of our people like if the matter allows for this kind of settlement. Government provides legal aids to poor, there is a fear of monetary loss during the time period which is why most people prefer Lok Adalats.

Solutions of family disputes : Family disputes like property acquisition and matrimonial issues are far better and faster solved by these Lok Adalats in comparison to courts. It saves time and expenses and also is easier for parties to make their claims which is

not the case when the matter is in court and witnesses are afraid of getting involved into legal matters.

Lesser pending cases : The number of cases that require jurisdiction is increasing at an alarming rate. We have far inadequate number of courts and judges in our country. If more and more people could understand the significance of Lok Adalats and resort to them for easy litigations, there would be lesser pending cases in the files gathering dust since years in courts.

Supplement to the work of courts : Lok Adalats can be a decent supplement to the work of courts and could contribute to justice in a good way only if awareness is increased and people are encouraged to opt for them.

Refundable expenses : Even if the case is filed in court, the expenses are refunded to the party when the case is solved by Lok Adalat which is another reason why people should be made more aware of this litigation system where there is no fee involved.

Less need of Advocates : There is no absolute need of advocates by the victim and the convict, who can either refer to have their cases pleaded by the lawyer or simply talk to the judge about the matter directly.

Ombudsman

The word 'Ombudsman' means delegate, officer or commissioner. The institution of Ombudsman exists in the Scandinavian countries. The office of the ombudsman originated in Sweden in 1809 AD, and adopted eventually by many nations as a bulwark of democratic government against the tyranny of officialdom. Ombudsman is a Swedish word that stands for an officer appointed by the legislature to handle complaints against administrative and judicial action. Traditionally the ombudsman is appointed based on unanimity among all political parties supporting the proposal. The incumbent, though appointed by the legislature, is an independent functionary-independent of all the three organs of the state, but reports to the legislature. The Ombudsman can act both on the basis of complaints made by citizens, or *suo moto*. It can look into allegations of corruption as well as mal-administration.

Powers and Duties

- He investigates into complaints made by citizens against abuse of discretionary power, malad-ministration or administrative inefficiency and takes appropriate actions. He has access to departmental files. The complainant is not required to lead any evidence before the Ombudsman to provide his case.

- It is the function and duty of the ombudsman to satisfy himself whether or not the complaint was justified.

- He can act *suo motu*.

- He can grant bail to the aggrieved person as unlike the powers of a civil court his power are limited.

LOKPAL AND LOKAYUKTA

The Indian Lokpal is synonymous to the institution of Ombudsman. The existing devices for checks on elected and administrative officials have not been effective, as the growing instances of corruption cases suggest. The Central Vigilance Commission (CVC) is designed to inquire into allegations of corruption by administrative officials only. The CBI, the premier investigating agency of the country, functions under the supervision of the Ministry of Personnel Public Grievances and Pensions (under the Prime Minister) and is therefore not immune from political pressures during investigation. Indeed, the lack of independence and professionalism of CBI has been castigated by the Supreme Court often in recent times. All these have necessitated the creation of Lokpal with its own investigating team in earliest possible occasion. Therefore, there is a need for a mechanism that would adopt very simple, independent, speedy and cheaper means of delivering justice by redressing the grievances of the people. Examples from various countries suggest that the institution of ombudsman has very successfully fought against corruption and unscrupulous administrative decisions by public servants, and acted as a real guardian of democracy and civil rights.

The Lokpal

The term 'Lokpal' was coined by Dr. L. M. Singhvi in 1963. In early 1960s, mounting corruption in public administration set the winds blowing in favour of an Ombudsman in India too. The Administrative Reforms Commission (ARC) set up in 1966 recommended the constitution of a two-tier machinery of a Lokpal at the Centre and Lokayukts in the states. The ARC while recommending the constitution of Lokpal was convinced that such an institution was justified not only for removing the sense of injustice from the minds of adversely affected citizens but also necessary to instill public confidence in the efficiency of administrative machinery. Following this, the Lokpal Bill was for the first time presented during the fourth Lok Sabha in 1968, and was passed there in 1969. However, while it was pending in the Rajya Sabha, the Lok Sabha was dissolved, resulting the first death of the bill. The bill was revived in 1971, 1977, 1985, 1989, 1996, 1998, 2001, 2004 and finally in 2011. In 2013, The Lokpal and Lokayuktas Act, 2013 was passed in 2013 and came into force from 16th January, 2014. The first Lokpal of India is Pinaki Chandra Ghose, retired Supreme Court Judge. He was appointed on 17 March 2019.

As per the Act, the Lokpal shall consist of :

- A chairperson who has been a Chief Justice of India or is or has been a Judge of 2 the Supreme Court or is an eminent judicial member of impeccable integrity and outstanding ability having special knowledge and expertise of not less than 25 years in matters relating to anti-corruption policy, public administration, vigilance or finance.

- The total members of Lokpal shall not exceed 8, out of whom 50% shall be the Judicial Members.

Under this Act, the bribery and corruption of charges against public-servants would be dealt with. The Act applies to the public servants in and outside India. The public servants include under the purview of Lokpal are :

- The current and ex-prime ministers of India (except in matters pertaining to international relations, external and internal security, public order, atomic energy and space

- Any person who is or has been a Minister of the Union and any person who is or has been a Member of either House of Parliament

- Includes any Group 'A', 'B','C' or 'D' official or equivalent from amongst the public servants defined in the Prevention of Corruption Act, 1988 when serving or who has served in connection with the affairs of the Union.

The enquiry shall be held in camera. If the Lokpal comes to the conclusion that the complaint should be dismissed, then the records of the inquiry shall not be published or made available to anyone. The Lokpal shall deal with allegation of corruption, declaration of assets by public-servants etc.

The Act has directed the States to institute Lokayuktas within one year of from the date of the commencement of The Lokpal and Lokayuktas Act, 2013. Odisha, Maharashtra, Delhi, Gujarat, Kerala, Andhra Pradesh, Karnataka, etc had Lokayuktas even before the enactment of the 2013 Act.

Summary

Adversial System–In an adversarial system, the parties in a legal proceeding develop their own theory of the case and gather evidence to support their claims. The parties are assisted by their lawyers who take a pro-active role in delivering justice to the litigants. The lawyers gather evidence and even participate in cross-examination and scrutiny of evidence presented by the other disputing party. The role of the judge/decision maker is rather passive as the judge decides the claims based solely on the evidences and arguments presented by the parties and their lawyers.

Advantages of Adversial System–The use of cross-examination can be an effective way to test the credibility of witnesses presented.

The parties may be more willing to accept the results when they are given effective control over the process.

Disadvantages of Adversarial System–The role of lawyers and the procedural formalities, e.g. cross-examination may 2 prolong the trial and lead to delays in several matters.

Judges play less active role, a judge is not duty bound to ascertain the truth but 2 only to evaluate the matter based on the evidences presented before him/her.

Inquisitorial System–In an inquisitorial system, the judge/decision maker takes a centre-stage in dispensing justice. The role of the judge/decision maker is active as he/she determines the facts and issues in dispute. The judge/decision maker also decides the manner in which the evidence must be presented before the court.

Advantages of Inquisitorial System–The system offers procedural efficiency as the active role of judges prevents 2 delays and prolonged trials.

The system preserves equality between the parties as even the stronger party 2 with more resources and expert lawyers may not be able to influence the judges.

The disadvantages of this model include :

- The judge is less impartial
- Judge is aware of character reports and past records.

Alternative Dispute Resolution (ADR)–Any method of resolving disputes other than by litigation. Abbreviated as ADR. Public courts may be asked to review the validity of ADR methods, but they will rarely overturn ADR decisions and awards if the disputing parties formed a valid contract to abide by them. Arbitration and mediation are the two major forms of ADR.

Need of ADR in India–The system of dispensing justice in India has come under great stress for several reasons mainly because of the huge pendency of cases in courts. In India, the number of cases filed in the courts has shown a tremendous increase years resulting in pendency and delays underlining the need for alternative dispute resolution methods.

Advantages of Alternate Dispute Resolution–The parties are free to discuss their difference of opinion without any fear of disclosure of this fact before any law courts.

- It is less time consuming.
- It is free from technicalities as in the case of conducting cases in law crouts.

Arbitration–Arbitration is a private arrangement of taking disputes to a less adversarial, less formal and more flexible forum and abiding by judgment of a selected person instead of carrying it to the established courts of justice.

Types of Arbitration–Domestic, foreign, Ad hoc, Instituional, Statutory and Internatioanal. These are the types of arbitration.

Administrative Tribunals–An administrative tribunal is an autonomous agency that is independent of the provincial government and is responsible for settling disputes between the Province of Ontario and its citizens. An administrative tribunal is also known as an agency, board or commission.

Mediation–Mediation is a method of ADR in which parties appoint a neutral third party who facilitates the mediation process in-order to assist the parties in achieving an acceptable, voluntary agreement. Mediation is premised on the voluntary will of the parties and is a flexible and informal technique of dispute resolution.

Types of Mediation–Evaluation, faciliating, transformative, mediation with arbitration and online mediation.

Conciliation–Conciliation is a process similar to mediation as parties out of their own free will appoint a neutral third party to resolve their disputes.

Lok Adalat–The institution of Lok Adalat in India, as the very name suggests, means, People's Court. 'Lok' stands for 'people' and the vernacular meaning of the term 'Adalat' is the court. India has a long tradition and history of such methods being practiced in the society at grass roots level. These are called panchayat and in the legal terminology, these are called arbitration.

The Benefits of Lok Adalat include :

- There is no court fee and even if the case is already filed in the regular court,
- The fee paid will be refunded if the dispute is settled at the Lok Adalat.
- There is no strict appliation of the procedural laws and the disputing parties can directly interact with the judges.
- The decision of Lok Adalat is binding on the parties and its order is capable of execution through legal process.

Ombudsman–An ombudsman or public advocate is usually appointed by the government or by parliament, but with a significant degree of independence, who is charged with representing the interests of the public by investigating and addressing complaints of maladministration or a violation of rights.

Lokpal–It is an anti-corruption authority or ombudsman who represents the public interest. The Lokpal has jurisdiction over all Members of Parliament and central government employees in cases of corruption. The Lokpal and Lokayuktas Act was passed in 2013 with amendments in parliament, following the Jan Lokpal movement led by Anna Hazare. The Lokpal is responsible for enquiring into corruption charges at the national level while the Lokayukta performs the same function at the state level.

Lokayuktas–The Lokayukta (appointed by the people) is a similar anti-corruption ombudsman organisation in the Indian states.

Multiple Choice of Questions

1. The term .... dispute resolution refers to the resolution of legal disputes through methods other than litigation, such as negotiation, mediation, arbitration, summary jury trials, mini-trials, neutral case evaluations and private trials.

    (a) Alternating   (b) Alternative

    (c) Qualified   (d) Quasi- judicial

2. In .... negotiation, each party seeks to maximize its own gain, while in .... negotiation, the parties seek joint gain.

    (a) Arbitrated; mediated

    (b) Mediated; arbitrated

    (c) Adversarial; problem-solving

    (d) Problem-solving; adversarial

3. Arbitration :

    (a) Involves the resolution of a dispute, by a neutral third party, outside the judicial setting

    (b) Is costlier and more time-consuming than mediation

    (c) Is costlier and more time-consuming than litigation

    (d) Is an specialized form of mediation

4. All of the following are advantages of arbitration except :

    (a) Arbitration is more efficient, although more expensive, than litigation.

    (b) Parties have more control over the process of dispute resolution through arbitration.

    (c) The parties can choose someone to serve as the arbitrator who has expertise in the specific subject matter of the dispute.

    (d) All of the above are advantages of arbitration.

5. In a binding arbitration clause :

    (a) A contractual provision gives the parties the opportunity to select arbitration, mediation, or litigation as the method of dispute resolution.

    (b) The losing party must be handcuffed and led out of the arbitration room, and immediately begin serving an arbitrator-imposed term of imprisonment.

    (c) A contractual provision mandates that all disputes arising under the contract must be settled by arbitration.

    (d) None of the above

6. What does ADR actually stand for ?

    (a) Alternative desperate resolution

    (b) Alternative dispite resolution

    (c) Alternative dispute resolution

7. What is the role of an arbitrated ?

    (a) Sit and talk

    (b) Acts like a judge

    (c) Acts like a jury

    (d) Acts like a police officer

8. Which of these statements is most accurate ?

    (a) Tribunals are superior to courts

    (b) Tribunals are equal to courts

    (c) Tribunals are inferior to courts

(d) Tribunals are completely different to courts in terms of their functions

9. What does an Ombudsman investigate ?

    (a) Complaints of maladministration

    (b) Allegations of political corruption

    (c) Complaints about judges' personal conduct

    (d) Both (b) and (c)

10. What is the role of the third party in conciliation ?

    (a) To make a decision on the facts of the matter

    (b) To suggest appropriate solutions

    (c) To act as judge

    (d) To tell each side what to argue

Long Answer Questions

1. What is Adversarial and Inquisitorial System ?

2. What are advantages and disadvantage of Adversarial and Inquisitorial System ?

3. What is arbitration ? Explain in detail the types and the procedure.

Short Answer Questions

1. What are administrative tribunals ?

2. How can one be sure mediation will produce a fair result ?

3. Are there some cases that should not be mediated ?

4. What kinds of cases can be mediated ?

5. How long does mediation take ?

6. What is conciliation ?

7. How is conciliation different from Mediation ?

8. What are the benefits of Arbitration ?

9. Write short notes :

    (a) Lokpal

    (b) Lokayuktas

    (c) Ombudman

Board Questions

1. Nitin, aged 15 years, agreed to sell his cottage for ₹10,00,000 to Mayank, aged 20 years. However, the market value of the cottage at the time of sale was ₹ 20,00,000. Nitin afterwards avoided the agreement of sale by saying that, he is a minor and a case was also pending before the court regarding the title of the cottage, at the time of sale. They both appointed Ms. Kriti (a mediator) for the settlement of their dispute. In this context, which one of the following is correct ?

    (a) The above dispute can be referred to a mediator, as contractual disputes are most suited for mediation.

    (b) The above dispute cannot be referred for mediation as case against specific classes of persons (minors, mentally challenged) have been excluded from the scope of mediation.

    (c) The above dispute cannot be referred for mediation as the consideration was not adequate and hence contact is void ab initio.

    (d) The above dispute can be referred to mediation, as property disputes are most suited for mediation.

2. When can a dispute be referred to Lok Adalat ? State any two powers of Lok Adalats.

3. A dispute arose between Kerry & Claire Co., a Netherland based Cosmetic Co. and Star Heaven Co., an Indian cosmetic company regarding money transactions. The parties to the dispute appointed Mr. Harry, a neutral third party, for settlement for their dispute. Mr. Harry acted as a guardian of the dispute resolution process and was focused on helping the parties to find solution to their dispute but failed to bring the parties to settlement. The disputing parties then approached an institution named Roger's Organisation for the settlement of their dispute. The Roger's Organisation appointed Mr. Jeff (Financial Transactions expert) to resolve the said dispute.

    (a) State the two types of Alternate Dispute Resolution Mechanism in the above situation.

4. Yashu, a student from Chandigarh, had approached Moon Life Insurance Company to get a policy that catered to the requirements of his admission to a University in U.S.A. for further studies. He paid a premium amount of ₹ 1 lakh and left for U.S.A. On reaching U.S.A., he realized that the policy that he is holding in his hands is worthless, as it is not recognized by the University. Moon Life Insurance Company in spirit of selling an insurance policy withheld crucial information that their policy is not valid overseas.

    (a) Identify the 'Ombudsman' with in India to investigate and resolve complaints related to Insurance and banking.

    (b) Can Yashu approach this Ombudsman as Moon Life Insurance is a private company ? Give reasons for your answer.

    (c) What method of dispute resolution is followed by the Ombudsman ?

    (d) Give one advantage and one limitation of an Ombudsman in India.

NCERT Questions

1. True & False
   (i) The adversarial system of adjudication is interventionist in nature.
   (ii) The judge/decision maker assumes a police-like role in an inquisitorial model.
   (iii) Judges may be more influenced by parties in an adversarial rather than an inquisitorial system of adjudication.
2. What is arbitration ? Describe its types.
3. Define the following terms :
   arbitration agreement; enforcement of arbitral award; setting aside of arbitral award.
4. Define Mediation. What are its types ?
5. What are the key differences between mediation and conciliation ?
6. What are the different ways in which mediation can be triggered in a given dispute/legal claim ?

Essay Type Questions

1. Discuss the advantages and disadvantages of the two models of adjudication within a legal system? Which model do you favour ? Explain with reasons.
2. What are the advantages of ADR over traditional forms of dispute resolution ? Discuss the similarities and differences between arbitration and litigation.
3. Compare and Contrast the processes of Arbitration, Mediation and Conciliation. Highlight the salient similarities and differences amongst them. Which ADR method appeals to you the most- Explain with reasons ?
4. What is the meaning of Ombudsman ? Can you identify equivalent institutions within India ? Discuss their roles and limitations.
5. Trace the progress and development of the contemporary Lokpal movement in India

Sample Questions

1. Rahul is facilitating an alternative dispute resolution in which parties appoint a neutral third party who facilitates the parties in achieving an acceptable, voluntary agreement, which is more formal than negotiation. What is Rahul facilitating ?
   (a) Arbitration
   (b) Mediation
   (c) Conciliation
   (d) Administrative Tribunal
2. Kapoor's and Bedi's are neighbours living on the first and second floor of ABCL Apartments. The issue between the two is that the water from the kitchen area of Bedi's seeps through and the wall of Kapoor's kitchen is drenching. The electric gadgets are fitted on that wall and it leads to electric shock. Kapoor's have been trying to draw the attention of Bedis to this problem. How can this issue between the two be resolved ?
3. Who is an Ombudsman? Identify the Ombudsman in India that brings the Members of Parliament, Union ministers and even the Prime Minister in its preview.
4. A frustrated judge in an English court finally asked a barrister after witnesses had produced conflicting accounts,' Am I never to hear the truth? 'No, my lord, merely the evidence', replied counsel. To which judicial system does this judge belong? What is his role in such a system ? Give two disadvantages of this system.
5. What is meant by Arbitration ? What is the procedure followed for administering justice by this mechanism ? Distinguish between foreign arbitration and International commercial arbitration.

❏❏

8

Human Rights

INTRODUCTION

Rights can be political, social and other advantages to which one has a just claim, morally or legally. Human rights are fundamental to the stability and development of countries all around the world. Human rights are the basic rights and freedom that belong to every person in the world from birth until death. They apply regardless of where you are from, what you believe or how you choose to live your life. They can never be taken away, although they can sometimes be restricted – for example if a person breaks the law, or in the interests of national security. These basic rights are based on values like dignity, fairness, equality, respect and independence. But human rights are not just abstract concepts – they are defined and protected by law. In Britain human rights are protected by the Human Rights Act 1998. The Hindu Vedas, the Babylonian Code of Hammurabi, the Bible, the Quran (Koran) and the Analects of Confucius are five of the oldest written sources which address questions of people's duties, rights and responsibilities. Human rights are relevant to all of us, not just those who face repression or mistreatment. The idea that human beings should have a set of basic rights and freedoms has deep roots in Britain. Landmark developments in Britain and USA include :

- the Magna Carta of 1215
- the Habeas Corpus Act of 1679
- the Bill of Rights of 1689
- the US Constitution (1787)
- the French Declaration of the Rights of Man and of the Citizen (1789)
- the US Bill of Rights (1791)

These documents are precursors of today's Human rights documents. The atrocities of the Second World War made the protection of human rights an international priority. The formation of the United Nations paved the way for more than 50 Member States to contribute to the final draft of the Universal Declaration of Human Rights, adopted in 1948. This was the first attempt to set out at a global level the fundamental rights and freedoms shared by all human beings. The Declaration formed the basis for the European Convention on Human Rights, adopted in 1950. It protects the human rights of people in countries that belong to the Council of Europe including the UK. The Human Rights Act 1998 made these right a part of our domestic law.

Magna Carta 1215

- In 1215, abuses by King John caused a revolt by nobles who compelled him to execute this recognition of rights for both noblemen and ordinary Englishmen.
- It established the principle that no one, including the king or a lawmaker, is above the law.
- Other rights include the right of the church to be free from governmental interference, the rights of all free citizens to own and inherit property and to be protected from excessive taxes.
- It established the right of widows who owned property to choose not to remarry, and established principles of due process and equality before the law.
- It also contained provisions forbidding bribery and official misconduct.
- Widely viewed as one of the most important legal documents in the development of modern democracy, the Magna Carta was a crucial turning point in the struggle to establish freedom.

The Bill of Rights (1689)

- The bill has framed the civil and constitutional rights to the people of England.
- It has given the Parliament more powers than monarch. It limits the power of kings and queens in England.
- It ensures democratic election.
- It creates separation of power.
- It paves the way for freedom of speech.

United States Declaration of Independence (1776)

- In 1776, Thomas Jefferson penned the American Declaration of Independence. On July 4, 1776, the

United States Congress approved the Declaration of Independence.

- The Declaration declared USA independence from Great Britain and announced that the thirteen American Colonies were no longer a part of the British Empire.

- Philosophically, the Declaration stressed two themes: individual rights and the right of revolution.

Declaration of the Rights of Man and of the Citizen (1789)

- In 1789, the people of France brought about the abolishment of the absolute monarchy and set the stage for the establishment of the first French Republic.

- The Declaration of the Rights of Man and of the Citizen (French: La D'claration des Droits de l'Homme et du Citoyen) was adopted by the National Constituent Assembly as the first step towards writing a constitution for the Republic of France.

- The Declaration proclaims that all citizens are to be guaranteed the rights of "liberty, property, security, and resistance to oppression".

- It argues that the need for law derives from the fact that "...the exercise of the natural rights of each man has only those borders which assure other members of the society the enjoyment of these rights".

- Thus, the Declaration sees law as an "expression of the general will, intended to promote the equality of rights and to forbid only actions harmful to the society".

The Universal Declaration of Human Rights (1948)

After bitter experience of two world wars human race become conscious to protect their right as the only means to save their identity. Under the dynamic chairmanship of Eleanor Roosevelt–President Franklin Roosevelt's widow, a human rights champion in her own right and the United States delegate to the UN– the Commission set out to draft the document that became the Universal Declaration of Human Rights.

- It was adopted by the United Nations on December 10, 1948.

- In its preamble it states that the recognition of the inherent dignity and of the equal and inalienable rights of all member of the human family is the foundation of freedom, justice and peace in the world.

- In Article 1, the Declaration unequivocally proclaims the inherent rights of all human beings as all human beings are born free and equal in dignity and rights.

- Universal Declaration of Human Rights consists of 30 Articles dealing with fundamental commitment for the protection of human rights.

- The Member States of the United Nations pledged to work together to promote the thirty Articles of human rights that, for the first time in history, had been assembled and codified into a single document.

Other international treaties :

- **Convention Relating to the Status of Refugees, 1954**

  The convention has granted several rights to refugees like non-discrimination, right to religion, access to courts, employment, rationing and housing, etc.

- **International Covenant on Civil and Political Rights, 1976 and International Covenant on Economic, Social and Cultural Rights, 1976**

  Both these conventions have granted the right of self-determination to every human being. The people can freely determine their political status and freely pursue their economic, social and cultural development.

- **Convention on the Elimination of All Forms of Discrimination Against Women, 1979**

  This Convention tries to bring the women into the focus of human rights concerns. Under Article 3, the Convention urges the States parties to take "all appropriate measures, including legislation, to ensure the full development and advancement of women, for the purpose of guaranteeing them the exercise and enjoyment of human rights and fundamental freedoms on a basis of equality with men."

- **Convention on the Rights of the Child, 1990**

  The convention has guaranteed special care, protection, assistance and development of all the children (below 18 years old) without any sort of discrimination such as race, colour, sex, language, religion, political or other opinion, national or social origin, property, birth or other status.

CONSTITUTIONAL FRAMEWORK AND RELATED LAWS IN INDIA

The Constitution of the Republic of India which came into force on 26th January, 1950 with 395 Articles and 8 Schedules is one of the most elaborate fundamental laws ever adopted.

- The Preamble to the Constitution declares India to be a Sovereign, Socialist, Secular and Democratic Republic.

- Sovereignty denotes that India is a free country and can take decisions on its own. It does not depend on any foreign country for making rules and regulations.

- The term 'democratic' denotes that the government gets its authority from the will of the people.

- Republic means there is no hereditary monarch of the country. The head of the country is selected by the people.

- Secularism means that India has no recognised religion as the religion of the State.

- Socialism here used in the means that production in the country is controlled wholly or partially by the government.

- Preamble also gives a feeling that all are equal "irrespective of the race, religion, language, sex and culture".

- The Preamble to the Constitution pledges justice, social, economic and political, liberty of thought, expression, belief, faith and worship, equality of status and of opportunity and fraternity assuring the dignity of the individual and the unity and integrity of the nation to all its citizens.

FUNDAMENTAL RIGHTS AND HUMAN RIGHTS

Introduction

Part-III of the Indian constitution from article 12 to 32 contains fundamental rights. Part-III of the Indian constitution is called corner stone of the constitution and together with Part-4 (directive principles and state policy) constitutes the conscience of the Constitution. This chapter of the Constitution has been described as the Magna Carta of India. Fundamental Rights are individual rights are enforced against the arbitrary invasion by the state except, in case of Article 15 (2), Article 17, Article 18(3-4), Article 23 and Article 24 where these can be enforced against private individuals also.

Fundamental rights are not absolute rights and parliament could put reasonable restriction. The grounds for the restriction may be advancement of SCs, STs, OBCs, women and children, general public order; decency, mortality, sovereignity and integrity of India; security of state, friendly relations with foreign sates, etc.

According to Article 12 'the state' includes

- Government and Parliament of India

- Government and Legislature of States

- All local or state authorities such as municipalities, panchayats, district boards, improvement trusts, etc. within the territory of India or under the control of Government of India.

Classification of Fundamental Rights

Originally Constitution provided for seven Fundamental Rights viz.

- Right to equality (Article 14-18)
- Right to freedom (Article 19-22)
- Right against exploitation (Article 23-24)
- Right to freedom of religion (Articles 25-28)
- Cultural and educational rights (Articles 29-30)
- Right to Property (Article 31)
- Right to Constitutional remedies (Article 32)

But, Right to property was removed from the list of the Fundamental Rights by the 44th Constitution amendment Act, 1978 and after amendment, it was made legal right under article 300-A in part-12 of the constitution.

➢ **Right to Equality (Articles 14-18)**

Article 14 (Equality before law)

- Article 14 says that state shall not deny to any person equality before the law or the equal protection of the laws within the territory of India.

- Article 14 is available to any person including legal persons viz. statutory corporation, companies, etc.

- Article 14 is taken from the concept of equal protection of laws has been taken from the constitution of USA.

- The concept of rule of law is a negative concept while the concept of equal protection of laws is a positive concept.

- The concept of equality before law is equivalent to the second element of the concept of the 'rule of law' propounded by A.V. Dicey, the British jurist. But certain exceptions to it are, the President of India, State Governors, Public servants, Judges, Foreign diplomats, etc., who enjoy immunities, protections and special privileges.

Article 15 (Prohibition of discrimination on grounds of religion,race,caste,sex or place of birth)

- Article 15 says that the state shall not discriminate against only of religion, race, sex, place of birth or any of them.

- Under article 15 (3) and (4), government can make special provisions for women and children and for group of citizens who are economically and socially backward.

Article 16 (Equality of opportunities in matters of public employment)

- Article 16 says that there shall be equality of opportunity for all citizens in matters relating to employment or appointment to any office under the state.

Article 17 (Abolition of Untouchability)

- Article 17 says that untouchability is abolished and its practice in any form is forbidden. The enforcement of any disability arising out of untouchability shall be an offence punishable in accordance with law.

Article 18 (Abolition of titles)

- Article 18 says that no title, not being a military or academic distinction, shall be conferred by the State.
- No citizen of India shall accept any title from any foreign state.
- The awards, Bharat Ratna, Padma Vibhuhan, Padma Bhusan and Padma Shri called as The National Awards would not amount to title within the meaning of Article 18(i).

➤ **Right to Freedom (Articles 19-22)**

Article 19 (Protection of certain rights regarding freedom of speech, etc.)

  Article 19 says that all citizens shall have the right to freedom of speech and expression
- to assemble peacefully and without arms.
- to form associations or unions.
- to move freely throughout the territory of India.
- to practice any profession or to carry on any occupation, trade or business.

Article 20 (Protection in respect of conviction for offences)

- Article 20 says that state can impose reasonable restrictions on the groups of security of the state, friendly relations with foreign states, public order, decency, morality, contempt of court, defamation etc.

Article 21 deals with protection of life and personal liberty.

- Article 21A states that that state shall provide free and compulsory education to all children of the age of 6-14 years.

Article 22 deals with protection against arrest and detention in certain cases.

➤ **Right against Exploitation (Articles 23-24)**
- Article 23 deals with the prohibition of traffic in human beings and forced labour.
- Article 24 deals with prohibition of employment of children in factories, etc.

➤ **Right to Freedom of Religion (Articles 25-28)**
- Article 25 deals with freedom of conscience and free profession, practice and propagation of religion.
- Article 26 deals with freedom to manage religious affairs.
- Article 27 deals with freedom as to payment to taxes for promotion of any particular religion.
- Article 28 deals with freedom as to attendance at religious instructions or religious worship in certain educational institutions.

➤ **Cultural and Educational Rights (Articles 29-30)**
- Article 29 deals with the protection of language, script and culture of minorities.
- Article 30 deals with the right of minorities to establish and administer educational institutions.

➤ **Right to Constitutional Remedies (Article 32)**
- Article 32 deals with the right to move to the Supreme Court for the enforcement of Fundamental Rights including the Writs of (i) Habeas corpus, (ii) Mandamus, (iii) Prohibition, (iv) Certiorari and (iv) Quo warranto.

Directive Principles of State Policy and Human Rights

  Part IV, Articles 36-51 of the Indian constitution constitutes the Directive Principles of State Policy which contain the broad directives or guidelines to be followed by the State while establishing policies and laws.

- The legislative and executive powers of the state are to be exercised under the purview of the Directive Principles of the Indian Constitution.
- The Indian Constitution was written immediately after India obtained freedom and the contributors to the Constitution were well aware of the ruined state of the Indian economy as well as the fragile state of the nation's unity. Thus they created a set of guidelines under the heading Directive Principles for an inclusive development of the society.
- Inspired by the Constitution of Ireland, the Directive Principles contain the very basic philosophy of the Constitution of India and that is the overall development of the nation through

guidelines related to social justice, economic welfare, foreign policy and legal and administrative matters.

- The Directive Principles are codified versions of democratic socialist order as conceived by Nehru with an admixture of Gandhian thought.

- However, the Directive Principles cannot be enforced in a court of law and the State cannot be sued for non-compliance of the same. This indeed makes the Directive Principles a very interesting and enchanting part of the Constitution because while it does stand for the ideals of the nation, these ideals have not been made mandatory.

Directive Principles consist of the following guidelines for the States :

- The State should strive to promote the welfare of the people.
- Maintain social order through social, economic and political justice.
- The State should strive towards removing economic inequality.
- Removal of inequality in status and opportunities.
- To secure adequate means of livelihood for the citizens.
- Equal work opportunity for both men and women.
- Prevent concentration of wealth in specific pockets through uniform distribution of the material resources amongst all the strata of the society.
- Prevention of child abuse and exploitation of workers.
- Protection of children against moral and material abandonment.
- Free legal advice for equal opportunities to avail of justice by the economically weaker section.
- Organisation of Village Panchayats which will work as an autonomous body working towards giving justice.
- Assistance to the needy including the unemployed, sick, disabled and old people
- Ensure proper working conditions and a living wage.
- Promotion of cottage industries in rural areas.
- The state should endeavour towards a uniform civil code for all the citizens of India.
- Free and compulsory education for children below the age of 14 years.
- Economic and educational upliftment of the SC and ST and other weaker sections of the society.

- Prohibition of alcoholic drinks, recreational drugs and cow slaughter.
- Preservation of the environment by safeguarding the forests and the wild life.
- Protection of monuments, places and objects of historic and artistic interest and national importance against destruction and damage.
- Promotion and maintenance of international peace and security, just and honourable relations between nations, respect for international law and treaty obligations, as well as settlement of international disputes by arbitration.

Fundamental Duties and Human Rights

Part IV (A) of the Constitution embodies the Eleven Fundamental Duties of every Indian citizen (Article 51-A). These are :

- To respect the Constitution and its institutions.
- To live by the noble ideals of the freedom struggle.
- To protect the sovereignty and integrity of India.
- To defend the country, to promote communal harmony.
- To renounce practices derogatory to the dignity of women.
- To preserve the cultural heritage.
- To protect and improve the natural environment.
- To have compassion for living creatures.
- To develop the scientific temper.
- To safeguard public property.
- To abjure violence.
- And to strive towards excellence in all spheres of individual and collective activity.

The Eighty sixth Constitutional Amendment 2002 inserted a new clause (k) in Article 51(A) instructing "a parent or guardian to provide opportunities for education to his child or as the case may be, ward between the ages of 6 and 14 years,

COMPLAINT MECHANISMS OF QUASI-JUDICIAL BODIES

National Human Rights Commission

The most important development in India is the creation of the National Human Rights Commission (NHRC) on 29th September, 1993 as the result of an ordinance promulgated by the President. Subsequently in the following year, the act of the Parliament provided this body a statutory status. Currently, H.L Dattu is the Chairperson of NHRC.

Composition

The National Human Rights Commission (NHRC) is consisting of a chairperson and seven other members. Out of the seven members, three are *ex officio* members and four others are appointed by the President on the recommendation of a Selection Committee. The Committee is consisting of the Prime Minister who is the chairman of this Committee, Union Home Minister, Deputy Chairman of the Rajya Sabha, Speaker of the Lok Sabha and the Leaders of the Opposition in both the Houses of Parliament.

The members of the NHRC are as follows :

- The Chairperson is a retired Chief Justice of the Supreme Court.
- One member is either a working or a retired judge of the Supreme Court.
- One member is either a working or a retired Chief Justice or a judge of a High Court.
- Two persons having knowledge or practical experience in matters relating to Human Rights.
- Besides them, the Chairpersons of the National Commission for Scheduled Castes and Scheduled Tribes, National Commission for Minorities and National Commission for Women shall be its *ex officio* members.

Tenure

The Chairperson and the members of the NHRC have a tenure of five years. But if any member attains the age of 70 years before the completion of his tenure, he or she has to retire from the membership.

Removal

The Chairperson or any other member of this commission can be removed by the President even before the expiry of their full term. They can be removed only on the charge of proved misbehavior or incapacity or both, if it is proved by an inquiry conducted by a judge of the Supreme Court.

Powers and Functions

The NHRC has the following functions :

(i) To investigate complaints regarding the violation of human rights either suo moto on its own motus or after receiving a petition.

(ii) To investigate the failure of duties on the part of any public official in preventing the violation of human rights.

(iii) To intervene in any judicial proceedings involving any allegation of violation of human rights.

(iv) To visit any jail or any other institution under the control of the State Government to see the living conditions of the inmates and to make recommendations thereon.

(v) To review the safeguards provided under the constitution or any law for the protection of the human rights and to recommend appropriate remedial measures.

(vi) To study treaties and other international instruments on human rights and to make recommendations for their effective implementation.

(vii) To undertake and promote research in the field of human rights.

(viii) To encourage the efforts of the non-governmental organisations working in the field of human rights.

(ix) To spread human rights literacy among various sections of society and to promote awareness of the safeguards available for the protection of these rights through publications, media, seminars and other means.

(x) To review all facts related to the activities of the terrorists which obstruct the way of the protection of human rights and to make recommendations for their effective implementation.

Complaint Mechanism

While making an inquiry into the complaints submitted to it, the commission enjoys the powers of a civil court. It can recommend to both the central and state governments to take appropriate steps to prevent the violation of human rights. It submits its annual report to the President of India who causes it to be laid before each House of Parliament. It usually sends a copy of the inquiry report to the petitioner and also to the concerned government. The government may be asked to inform it about the action taken or proposed to be taken on the concerned complaints. The Protection of Human Rights Act, 1993, empowered the State Governments to set up their own commission for such a purpose. The chairman and the members of such State Commission are appointed by the Governor in consultation with the Chief Minister, Home Minister, Speaker and Leader of the Opposition in the State Legislative Assembly. The National Human Rights Commission, so far in India has successfully demonstrated its willingness to act as an effective organisation in the protection of human rights.

Guidelines on How to File Complaint with the NHRC

(i) Complaint may be made to the Commission by the victim or any other person on his behalf.

(ii) Complaint should be in writing either in English or Hindi or in any other language included in the eighth schedule of the Constitution. Only one set of complaint needs to be submitted to the Commission.

(iii) Complaint may be sent either by Post or Faxed at Nos. 91-11-23382911/23382734 or through email covdnhrc@nic.in

(iv) No fee is chargeable on such complaints.

(v) The complaint shall disclose (i) violation of human rights or abetment thereof or; (ii) negligence in the prevention of such violations, by a public servant.

(vi) The jurisdiction of the Commission is restricted to the violation of human rights alleged to have been committed within one year of the receipt of complaint by the Commission.

(vii) Documents, if any enclosed in support of the allegations in the complaint must be legible.

(viii) Name of the victim, his/her age, sex, religion/caste, State and District to which the incident relates, incident date etc. should invariably be mentioned in the complaint.

(ix) Please submit the complaint preferably in the enclosed format.

(x) Following types of Complaint(s) are not ordinarily entertained:

● Illegible

● Vague, anonymous or pseudonymous;

● Trivial or frivolous in nature;

● The matters which are pending before a State Human Rights Commission or any other Commission;

● Any matter after the expiry of one year from the date on which the act constituting violation of human rights is alleged to have been committed;

● Allegation is not against any public servant;

● The issue raised relates to civil dispute, such property rights, contractual obligations, etc;

● The issue raised relates to service matters;

● The issue raised relates to labour/industrial disputes;

● Allegations do not make out any specific violation of human rights;

● The matter is sub-judice before a Court/Tribunal;

● The matter is covered by judicial verdict/decision of the Commission.

(xi) As far as possible complainants are encouraged to make use of the format given above to file their complaints. The guidelines indicate the kind of information, which would facilitate in processing a complaint.

The NHRC has been accredited with 'A status' by the International Coordinating Committee of National Human Rights Institutions (the ICC), indicating that it is in conformity with the Paris Principles – a broad set of principles agreed upon by a conference of experts on the promotion and protection of human rights, in Paris in October 1991, and subsequently endorsed by the UN General Assembly. The Commission is thus entitled to participate in the ICC and in its regional sub-group, the Asia Pacific Forum, and may take part in certain sessions of the UN human rights committees.

NATIONAL COMMISSION FOR MINORITIES

The Union Government set up the National Commission for Minorities (NCM) under the National Commission for Minorities Act, 1992. Six religious communities, viz; Muslims, Christians, Sikhs, Buddhists, Zoroastrians (Parsis) and Jains have been notified as minority communities by the Union Government. Shri Syed Ghayorul Hasan Rizvi is currently Chairperson, National Commission for Minorities.

Functions :

The Commission has the following functions :

(i) Evaluate the progress of the development of minorities under the Union and States.

(ii) Monitor the working of the safeguards provided in the Constitution and laws enacted by Parliament and the State Legislatures.

(iii) Make recommendations for the effective implementation of safeguards for the protection of the interests of minorities by the Central Government or the State Governments.

(iv) Look into specific complaints regarding deprivation of rights and safeguards of the minorities and take up such matters with the appropriate authorities.

(v) Case studies to be undertaken into problems arising out of any discrimination against minorities and recommend measures for their removal.

(vi) Conduct studies, research and analysis on the issues relating to socio-economic and educational development of minorities.

(vii) Suggest appropriate measures in respect of any Minority to be undertaken by the Central Government or the State Governments.

(viii) Make periodical or special reports to the Central Government on any matter pertaining to minorities and in particular the difficulties confronted by them.

(ix) Any other matter which may be referred to it by the Central Government.

The Commission has the following Powers :

(i) Summoning and enforcing the attendance of any person from any part of India and examining him on oath.

(ii) Requiring the discovery and production of any document.

(iii) Receiving evidence on affidavit.

(iv) Requisitioning any public record or copy thereof from any court or office.

(v) Issuing commissions for the examination of witnesses and documents.

Composition of Commission

The Commission shall consist of a Chairperson, a Vice Chairperson and five Members to be nominated by the Central Government from amongst persons of eminence, ability and integrity; provided that five Members including the Chairperson shall be from amongst the minority communities.

Complaint Mechanisms

There are many grounds on which the commission typically declines admitting the complaint :

- Firstly, it does not entertain or admit cases or complaints that do not relate to minority status or rights.

- Secondly, the complaint should not be pending before another court or commission, i.e., matters that are sub judice.

- Thirdly, where the complainant has not availed of other ordinary judicial/quasi-judicial/administrative institutions that are available for redressal, the commission does not admit such matters unless the complainant has reasonable justification.

- Fourthly, the complaint should not relate to events that are more than one-year old.

- Fifthly, complaint should not be vague, anonymous, pseudonymous or frivolous.

- Lastly, commission does not entertain complaints that are not directly addressed to it.

NATIONAL COMMISSION FOR WOMAN

Introduction

The National Commission for Women was set up as statutory body in January 1992 under the National Commission for Women Act, 1990 (Act No. 20 of 1990 of Govt.of India) to :

- review the constitutional and legal safeguards for women;

- recommend remedial legislative measures;

- facilitate redressal of grievances and

- advise the government on all policy matters affecting women.

The first commission was constituted on 31st January 1992 with Mrs. Jayanti Patnaik as the Chairperson. The second commission was constituted on July 1995 with Dr. (Mrs.) Mohini Giri as the Chairperson. The third commission was constituted on January 1999 with Mrs. Vibha Parthasarathy as the Chairperson. The fourth commission was constituted on January 2002 and the government had nominated Dr. Poornima Advani as the Chairperson. The fifth commission was constituted on February 2005 Dr. Girija Vyas as the Chairperson. The sixth commission was constituted on August 2011 with Mrs. Mamta Sharma as the Chairperson. The seventh commission has been constituted in 2014 with Ms. Lalitha Kumaramanglam as Chairperson. Currently, Rekha Sharma is the Chairperson.

CONSTITUTION OF THE COMMISSION

The Central Government shall constitute a body to be known as the National Commission for Women to exercise the powers conferred on and to perform the functions assigned to, it under this Act.

The Commission shall consist of :

(i) A Chairperson, committed to the cause of women, to be nominated by the Central Government.

(ii) Five members to be nominated by the Central Government from amongst persons of ability, integrity and standing who have had experience in law or legislation, trade unionism, management of an industry potential of women, women's voluntary organisations (including women activist), administration, economic development, health, education or social welfare;

Provided that at least one member each shall be from amongst persons belonging to the Scheduled Castes and Scheduled Tribes respectively;

(iii) A Member-Secretary to be nominated by the Central Government who shall be :

An expert in the field of management, organisational structure or sociological movement, or

An officer who is a member of a civil service of the Union or of an all-India service or holds a civil post under the Union with appropriate experience.

Functions

(i) Shall be the coordinating agency to receive and process all the complaints related to Indian Women deserted by their Overseas Indian husbands.

(ii) Shall render all possible assistance to the complaints including conciliation and mediation between the parties and advising the complainant on related issues.

(iii) Associating, networking with NGO's, community organisations in India and abroad and State Women Commissions for wider area coverage, so as to facilitate easy reach and provide support services.

(iv) Shall endeavor towards a coordinated response amongst various government agencies/ organisations such as State Governments, The National Human Rights Commission, Indian Embassies and Mission, concerned Ministries etc.

(v) Providing assistance to the aggrieved woman in litigation and other issues pertaining to the complainant/case.

(vi) Shall maintain a data bank record of cases registered.

(vii) Seek reports from the State Government and other authorities on the complaints filed and action taken thereon.

(viii) Shall advice and recommend the government on any policy or issue relating to the NRI marriages.

(ix) Analyse various legal treaties on the issue and advice the government on the subject, wherever and whenever required.

(x) Shall constitute an advisory committee panel of reputed advocates/NGOs, both in India as well as abroad, which shall periodically review the functioning of the cell, cases filed and policy issues.

(xi) Shall constitute a panel of experts (All India) to assist the aggrieved wife and rendering legal services and other assistance, including mediation and conciliation

(xii) Planning of training modules and carrying out training on sensitisation on the subject to the various agencies entrusted with the task of providing justice, viz. Judiciary, police, administration, etc.

(xiii) Shall carry out awareness campaigns for the masses on the issue. For this, all the available media services would be utilised by the cell.

(xiv) Shall encourage/support research and study in the related field like issues of grievances associated with dual citizenship, enactment of new legislation or signing of international treaties, marriage laws of other countries ,etc .

(xv) Shall look into complaints and take suo-moto notice on any issue brought to the notice of the NRI Cell in accordance with Section 10 (1)(f) of the National Commission for Women Act, 1990 read with sub-section 4 of Section 10 and Section 8 of the Act.

(xvi) The cell shall regulate its own procedures in accordance with the National Commission for Women Act 1990

(xvii) Perform any other function as assigned to it by the Commission/Central Government.

National Commission for Scheduled Caste

The National Commission for Scheduled Castes plays a crucial role to investigate and monitor all matters relating to Scheduled Castes under the Constitution. The National Commission for Scheduled Caste has been set up under Article 338 on the bifurcation of the erstwhile National Commission for Scheduled Castes and Scheduled Tribes to oversee the implementation of various safeguards provided to Scheduled Tribes under the Constitution. The Commission comprises a Chairperson, a Vice-Chairperson and three full time Members (including one lady Member).

National Commisson for Schedule Tribes

On the 89th Amendment of the Constitution coming into force on 19th February 2004, the National Commission for Scheduled Tribes has been set up under Article 338A on the bifurcation of the erstwhile National Commission for Scheduled Castes and Scheduled Tribes to oversee the implementation of various safeguards provided to Scheduled Tribes under the Constitution. The Commission comprises a Chairperson, a Vice-Chairperson and three full time Members (including one lady Member).

Complaint Mechanism for Schedule Caste and Schedule Tribe are as follows :

- To investigate and monitor all matters relating to the safeguards provided for the Scheduled Castes and Scheduled Tribes under this Constitution or under any other law for the time being in force or under any order of the government and to evaluate the working of such safeguards.
- To inquire into specific complaints with respect to the deprivation of rights and safeguards of the Scheduled Castes and Scheduled Tribes.
- To participate and advise on the planning process of socio-economic development of the Scheduled Castes and Scheduled tribes and to evaluate the progress of their development under the Union and any State.
- To present to the President, annually and at such other times as the Commission may deem fit, reports upon the working of those safeguards.
- To make in such reports recommendations as to the measures that should be taken by the Union or any State for the effective implementation of those safeguards and other measures for the protection, welfare and socio-economic development of the Scheduled Castes and Scheduled Tribes and
- To discharge such other functions in relation to the protection, welfare and development and advancement of the Scheduled Castes and Scheduled tribes as the President may, subject to the provisions of any law made by Parliament, by rule specify.

Powers of the Commission

While investigating the matters referred to in sub-clause (a) to inquire into any complaint referred to in sub-clause (b) of clause 5, the commission have all the powers of a Civil Court trying a suit and in particular in respect of the following matters :

- Summoning and enforcing the attendance of any person from any part of India and examining him on oath.
- Requiring the discovery and production of any documents.
- Receiving evidence on affidavits.
- Requisitioning any public record or copy thereof from any court or office.
- Issuing summons/communications for the examination of witnesses and documents.
- Any other matter which the President may by rule determine.
- Other Functions of Scheduled Tribes.

- The Commission shall discharge the following other functions in relation to the protection, welfare
- and development and advancement of the Scheduled Tribes :
- Measures that need to be taken over conferring ownership rights in respect of minor forest produce. Measures to be taken to safeguard rights of the tribal communities over mineral resources, water resources, etc. as per law.
- Measures to be taken for the development of tribals and to work for more viable livelihood strategies.
- Measures to be taken to improve the efficacy of relief and rehabilitation.
- Measures for tribal groups displaced by development projects.
- Measures to be taken to prevent alienation of tribal people from land and to effectively rehabilitate such people in whose case alienation has already taken place.
- Measures to be taken to elicit maximum co-operation and involvement of tribal communities for protecting forests and undertaking social afforestation.
- Measures to be taken to ensure full implementation of the Provisions of Panchayats (Extension to the Scheduled Areas) Act, 1996 (40 of 1996).
- Measures to be taken to reduce and ultimately eliminate the practice of shifting cultivation by tribals that lead to their continuous disempowerment

Summary

Introduction–Human rights are moral principles or norms, which describe certain standards of human behaviour and are regularly protected as legal rights in municipal and international law. They are commonly understood as inalienable fundamental rights "to which a person is inherently entitled simply because she or he is a human being," and which are "inherent in all human beings" regardless of their nation, location, language, religion, ethnic origin or any other status. They are applicable everywhere and at every time in the sense of being universal and they are egalitarian in the sense of being the same for everyone. They require empathy and the rule of law and impose an obligation on persons to respect the human rights of others. They should not be taken away except as a result of due process based on specific circumstances; for example, human rights may include freedom from unlawful imprisonment, torture and execution.

History of International Human Rights–The modern concept of human rights emerged from the Western politics and philosophy. Under this topic you will read about the The Cyrus Cylinder (539 B.C.), The Magna Carta (1215) ,The Petition of Right (1628), United States Declaration of Independence (1776),The Constitution of the United States of America (1787) and Bill of Rights (1791),Declaration of the Rights of Man and of the Citizen (1789), The First Geneva Convention for the Amelioration of the Condition of the Wounded in Armies in the Field (1864), The United Nations (1945) and The Universal Declaration of Human Rights (1948).

Fundamental Rights–Articles 12-35 in Part III of the Constitution contain the provisions on fundamental rights. Fundamental Rights are largely civil and political rights and consist of the Right to equality (Articles 14-18), Right to freedom (Arts. 19-22), Right against exploitation (Arts. 24 and 25), right to freedom of religion (Arts. 25-28), Cultural and Educational rights (Arts. 29-30) and right to constitutional remedies (Arts. 32-35).

Directive Principles of State Policy–Articles 36-51 in Part IV of the Constitution lay down the guiding principles of governance for the State are called the 'Directive Principles of State Policy'.

Fundamental Duties–Part IV(A) Article 51A of the Constitution prescribes fundamental duties of every citizen. In that, certain conduct and behaviour are expected of the citizens. The salient features of fundamental duties are :

● The fundamental duties cannot be enforced in a court of law for violation of the duties and no one can be punished for the violation.

● Fundamental duties contain standards to be followed by the citizens.

● They remind citizens not to be have irresponsibly but help building a free, democratic and strong society.

National Human Rights Commission–The specific legislation called the Protection of Human Rights Act was enacted by the Parliament in 1993, which in turn established the National Human Rights Commission as an independent institution with powers and functions to promote and protect human rights. This act also provides for the constitution of State Human Rights Commissions at state levels for access to complaint mechanisms at the state level.

National Commission for Minorities–National Commission for Minorities Act, 1992 was enacted by the Parliament to create the National Commission for Minorities to safeguard the human rights of minorities including protection against inequality and discrimination.

National Commission for Woman–In 1992, the National Commission for Women was established under the National Commission for Women Act, 1990.

National Commission for Scheduled Castes and Scheduled Tribes–Article 338 of the Constitution of India provides for establishing a Special Officer for the Scheduled Castes and Scheduled Tribes to investigate all matters relating to the safeguards provided for the Scheduled Castes and Scheduled Tribes in the Constitution and report to the President. The two commissions, the National Commission for Scheduled Castes and the National Commission for Scheduled Tribes were instituted in fulfillment of Art.338 of the Constitution to protect their human rights and prevent their exploitation and to encourage and defend their social, educational, economic and cultural securities as provided in the Constitution and other legislations.

Multiple Choice of Questions

1. Which one of the following was wrongly listed in the group of freedom under article 19 ?
    (a) Freedom of assembly
    (b) Freedom of religion
    (c) Freedom of movement
    (d) Freedom of residence

2. When did the Human Rights Act come into effect ?
    (a) 1951 (b) 1966
    (c) 1989 (d) 1991

3. Magna Carta was :
    (a) An agreement in 1689 which guaranteed freedom of speech in Parliament.
    (b) A document setting and a complete Bill of Rights for England.
    (c) A constitutional document in the 19th century guaranteeing the right to vote.
    (d) An agreement in 1215 between the King and his barons, which guaranteed certain protections for subjects.

4. Which of the following best describes the concept of human rights ?
    (a) Laws about rights contained in the Australian Constitution.

(b) The existence of UN peacekeeping forces around the world.

(c) Basic rights and freedoms to which all humans are entitled.

(d) The rights to freedom of speech and religion.

5. Which of the following best describes a Bill of Rights ?

(a) A document outlining the responsibilities of citizens in a community.

(b) A document proposing that Australia reduce immigration.

(c) A bill from the UN for Australia's contribution to UN peacekeeping forces addressing human rights breaches around the world.

(d) Legal document enshrining human rights in a country.

Short Answer Questions

1. Give a breif history of international human rights.

2. What are fundamental rights ? Name and explain a few.

3. Explain the national commission for woman miniorities.

4. What is NHRC ?

Long Answer Questions

1. Describe any two examples of historical developments on human rights that occurred in the Western world.

2. In two to three sentences, describe any two international human rights laws or treaties or declarations.

3. Identify any two features in the Preamble of the Indian Constitution that indicate its objective of protecting human rights.

4. Describe in two to three sentences any three salient features of fundamental rights in the Indian Constitution.

5. Why do you think the practice of untouchability was abolished, explain in one to two sentences ?

Board Questions

1. There was a treaty between two neighbouring countries 'Sodoland' and 'Borway', to stop the killing of Olive Ridly Turtle. A dispute arose between them regarding fulfilment of certain terms and conditions of this treaty obligation. Sodoland became member of United Nations in the year 1946 whereas Borway is not a member of United Nations. Sodoland refused to fulfil its treaty obligations. Aggrieved by this, Borway approached International Court of Justice to resolve this dispute.

(a) Can Borway approach International Court of Justice ? If yes, under which provision of United Nations charter ?

(b) Explain the jurisdiction of International Court of Justice.

2. Babulal was arrested and detained by police authorities on 26-11-2015 at 1 p.m., under the preventive detention law MACOCA (Maharashtra Control of Organised Crime Act, 1999). He was produced before the magistrate on 28-11-2015 at 1 p.m. He was not allowed to consult his lawyer during the period of detention in police custody. So Babulal applied for writ under Article 226 of the Indian Constitution on the ground that his fundamental right under Article 22 has been violated.

(a) State the provisions of Article 22 of the Indian Constitution.

(b) Are the authorities (police) justified in their action ? Give reasons for your answer.

(c) State any one value communicated by the provisions of Article 22.

3. Explain the powers, functions and complaint mechanism of National Commission for Scheduled Castes and Scheduled Tribes.

NCERT Questions

1. In one or two sentences explain what judicial remedies are available for the enforcement of fundamental rights.

2. In one or two sentences, describe any one salient feature of the Directive Principles of State Policy. Give one example of directive principle.

3. Give any one example of fundamental duties provided in the Constitution.

4. Explain any one power or function of the National Human Rights Commission.

5. Who are minorities whose interests the National Commission for Minorities intend to protect ?

6. Give one ground that disqualifies one's complaint from being admitted by the National Commission for Minorities.

7. Explain any one power or function of the National Commission for Women.

8. Why were the National Commission for Scheduled Castes and the National Commission for Scheduled Tribes created ? Explain any one power or function of the National Commissions for Scheduled Castes and Scheduled Tribes.

Sample Questions

1. With regards to International Human Rights 'ICCPR' stands for :

    (a) International Covenant on Civil and Political Rights.

    (b) International Covenant on Criminal and Penal Rights.

    (c) International Charter on Civil and Political Rights.

    (d) International Committee on Civic and Public Rights.

2. A public authority was given the duty to construct a community centre for public in Uddeshya nagar and land was also allotted for this purpose. But instead of constructing community centre, the public authorities started constructing shops on that allotted land. What remedy is available to the citizens of Uddeshyanagar under Indian Constitution ?

3. Article 14 of the Constitution provides to all the right to equality. Article 16 provides for Reservation and affirmative action for government jobs to backward classes. Are these two provisions contradictory to each other ? Explain giving reasons.

❑❑

9

Legal Profession in India

INTRODUCTION

The Indian legal profession is one of the largest in the world with over 1.4 million enrolled advocates nationwide. The legal profession, evolving as it has done from colonial India, has undergone a huge transformation since its independence. The efforts of the members of the bar to achieve excellence in all spheres of their practise through stiff competition is not only apparent in their every dealing with newer challenges due to technological and other developments, but also in the recognition earned by them in a globalised world.

Why do we need a legal system ?

We need a legal system as a centripetal force for the following reasons :

(i) To regulate the behaviour of mankind.

(ii) To institutionalise the social norms blended with the colour of cultural manifestation.

(iii) To organise a political system to make sets of rules binding in nature.

(iv) To form an efficient judicial system to enforce those sets of rules.

HISTORY OF LEGAL PROFESSION

- The history of the legal profession in India can be traced back to the establishment of the First British Court in Bombay in 1672 by Governor Aungier. The admission of attorneys was placed in the hands of the Governor-in-Council and not with the Court.

- Prior to the establishment of the Mayor's Courts in 1726 in Madras and Calcutta, there were no legal practitioners.

- In 1791, Judges felt the need of experience, and thus the role of an attorney to protect the rights of his client was upheld in each of the Mayor's Courts.

- A second principle was also established during the period of the Mayor's Courts. This was the right to dismiss an attorney guilty of misconduct. The first example of dismissal was recorded by the Mayor's Court at Madras which dismissed attorney Jones.

- The Supreme Court of Judicature was established by a Royal Charter in 1774. The Supreme Court was established as there was dissatisfaction with the weaknesses of the Court of the Mayor. Similar Supreme Courts were established in Madras in 1801 and Bombay in 1823. The first barrister appeared in India after the opening of the Supreme Court in Calcutta in 1774. As barristers began to come into the Courts on work as advocates, the attorneys gave up pleading and worked as solicitors. The two grades of legal practice gradually became distinct and separate as they were in England. Madras gained its first barrister in 1778 with Mr. Benjamin Sullivan. Thus, the establishment of the Supreme Court brought recognition, wealth and prestige to the legal profession.

- Bengal Regulation VII of 1793 was enacted as it was felt that in order to administer justice, Courts must have pleading of causes administered by a distinct profession. Only men of character and education, well versed in the Mohammedan or Hindu law and in the Regulations passed by the British Government, would be admitted to plead in the Courts. They should be subjected to rules and restrictions in order to discharge their work diligently and faithfully by upholding the client's trust.

- In 1862, the High Courts, started by the Crown were established at Calcutta, Bombay and Madras. The High Court Bench was designed to combine Supreme Court and Sadar Court traditions. This was done to unite the legal learning and judicial experience of the English barristers with the intimate experience of civil servants in matters of Indian customs, usages and laws possessed by the civil servants. Each of the High Courts was given the power to make rules for the qualifications of proper persons, advocates, vakils and attorneys at Bar. The admission of vakils to practice before the High Courts ended the monopoly that the barristers had enjoyed in the Supreme Courts. It greatly extended the practice and prestige of the Indian laws by giving them opportunities and privileges equal to those enjoyed for many years by the English lawyers.

● There were six grades of legal practice in India after the founding of the High Courts : (i) Advocates (ii) Attorneys (Solicitors) (iii) Vakils of High Courts (iv) Pleaders (v) Mukhtars (vi) Revenue Agents.

● The Legal Practitioners Act of 1879 in fact brought all the six grades of the profession into one system under the jurisdiction of the High Courts. The Legal Practitioners Act and the Letters Patent of the High Courts formed the chief legislative governance of legal practitioners in the sub-ordinate Courts in the country until the Advocates Act, 1961 was enacted.

● In order to be a vakil, the candidate had to study at a college or university, master the use of English and pass a vakil's examination. By 1940, a vakil was required to be a graduate with an LL.B. from a recognised university in India in addition to three other certified requirements. The certificate should be a proof that he had passed in the examination read in the chamber of a qualified lawyer and was of a good character. In fact, Sir Sunder Lal, Jogendra Nath Chaudhary, Ram Prasad and Moti Lal Nehru were all vakils who were raised to the rank of an Advocate.

● The Indian Bar Councils Act, 1926 was passed to unify the various grades of legal practice and to provide self-government to the Bars attached to various Courts. The Act required that each High Court must constitute a Bar Council made up of the Advocate General, four men nominated by the High Court of whom two should be Judges and ten elected from among the advocates of the Bar. The duties of the Bar Council were to decide all matters concerning legal education, qualification for enrolment, discipline and control of the profession. It was favourable to the advocates as it gave them authority previously held by the judiciary to regulate the membership and discipline of their profession.

The Advocates Act, 1961

In India, the Advocates Act, 1961 governs legal profession and the rules framed there under by the Bar Council of India. It is a law relating to legal practitioners and provides for the constitution of State Bar Councils and Bar Council of India. A person enrolled as an advocate under the Advocates Act, 1961, is entitled to practice law throughout the country. An advocate on the roll of a State Bar Council may apply for transfer to the roll of any other State Bar Council in the prescribed manner. No person can be enrolled as an advocate on the rolls of more than one State Bar Council.

There are two classes of advocates, namely, senior advocates and other advocates. An advocate with his consent, may be designated as a senior advocate, if the Supreme Court or a High Court is of the opinion that by virtue of his ability, standing at the Bar or special knowledge or experience in law, he deserves such distinction.

A senior advocate cannot appear without an advocate-on-record in the Supreme Court or without some other advocate on the State Roll in any other court or tribunal. The Advocate- on- Record (AOR) is another category of Advocate in the Supreme Court.

After the enactment of the Advocates Act, 1961 all the old categories of practitioners (vakils, barristers, pleaders of several grades, and mukhtars) were abolished and consolidated into a single category called 'advocates' who enjoy the right to practice in courts throughout India.

The Act has created a State Bar Council in each State with the Advocate General of the State as an ex-officio member, and 15-25 advocates elected for a period of five years. The State Council's main functions include :

(i) Admitting law graduates on its Roll,

(ii) Determining cases of misconduct against Advocates on the Roll and

(iii) Organising legal aid, among other functions.

Application for enrolment is therefore made to the State Bar Council. State Council rules need to be approved by the Bar Council, however the Central Government has overriding power to make rules. State Bar Councils have disciplinary jurisdiction over advocates whose names appear on their rolls. This is subject to right of appeal to the Bar Council of India and a further right of appeal to the Supreme Court of India.

Bar Council of India

The Bar Council of India is a statutory body established under the section 4 of advocates Act 1961 that regulates the legal practice and legal education in India. Its members are elected from amongst the lawyers in India and represents the Indian bar. It prescribes standards of professional conduct, etiquettes and exercises disciplinary jurisdiction over the bar. It also sets standards for legal education and grants recognition to Universities whose degree in law will serve as a qualification for students to enroll themselves as advocates upon graduation. The Council regulates the content, syllabus, duration of the law degree, subject to which every University can lay down its own provisions. The Council has a Legal Education Committee for this purpose.

Functions

Section 7 of the Advocates Act, 1961 lays down the Bar Council's regulatory and representative mandate. The functions of the Bar Council are to :

(i) Lay down standards of professional conduct and etiquette for advocates.

(ii) Lay down procedure to be followed by disciplinary committees.

(iii) Safeguard the rights, privileges and interests of advocates.

(iv) Promote and support law reform.

(v) Deal with and dispose of any matter which may be referred by a State Bar Council.

(vi) Promote legal education and lay down standards of legal education.

(vii) Determine universities whose degree in law shall be a qualification for enrollment as an advocate.

(viii) Conduct seminars on legal topics by eminent jurists and publish journals and papers of legal interest.

(ix) Organise and provide legal aid to the poor.

(x) Recognise foreign qualifications in law obtained outside India for admission as an advocate.

(xi) Manage and invest funds of the Bar Council.

(xii) Provide for the election of its members who shall run the Bar Councils.

(xiii) Organise and provide legal aid to the scheduled cast.

Constitution

As per the Advocates Act, the Bar Council of India consists of members elected from each state bar council, the Attorney General of India and the Solicitor General of India who are ex officio members. The members from the state bar councils are elected for a period of five years. The council elects its own Chairman and Vice- Chairman for a period of two years from amongst its members. It is assisted by the various committees of the Council, the chairman acts as the chief executive and director of the Council.

Enrollment of advocates

In order to be eligible for enrolment, an Advocate must be :

- citizen of India,
- At least 21 years of age and
- Must have an LL.B. degree from an Indian University.

Eligible persons having a recognised law degree are admitted as advocates on the rolls of the state bar Councils. The Advocates Act, 1961 empowers state bar councils to frame their own rules regarding enrollment of advocates. The Council's enrollment committee may scrutinise a candidate's application.

There is an additional requirement of an All India Bar Examination since 2010, which Advocates must clear in order to be able to start practice. Those admitted as advocates by any state bar council are eligible to take the All India Bar Examination which is conducted by the Bar Council of India. Passing the All India Bar Examination awards the state-enrolled advocate with a 'Certificate of Enrolment' which enables the state-enrolled advocate to practice law as an advocate in any High Court and lower court within the territory of India. However to practise Law before the Supreme Court of India, Advocates must first appear for and qualify in the Supreme Court Advocate on Record Examination conducted by the Supreme Court.

A foreign national may be enrolled on a reciprocal basis with the country of his citizenship, and his foreign degree may be recognised by the Council for the purpose. In the absence of such reciprocity, foreign nationals cannot practice law in India. The Council has released a list of foreign degrees that it recognises.

Rules on an Advocate

Act in a dignified manner : During the presentation of his case and also while acting before a court, an advocate should act in a dignified manner.

Respect the court : An advocate should always show respect towards the court.

Not communicate in private : An advocate should not communicate in private to a judge with regard to any matter pending before the judge or any other judge. An advocate should not influence the decision of a court in any matter using illegal or improper means such as coercion, bribe etc.

Refuse to act in an illegal manner towards the opposition : An advocate should refuse to act in an illegal or improper manner towards the opposing counsel or the opposing parties.

Refuse to represent clients who insist on unfair means : An advocate shall refuse to represent any client who insists on using unfair or improper means. He shall be dignified in use of his language in correspondence and during arguments in court. He shall not use unparliamentary language during arguments in the court.

Appear in proper dress code : An advocate should always appear in court only in the dress prescribed under the Bar Council of India Rules and his appearance should always be presentable.

Refuse to appear in front of relations : An advocate should not enter appearance, act, plead or practice in any way before a judicial authority if the sole or any member of the bench is related to the advocate.

Not to wear bands or gowns in public places : An advocate should not wear bands or gowns in public places other than in courts, except on such ceremonial occasions and at such places as the Bar Council of India or as the court may prescribe.

Advocate should not represent establishments of which he is a member : An advocate should not appear in or before any judicial authority, for or against any establishment if he is a member of the management of the establishment.

Not appear in matters of pecuniary interest : An advocate should not act or plead in any matter in which he has financial interests. He should also not accept a brief from a company of which he is a Director.

Not stand as surety for client : An advocate should not stand as a surety, or certify the soundness of a surety that his client requires for the purpose of any legal proceedings.

Legal Advertising

In India, the cumulative effect of the Advocates Act, the Rules of the Bar Council of India and other professional bodies is that lawyers are prohibited to advertise their services. Lawyers may not solicit clients and cannot do anything that might influence the decision of a potential litigant from engaging one or the other lawyer.

In India, according to Rule 36 of the Bar Council of India,

- An Advocate shall not solicit work or advertise, except through a medium maintained by the Bar Council of India, either directly or indirectly, whether by circulars, advertisements, touts, personal communications, interviews not warranted by personal relations, furnishing or inspiring newspaper comments or producing his/her photographs to be published in connection with cases in which he/she has been engaged or concerned.

- His/her sign-board or name-plate should be of a reasonable size. The sign-board or name-plate or stationery should not indicate that he/she is or has been a President or Member of a Bar Council or of any Association or that he/she has been associated with any person or organisation or with any particular cause or matter

- he/she specialises in any particular type of work

- he/she has been a Judge or an Advocate General.

Soliciting work or advertise as used in this clause of the Code would not mean and include setting up of a website by an advocate or a law firm giving only basic information about the names and number of lawyers in a law firm, the contact details and areas of practice. This would apply similarly to lawyers' brochures and law directories. Under the amended rule, advocates can mention in their chosen websites, their names, telephone numbers, e-mail ID, professional qualification and areas of specialisation.

OPPORTUNITIES FOR LAW GRADUATES

There are a plethora of opportunities for a law graduate. One can either practice as an advocate in a court of law or work with corporate firms. By clearing exams conducted by Public Service Commissions, a law graduate can become a judge. After gaining experience, a law graduate can hope to become Solicitor General, a Public Prosecutor or offer services to government departments and ministries. One can also work as a legal adviser for various organisations. Teaching in colleges, working with NGOs and working as a reporter for newspapers and television channels are other attractive options.

Names and Roles of Advocate

- **Criminal Lawyer :** Specialises in criminal laws CrPC, IPC, Evidence Act and various other penal laws.

- **Civil Litigation Lawyer :** Specialises in civil laws *e.g.,* taxation laws and excise laws.

- Legal Analyst : Works for corporate firms or law firms and analyses laws pertaining to the sphere of the company and its operation.

- **Document Drafting Lawyer :** Specialises in drafting various documents containing agreements, terms and conditions, case material, etc.

- **Legal Journalist :** Covers crime beats, legal proceedings in courts, arbitration courts, international courts and arbitration events.
- **Legal Advisor :** Offers consultancy to corporate firms regarding their legal obligations, duties, legal relations with other firms.
- **Government Lawyer :** Works for the government and in close coordination with the police.
- **Judge :** Offers judgment after conducting the court proceedings and hearing all the concerned parties.

LEGAL EDUCATION IN INDIA

Students interested in making a career in law can either do a 3-year law course after graduation in any discipline or a 5-years' course after 12th class. The LL.B. course is regulated by the Bar Council of India which sets rules and regulations regarding legal practice in the country. Any specialisation is done at masters, M.Phil. or Ph.D. stage. A higher degree helps candidates getting jobs in academics.

A candidate can start preparing for law entrance exam conducted at national level for 5 years' B.A., LL.B. at various National Law Schools soon after completing the senior secondary exam. The national law entrance exam, CLAT (Combined Law Admission Test) basically tests the student's general English, legal aptitude, general awareness, logical skills, etc. Some universities have their own law entrance exams. Some universities which offer the three years' LLB conduct entrance exam which have a syllabus on the same lines.

Nature of the Job

Decades ago, Legal Profession was meant for those from a well-to-do family. Almost all the leadership of pre-Independence India comprised lawyers. Gandhi, Nehru, Jinnah were all lawyers. Lawyers had a significant impact on the destiny of this nation. The present is not as glorious as past but it is not bleak either. The social acceptability is there so is the wealth, honour and recognition provided you excel in your work. The degree of competition that prevails in the profession is very high. A large numbers of law graduates pass every year. They are allowed to enroll and practice in any court in any part of the country.

To be a good lawyer one
- must have good knowledge of what one is practicing.
- must have the capacity to patiently convince the judge of the point of law which one is propagating.

Liberalisation of the Legal Profession

Legal services encompass numerous activities of economic and social consequences. Most of the demand for legal services comes from business and organisations. Recently, increasing activities such as corporate restructuring, intellectual property rights and cross border mergers and acquisitions have forced the industry to come up with sophisticated legal services. The national character of law has created some obstacles for cross-border trade in legal services.

While there has been different opinion on the issue of opening up, many developments over the years have brought up the need to liberalise the sector. Some of them are:
- Increasing transnational deals
- Specialised advisory
- Reciprocity interests
- Positive Impact on other sectors
- Professionalising the industry

In 2011, a public interest litigation (PIL) was filed by Lawyer's Collective, a non-profit organisation on the issue of permitting foreign law firms to open office in India. The Bombay High Court didn't permit foreign law firms to set up liaison offices in India. On the other hand, in response to the PIL filed by A. K. Balaji, Madras High Court allowed foreign lawyers to practice in India on a fly in fly out basis.

Women and the Legal Profession in India

Legal practice in India, as in most other countries, is a male dominated profession. In 1916, the Calcutta High Court, and in 1922, the Patna High Court had held that women otherwise qualified were not entitled to be enrolled as Vakil or Pleader. In the Patna High Court case, Ms. Hazra, the petitioner, secured a B.L. degree from Calcutta University. She was refused enrolment as a Pleader. She challenged this in the High Court of Patna. The Court rules that the sections of the Legal Practitioner's Act referred to males and not females. Since 1793, no woman had ever been admitted to the roll of pleaders. To remove doubts about the eligibility of women to be enrolled and to practise as legal practitioners, the Legal Practitioners (Women) Act, III of 1923, was enacted to expressly provide that no woman would by reason only of her sex disqualified from being admitted or enrolled as a legal practitioner or from practising as such. The Allahabad High Court took the lead by enrolling Ms. Cornelia Sorabji as the first Indian lady Vakil of Allahabad High Court on 24 August, 1921 by a decision of the English Committee of the Court (as the Administrative Committee was then called), consisting of Chief Justice Sir Grim Wood Meers. Since then, although the number of women entering into the profession has increased gender bias still pervades the profession. A recent survey found that the percentage of successful women candidates for the Common Law Admission Test was 47%, however 36% of women lawyer in another survey stated that they had faced some sort of gender bias at work. There have been only 5 women Senior Advocates since 1962 of the 397 designated Senior Advocates. However, recent studies have indicated that gender based disadvantages are gradually being eliminated, especially in the corporate law sector.

LEGAL PROFESSION IN OTHER COUNTRIES

Globalisation of Legal Profession

As globalisation increases the flow of people and information across borders, there are increasing opportunities for trained lawyers. Typically, the opportunities are available in Common Law based jurisdictions such as the United States and the United Kingdom and to an extent Australia and Canada. However, unlike many other professions, lawyers trained and licensed in one jurisdiction may not be licensed to practice in other jurisdictions. Lawyers trained in other jurisdictions will have to requalify in order to practice in the foreign jurisdictions. Given the globalisation of legal profession, a number of lawyers have dual qualifications.

Legal Education in the United States

In the United States, students after completing a four- year undergraduate degree in any discipline, can appear in the Law School Admission Test (LSAT) exam. Thereafter, they can apply to a law school and enrol in a three- year J.D. (Juris Doctor) programme. The pedagogical method adopted in law schools involves the case study method as well as the Socratic Method.

Licensing Requirements

Each state in the United States separately administers a mandatory Bar Exam. Typical first-time passage rates are: 72% (New York, 2009), 50% (CA, 2010), and 88% (MA 2008). Bar applicants must also satisfy the character and fitness requirements of the state. Most states also have mandatory or minimum continuing legal education (CLE) require-ments. CLE is professional education of lawyers that takes places after they are admitted to the Bar and entails minimum hourly commitments which lawyers must undertake in order to maintain their license.

Nearly all states require candidates to pass the Multistate Bar Examination (MBE) and the Multistate Professional Responsibility Examination (MPRE). Some states also require the passing of the Multistate Essay Examination (MEE) and/or the Multistate Performance Test (MPT).

The American Bar Association (ABA)

At a federal level, the American Bar Association acts as a voluntary professional body for US lawyers. With over 400,000 members it is the largest voluntary professional body in the world and has a significant international profile. Members of the legal profession in other countries can become international associates of the ABA. Founded in 1878, the ABA supports the legal profession with practical resources for legal professionals while improving the administration of justice, accrediting law schools, establishing model ethical codes, and more. Membership is open to lawyers, law students, and others interested in the law and the legal profession.

Its goals include :

- Serving the members,
- Improving the profession,
- Eliminating bias,
- Enhancing diversity,
- Advancing the rule of law.

One of its most important responsibilities is the creation and maintenance of a code of ethical standards for lawyers. The Model Code of Professional Responsibility, 1969 and the newer Model Rules of Professional Conduct, 1983 have been adopted in 49 states, D.C. and in the Virgin Islands. The only exception is state of California. The ABA has been accrediting schools since 1923 and even publishes the internationally reputed ABA Journal.

Regulation of Legal Profession by State Bar Associations

Lawyers are regulated at state not federal level by the state bar or the highest court. Bar associations in the US are divided into two categories: unified and nonunified :

(i) In states with a unified bar, the responsibilities of regulating lawyers (admission, discipline and so on) with activities to support their members as a professional body. Membership is mandatory in order to practice in such states. There are 32 states with unified bars, including California, Texas and Florida.

(ii) In states with a non-unified bar, responsibility for admitting and regulating lawyers lies with the state Supreme Court or board of bar examiners. In such states, the state bar is a voluntary professional body with activities that can include professional development, lobbying, networking and charitable programmes. States with non-unified bars include New York, Washington D.C. and Illinois.

LEGAL EDUCATION IN U.K

Legal education in the UK consists of a three-year LL.B., directly after secondary school. Graduates from fields other than law and non-graduates can become solicitors, but the LL.B. is the most straight-forward path. Clinical education continues after the LL.B., through the Legal Practice Course (LPC) and training contracts.

To become a Barrister, graduates are required to complete the Bar Vocational Course (BVC) instead of the LPC and then seek a 'pupillage' instead of a training contract. Though there are a number of differences between barristers and solicitors, the most significant one is that barristers can appear in all courts while solicitors can only appear in higher courts if they qualify to become solicitor advocates.

Legal education in Scotland is slightly different from the rest of the UK, and LL.B. degrees awarded in other parts of the UK are not recognised as part of the qualification process in Scotland (and vice-versa).

As stated, the most conventional route to become a lawyer is by reading law as an undergraduate. To qualify as a barrister or solicitor students are required to obtain a 'qualifying law degree'. For an LLB to meet the requirements of a 'qualifying law degree' the course must cover legal research skills and the seven foundation subjects:

- Obligations I (Contract Law) 2
- Obligations II (Tort Law) 2
- Foundations of Criminal Law 2
- Foundations of Equity & the Law of Trusts 2
- Foundations of the Law of the European Union 2
- Foundations of Property Law 2
- Foundations of Public Law 2

The requirement for completion of the academic stage is a lower second class UK Honours degree. Students who have not taken an undergraduate degree in law can still become lawyers. For students with undergraduate degrees in subjects besides law, it is possible to enrol in the Graduate Diploma in Law course (GDL), which is commonly known as Common Professional Examination (CPE) or a conversion course. This is a one year full-time or two years part-time course, which covers the seven foundation subjects, and results in an LLB on passing.

Law firms do not look unfavourably on students with non-Law undergraduate degrees when recruiting trainees.

Solicitors

To become a solicitor, it is necessary to take the Legal Practice Course (LPC), which is a one year full-time or two years part-time course. In some cases, students may be fortunate enough to have a training contract offer from a law firm at this stage. The LPC is a vocational course tailored to prepare students for a career in a law firm. Customarily, students will have to complete at least one vacation scheme at a solicitors' firm, during their academic or vocational training, prior to applying for a training contract. Following the LPC, students must obtain a training contract; this is two years training period spent in an authorised training establishment, usually a solicitors' firm, under the supervision of a training principal. Solicitors are organised through the Law Society of England and Wales. From negotiating with and lobbying the profession's regulators, government and others, to offering training and advice, the Society helps, protects and promotes solicitors across England and Wales.

Barristers

With far fewer spaces for potential barristers, this route is more competitive than that of a solicitor. Chambers often require first class degrees from students. All barristers must be a member of one of the four Inns of Court (Lincolns Inn, Gray's Inn, Middle Temple and Inner Temple) as one can only become a barrister if one has been 'called to the bar' by an Inn of Court. Before students can be 'called to the bar' by their Inn they are expected to complete 12 qualifying sessions at their Inn, which consists of collegiate and educational activities such as dinners, moots, lectures and residential courses. The Inns can provide financial support through scholarships, as well as providing important help and advice to aspiring barristers. All students are expected to join an Inn before commencing their Bar Professional Training Course. Graduates must complete the Bar Professional Training Course (BPTC) - formerly the Bar Vocational Course (BVC) - which is one year full-time or two years part-time course. Only 67% of applicants obtain a place at 'Bar School', while only 76% of enrolees were successful in passing the course in 2009. Customarily students will have to complete a number of 'minipupillages' during their academic and vocational training, and possibly have carried out some marshalling (which involves shadowing a judge), prior to applying for pupillage. After successfully passing the BPTC, prospective barristers are expected to obtain pupillage, which is one year spent in an authorised pupillage training organisa-tion, usually a barristers' chambers, being trained by their pupil master. Finally, one must obtain tenancy in a set of barristers' chambers, or go into employed practice with an organisation which employs barristers.

Foreign Lawyers and Practicing in the U.K.

For qualified lawyers coming from outside England and Wales, it is still possible to practice. The Solicitors Regulation Authority (SRA) does not impose any formal experience requirements in order to re-qualify as solicitors in England and Wales. Some law firms may express their own requirements which can differ from the SRA guidelines. Candidates can take the qualified Lawyers Transfer Scheme in order to qualify under this jurisdiction. Lawyers coming from EU Member States can rely on EU Directive 77/249 in this area. European lawyers can practice to the same level as they could in their own country. However, it is not possible to be a barrister and solicitor simultaneously.

France

The French legal profession (advocates) includes over 51,800 lawyers as of 2010. Almost half of the profession practise legal in the Paris region. Notaries (civil law notaries) play an important role to play in the French legal system for conveyancing, probate and related family matters. Regulation of the profession lies with the 181 Barreaux (local bar associations). Registration is mandatory to be able to practice. The Paris Bar, with over 21,000 advocates, is by far the most influential bar association of all French bars. The Conceal National des Barreaux, created in 1990, is the overarching national body for all French bars. Solicitors of England and Wales as well as European/EEA/Swiss lawyers may apply for registration as European lawyers. France implemen-ted the Establishment Directive 98/5/EC. Establish-ment is permitted for EU, EEA and Swiss nationals who are qualified in these countries. It allows them to give advice in international law, the law of their home country as well as French law. Foreign lawyers can requalify in France, under conditions of reciprocity, by sitting the relevant equivalence examination administered by the Conseil National des Barreaux.

Germany

German legal education consists of a four-year undergraduate degree completed following comple-tion of secondary school and passage of the university entrance exam. Students then take the First Examination, a comprehensive set of exams that emphasizes academic knowledge of the law. This is followed by a two-year practical training period (Referendarzeit). Students then must pass the Second Examination, a comprehensive set of exams that emphasizes practical legal skills. Upon passage, students are entitled to work in any legal profession. German legal education has a strong practical emphasis. Students are qualified to work in any legal profession once they pass both the First Examination and the Second Examination. To practice as a private attorney (Rechtsanwalt), a student must apply to join a state branch of the Federal Chamber of Lawyers (Bundesrechtsanwaltskammer). However, there is no separate bar exam, and an applicant can only be rejected under a narrow set of circumstances (primarily ethical or criminal grounds). European attorneys may requalify either by continually practicing in Germany for three years, or by sitting the relevant equivalence exam.

Singapore

Singapore has a fused legal profession of 'advocates and solicitors'. Admission to the Singapore Bar is governed by the Legal Profession Act and determinations of admission are made by the Board of Legal Education. The Law Society of Singapore determines fitness of character for admission after applications have been filed. The Law Society is the representative body for lawyers in Singapore. Foreign lawyers practicing in Singapore are regulated by the Legal Profession (International Services) Secretariat of the Attorney-General's Chambers. Foreign lawyers may work as employees, partners or directors in one of the following practice vehicles :

● As a qualifying Foreign Law Practice

● As a foreign law firm

● A Joint Law Venture

● A Formal Law Alliance

● As a foreign lawyer in a Singapore law firm

Registration in each case is required with the Attorney General's Chambers. In some cases, a non-Singapore citizen can qualify as Singapore advocate and solicitor, as long as he or she meets the requirements under the Legal Profession Act.

People's Republic of China

Students complete an integrated four-year bachelor of law (LL.B.) course directly after secon-dary school. Graduates holding bachelor's degrees in fields other than law may also sit for the PRC national judicial examination. The national core curriculum consists of 14 courses :

(i) Legal theory

(ii) Chinese legal history

(iii) Constitutional law

(iv) Administrative law

(v) Criminal law

(vi) Law of criminal procedure

(vii) Civil procedure

(viii) Civil law

(ix) Commercial law

(x) Economic law

(xi) Intellectual property

(xii) Private international law,

(xiii) International law

(xiv) International economic law.

Three additional degrees are offered, but the completion of an LL.B. is sufficient to become a practicing attorney. The Master of Law (L.L.M.) degree may be completed in two or three years, depending on the school. A three-year Juris Master (J.M.) course is also available for graduates who have obtained bachelor's degrees in other fields. Subject to the completion of an L.L.M or J.M., students may pursue a Juris Science Doctor degree (L.L.D.), which is completed in three to six years depending on the school.

Since 2002, the PRC Ministry of Justice, in consultation with the Supreme People's Court and the Supreme People's Procuratorate, has administered a 'uniform national judicial examination' on an annual basis. Anyone who wishes to become a judge, procurator, lawyer, or notary public must pass such examination. Average passage rate between 2002 and 2010 was 18.3%. Candidates must also be willing to uphold the constitution of the PRC, complete a one-year internship with a law firm and be a person of good character and conduct. Generally, foreign nationals cannot be admitted to practice in the P.R.C. Mainland.

However, foreign law firms can establish a representative office to provide legal advice concerning the legislation in its admitted jurisdiction, and the application of international treaties and practices. They can also represent clients from their admitted jurisdiction in transnational cases, etc. According to the regulations, the chief representative, the representative and the resident foreign lawyers (a consecutive

stay for at least 90 days) of the firm need to register with the All China Lawyers Association (ACLA).

Australia

Legal education in Australia first requires the completion of an integrated Bachelor of Laws (LL.B.) degree, often conferred along with a post-secondary degree. This degree requires a minimum of four years' coursework, although most students complete a five-year program including study of another discipline (such as business, engineering, or medicine). Some law schools have begun to offer a three-year J.D., available only to those with prior four-year university degrees. Some top schools, such as the University of Melbourne, have ceased offering the LL.B. and now offer only the J.D.Completion of the LL.B. is followed by a period of practical legal training (PLT) that may take the form of a practical training course at a law school, an apprenticeship with a legal practitioner (known as 'articles of clerkship'), or a combination of the two.

Licensing requirements are enacted by each state or territory, although the Law Council of Australia's model professional rules have been adopted by nearly every jurisdiction. There is general reciprocity throughout Australia (and often New Zealand). This is a two step process for admission to practice. Graduates must first obtain admission as a lawyer in the state / territory, which requires both possession of a recognised law degree and good character, plus completion of a post-graduate PLT course. Lawyers then apply to the applicable state private legal organisation for certificates of practice as either solicitors (requiring nothing further, beyond the application) or barristers (requiring a passing score on the state bar exam).

Barristers, who are traditionally sole practitioners, serve as advocates for clients in court and generally obtain work through references from solicitors. Solicitors may perform a wide variety of functions, from advising clients to negotiating and may work in a range of settings, from large firms to government offices to solo practice. Although there is a nominal distinction between solicitors and barristers, today the professions are largely fused. Where the distinction persists in practice (e.g., New South Wales), solicitors who wish to appear in court must meet the same requirements as barristers. Initial admission is usually on a restricted basis, requiring supervision by a senior practitioner for up to 24 months. English law degrees are generally recognised in Australia; however, each state may have its own additional requirements.

Summary

Introduction–The legal profession, evolving as it has done from colonial India, has undergone a huge transformation since its independence. The efforts of the members of the bar to achieve excellence in all spheres of their practice through stiff competition is not only apparent in their every dealing with newer challenges due to technological and other developments, but also in the recognition earned by them in a globalised world.

Advocates Act, 1961–The Advocates Act of 1961 amended and consolidated the law relating to legal practitioners and provided for the constitution of the State Bar Councils and an All-India Bar - the Bar Council of India as its apex body.

All India Bar Examination–All India Bar Examination (AIBE) is to examine an advocate's capability to practice the profession of law in India. The AIBE will assess skills at a basic level, and is intended to set a minimum benchmark for admission to the practice of law; it addresses a candidate's analytical abilities and understanding basic knowledge of law. After passing the examination candidate will be awarded 'Certificate of Practice' by the Bar Council of India. AIBE will be conducted in 40 cities all across India.

Legal advertising–Advertising by lawyers has been strictly restricted by the Bar Council of India. An advocate is prohibited from promoting himself through circulars, advertisements, touts, personal communications, interviews other than through personal relations, furnishing or inspiring newspaper comments or producing his photographs to be published in connection with cases in which he has been engaged or concerned. An amendment to this rule allows advocates to furnish certain information on their websites after intimating and taking approval from the Bar Council of India.

Opportunities for law graduates–Law graduates in India have various options and opportunities open to them after their graduation. A law degree, in addition to being a professional degree, is now considered to be training in a discipline which trains the mind to think analytically and communicate systematically.

Legal education in India–Legal education in India is regulated by the Bar Council of India. There are two ways to obtain a degree to practice law and enrol with the Bar Council: (1) a 3-year LL.B. program which requires a prior undergraduate degree and (2) a 5-year integrated B.A., LL.B./BBA.,LL.B./B.Sc., LL.B program which commences immediately after secondary school.

Liberalisation–India had signed the WTO Treaty in the 1990s leading to economic liberalisation, it is also expected to liberalise the legal services sector under the GATS (General Agreement on Trade and Services) and services negotiations under various free trade agreements/ economic partnership agreements. The Bar Council of India has consistently passed several resolutions between 2002 and 2007 opposing the opening up of the Indian legal profession to foreign lawyers or foreign law firms.

Women and legal profession in India–The number of women entering into the profession has increased gender bias still pervades the profession. There have been only 5 women Senior Advocates since 1962 of the 397 designated Senior Advocates. However, recent studies indicates that gender based disadvantages are gradually being eliminated, especially in the corporate law sector.

Globalisation of legal profession–As globalisation ncreases the flow of people and information across borders, there are increasing opportunities for trained lawyers. The opportunities are available in Common Law based jurisdictions such as the United States and the United Kingdom and to an extent Australia and Canada. However, unlike many other professions, lawyers trained and licensed in one jurisdiction may not be licensed to practice in other jurisdictions. Lawyers trained in other jurisdictions will have to requalify in order to practice in the foreign jurisdictions. Given the globalisation of legal profession, a number of lawyers have dual qualifications.

The chapter concludes by legal education for different countries like the US, UK, France, Germany, etc.

Multiple Choice of Questions

1. Who is the Legal Advisor to the Government of a State in India ?
   (a) The Solicitor General
   (b) The State Chief Legal Officer
   (c) The High Court
   (d) The Advocate General

2. Which of the following best describes the legal phrase **amicus curiae** ?
   (a) Let the buyer beware
   (b) Friend of the court
   (c) At one's own risk
   (d) On what authority

3. Which of the following is entrusted with a statutory duty of laying down the standards of professional conduct and etiquette for advocates in India ?

(a) Supreme Court of India

(b) Bar Association of India

(c) Bar Council of India

(d) Delhi Bar Council

4. Which of the following is the oldest High Court in India ?

(a) High Court of Madras

(b) High Court of Calcutta

(c) High Court of Delhi

(d) High Court of Allahabad

5. What is the total number of High Courts in India?

(a) 21   (b) 22

(c) 24   (d) 19

Short Answer Questions

1. Write a brief history about the legal profession in India.

2. What are rules on an advocate ?

3. What is a role of judge ?

Long Answer Questions

1. What were the different classes of practitioners who were permitted to practice in Indian courts prior to the Advocates Act and after the Advocates Act ?

2. How is the Bar Council of India organised ? What are its roles and functions ? Trace the history of the Bar Council.

3. Write a short note on advertising by legal professionals in India ?

Board Questions

1. Smith is a citizen of United Kingdom. He had completed LL.B. from recognised University of United Kingdom. He wants to practice as a 'Barrister' here. In order to practice as a 'Barrister', Smith is required to complete which of the following course ?

(a) Legal Practice Course (LPC)

(b) Legal Professional Training Course (LPTC)

(c) Bar Professional Training Course (BPTC)

(d) Bar Professional Course (BPC)

2. Rohan is a citizen of India and a resident of Mumbai. He is qualified Legal Practitioner and practicing law since 1992, in the Bombay High Court; where he only prepares the case but do not argue in the Court. He belongs to a separate class of legal practitioners, known as :

(a) Barristers   (b) Attorneys

(c) Advocates   (d) Solicitors

3. Compare the rules regarding Legal Education in India and The United Kingdom.

4. 'When a person becomes an advocate his relation with people in general is governed by the general rules of law but his conduct as an advocate is governed by the special rules of professional ethics of Bar Council of India.'

In the light of the above statement, answer the following :

(a) Duties and Responsibilities of an advocate, as laid down by the Bar Council of India.

(b) Rules regarding advertisement by Legal Professionals, as laid down by the Bar Council of India

NCERT Questions

I. Find Out :

1. Can you name any renowned senior advocates currently in practice ? Do you know what leading cases they are associated with ?

2. Who is the current Attorney General of India, Solicitor General of India and Additional Solicitor General's of India ?

II. Debate/Discuss :

1. Should lawyers in India be allowed to advertise ? What is your general view in allowing professionals to advertise ? What are the moral and ethical arguments involved in this debate ?

2. Should foreign law firms be allowed to establish offices and practice in India ? How will that decision impact the legal profession in India ?

III. Write short notes on the following :

1. Women and the Legal Profession.

2. Professional Ethics for lawyers.

3. Eligibility and qualification to practice as an Advocate in India.

4. Legal Education in India.

IV. Fill in the blanks :

1. Ms. Hazra challenged the rules against enrolment of _______ as ______ in the High Court of _____ .

2. Eligible graduates are enrolled in the Rolls of _________ .

3. Bar Council of India laws down standards for _________ .

4. Advocates are not permitted to _________ in _________, television and other media.

5. Person must be atleast ______ years of age and a _________ of India to be able to practice as an advocate in India.

6. The _________ is the organisation that represents and acts for solicitors in the UK.

Sample Questions

1. What changes did the Advocates Act 1961 bring in legal profession in India ?

2. "Law is an exciting and challenging profession." In the light of the above statement evaluate the opportunities for law graduates in India.[Any 5].

3. What are the regulatory and representative functions performed by the Bar Council of India ? Also state its statutory functions.

❏❏

INTRODUCTION

Legal aid implies giving free legal services to the poor and needy who are unable to afford legal representation and access to the court system. Legal aid is regarded as central in providing access to justice by ensuring equality before the law, the right to counsel and the right to a fair trial. This chapter describes the development of legal aid and its principles. A number of delivery models for legal aid have emerged, including duty lawyers, community legal clinics and the payment of lawyers to deal with cases for individuals who are entitled to legal aid.

Legal aid is essential to guaranteeing equal access to justice for all, especially for citizens who do not have sufficient financial means, the provision of legal aid to clients by governments will increase the likelihood, within court proceedings, of being assisted by legal professionals for free (or at a lower cost) or of receiving financial aid. One need not be a litigant to seek legal aid. **Justice Blackmun** in **Jackson V/s Bishop** held that the concept of seeking justice cannot be equated with value of dollars. Money plays no role in seeking justice.

HISTORY OF LEGAL AID

Legal aid has a close relationship with the welfare state, and the provision of legal aid by a state is influenced by attitudes towards welfare. Legal aid is a welfare provision by the state to people who could otherwise not afford counsel from the legal system. Legal aid also helps to ensure that welfare provisions are enforced by providing people entitled to welfare provisions, such as social housing, with access to legal advice and the courts.

Historically legal aid has played a strong role in ensuring respect for economic, social and cultural rights which are engaged in relation to social security, housing, social care, health and education service provision, which may be provided publicly or privately, as well as employment law and anti-discrimination legislation. Jurists such as **Mauro Cappelletti** argue that legal aid is essential in providing individuals with access to justice, by allowing the individual legal enforcement of economic, social and cultural rights. His views developed in the second half of the 20th century, when democracies with capitalist economies established liberal welfare states that focused on the individual. States acted as contractors and service providers within a market-based philosophy that emphasised the citizen as consumer. This led to an emphasis on individual enforcement to achieve the realisation of rights for all.

Prior to the mid 20th century, literature on legal aid emphasised the collective enforcement of economic, social and cultural rights. As classic welfare states were built in the 1940s and following World War II, an underlying principle was that citizens had collective responsibility for economic, social and cultural rights; and the state assumed responsibility for those unable to provide for themselves through illness and unemployment. The enforcement of economic, social and cultural rights was to be collective, through policies rather than individual legal action. Laws were enacted to support welfare provisions, though these were regarded as laws for planners, not lawyers. Legal aid schemes were established, as it was assumed that the state had a responsibility to assist those engaged in legal disputes, but they initially focused primarily on family law and divorce.

In the 1950s and 1960s, the role of the welfare state changed, and social goals were no longer assumed to be common goals. Individuals were free to pursue their own goals. The welfare state in this time expanded, along with legal aid provisions, as concerns emerged over the power of welfare providers and professionals. In the 1960s and 1970s, demand rose for the right of individuals to legally enforce economic, social and cultural rights and the welfare provisions they as individuals were entitled to. Mechanisms emerged through which citizens could legally enforce their economic, social and cultural rights, and welfare lawyers used legal aid to advise those on low income when dealing with state officials. Legal aid was extended from family law to a wide range of economic, social and cultural rights.

In the 1980s, the role of the classic welfare state was no longer regarded as necessarily positive, and welfare was increasingly provided by private entities. Legal aid was increasingly provided through private providers, but they remained focused on providing assistance in court cases. Citizens were increasingly regarded as consumers, who should be able to choose among services. Where it was not possible to provide such a choice, citizens were given the right to voice their dissatisfaction through administrative complaints processes. This resulted in tension, as legal aid was not designed to offer advice to those seeking redress through administrative complaints processes. Tensions also began to emerge as states which emphasised individual enforcement of economic, social and cultural rights, rather than collective enforcement through polices, reduced funding for legal aid as a welfare state provision. Individual enforcement of welfare entitlement requires the kind of legal aid funding states emphasising collective enforcement were more likely to provide.

Legal Background

In a participatory democracy, it is essential that citizens have faith in their institution. A fair and independent judiciary is an important component in sustaining their trust and confidence. An impartial independent judiciary is the guardian of the individual rights in a democratic society. In order for citizens to have faith in their court system, all people must have access to the courts when necessary. Citizens agree to a limitation on their freedom in exchange for peaceful coexistence and they expect that when conflicts between citizens or between the state and citizens arise, there is a place that is independent from undue influence, that is trustworthy, and that has an authority over all the parties to solve the disputes peacefully. It is also the responsibility of the State to ensure that fair and impartial justice is made available at the door steps of the poor and economically weaker sections irrespective of their caste, creed, religion, and geographical position at free of cost.

The fundamental value of Indian system of justice is that the stability of our society depends upon the ability of the people to readily obtain access to courts, because the court system is the mechanism recognised and accepted by all to peacefully resolve disputes. Denying access to the courts forces dispute resolution into other arenas and results in vigilantism and violence. As envisaged under **Article 15 of the Constitution of India**, the State shall not discriminate against any citizen on grounds of religion, race, caste,

sex, place of birth or any of them. Based on this cardinal principle, no citizen shall on the grounds only of religion, race, caste, sex, place of birth or any of them, be subject to any disability. **Article 14 of the Constitution of India** provides that the State shall not deny to any person equality before the law or the equal protection of the laws within the territory of India.

Human rights and human dignity form the premises for socio-legal foundations of free legal aid. As part of the human rights, it is necessary to recognise the principle of equality and ensure access to justice. These foundations reflect the incorporation of legal obligation in the international treaties, regional treaties, the working of monitoring bodies under these treaties or in the national legal systems.

FREE LEGAL AID UNDER INTERNATIONAL LAW

Access to justice is one of the most critical issues facing the legal community worldwide. Poor people from all over the world do not have access to the tools they need to protect and promote their rights and interests. In short, no legal system has escaped the difficulties to providing the justice system to poor people. If equality before the law is more than an empty promise, States must accept the task of guaranteeing all citizens an equal opportunity to protect their rights and promote their interests. Legal aid is undergoing profound changes around the globe. It is of course no accident that these changes are occurring simultaneously. Members of the legal profession are alarmed at the decline of state legal aid and are attempting to fill, at least partially; the resulting vacuum. Equal justice became more attainable when many governments established state legal aid schemes in the post- Second World War era. These schemes represented one of a variety of welfare state programs in health, housing, income support and increased funding to pay lawyers to undertake legal aid cases at a rate approaching the market price.

Europoean Convention for protection of Human Rights (1950) : The convention guaranteed the right to free legal aid to a person charged with a criminal offence, to enable him to defend himself.

United Nation Conference, 1965 : The conference realised the need for legal aid. Providing legal aid for accused and convicted was discussed. Lack of adequate legal aid system tends to increase recidivism.

International law addresses the provision for free legal service from the perspective of human rights. An explicit provision for legal services is incorporated in the International Covenant on Civil and Political Rights (ICCPR) (1966) and its protocol. Article 14(3) (d) of the International Covenant on Civil and Political Rights outlines the requirement for free legal assistance as follows: *In the determination of any criminal charge against him, everyone shall be entitled to the following minimum guarantees, in full equality to be tried in his presence, and to defend himself in person or through legal assistance of his own choosing to be informed if he does not have legal assistance, of this right and to have legal assistance assigned to him, in any case where the interests of justice require, and without payment by him in any such case if he does not have sufficient means to pay for it.*

A number of international treaties like International Covenant on Economic, Social and Cultural Rights (ICESCR), Convention on Elimination of Discrimination Against Women (CEDAW) and International Convention on Elimination of All Forms of Racial Discrimination may be interpreted as implicitly referring to the need for free legal services while aiming at effective legal remedy and access to justice.

There are a number of declarations and principles adopted by the UN which refer to effective legal remedy, of which free legal services (in genuine cases) form an essential component. For instance, Article 8 of the Universal Declaration on Human Rights (UDHR) provides that everyone has the right to an effective remedy by the competent national tribunals for acts violating the fundamental rights granted by the Constitution or by the law. Being a General Assembly resolution, some international law scholars describe UDHR as a soft law in terms of declaration and encapsulating lofty idealistic notions about human rights. Legal aid is sine qua non (an essential condition) for achievment of ideals enshrined in the preamble of the Declaration of Human rights. Still, it creates right centric obligations of norm creating character for the members of the international community.

Tehran Conference

The conference adopted the resolution on legal aid which declare that the government should encourage the development of comprehensive legal aid system for the protection of human rights and fundamental freedom.

American Convention on Human Rights (1969)

All persons are equal before the law and are entitled without any discrimination to equal protection of law. Every indigent person is entitled with full equality, the inalienable right to be assisted by counsel provided by the state.

Standard Minimum Rules for the Treatment of Prisoners

Under Rule 93, an untried prisoner can apply for free legal aid and receive visits from his legal advisor with a view to his defence and to prepare and hand to him confidential instructions.

Convention on Internatinal Access to Justice (1980)

Irrespective of nationality of the persons who habitually resident of contracting state is entitled to legal aid for the court proceeding in civil and commercial matters as if they were nationals of state.

LEGAL AID MOVEMENT IN INDIA AND THE INDIAN CONSTITUTION

After Independence schemes of legal aid was developed under the aegis of Justice N.H. Bhagwati, then of Bombay High Court and Justice Trevore Harris of Calcutta High Court. The matter of legal aid was also referred to the Law Commission to make recommendations for making the legal aid program an effective instrument for rendering social justice. Coming up with recommendation in its XIV report, under the leadership of leading jurist M.C. Setalvad, the Commission opined that free legal aid is a service which should be provided by the State to the poor. The State must, while accepting the obligation, make provision for funds to provide legal aid.

The legal community must play a pivotal role in accepting the responsibility for the administration and working of the legal aid scheme. It owes a moral and social obligation and therefore the Bar Association should take a step forward in rendering legal aid voluntarily. These would include representation by lawyers at government expenses to accused persons in criminal proceedings, in jails and appeals. "The Commission also recommended the substitution in Order XXXIII, Civil Procedure Code of the word 'pauper' with 'poor persons'. Acting on the recommendations of the Law Commission, the Government of India in 1960 prepared a national scheme of legal aid providing for legal aid in all courts including tribunals. It envisaged the establishment of committees at the State, District and Tehsil level. However due to the inability of States to implement the scheme because of lack of finances the scheme did not survive.

Meanwhile the judicial attitude towards legal aid was not very progressive. In *Janardhan Reddy vs. State of Hyderabad and Tara Singh vs. State of Punjab,* the court, while taking a very restrictive interpretation of statutory provisions giving a person the right to lawyer, opined that this was, "a privilege given to accused and it is his duty to ask for a lawyer if he wants to engage one or gets his relations to engage one for him. The only duty cast on the Magistrate is to afford him the necessary opportunity (to do so)". Even in capital punishment cases the early Supreme Court seemed relentless when it declared that "it cannot be laid down in every capital case where the accused is unrepresented the trial is vitiated."

Accepting this recommendation in the 1976, Article 39-A was introduced in the Directive Principles of State Policy by 42nd Amendment of the Constitution. With the object of providing free legal aid, the Government of India had, by a resolution dated 26th September, 1980 appointed a Committee known as "Committee for Implementing Legal Aid Schemes" (CILAS) under the chairmanship of Chief. Justice P.N. Bhagwati to monitor and implement legal aid programs on a uniform basis in all the States and Union Territories. 'CILAS' evolved a model scheme for legal aid programs applicable throughout the country by which several legal aid and advice Boards were set up in the States and Union Territories.

Although legal aid was recognised by the Courts as a fundamental right under Article 21 reversing their earlier stance, the scope and ambit of the right was not clear till this time. The step was taken in Sunil Batra *vs.* Delhi Administration, where the two situations in which a prisoner would be entitled for legal aid was given. First to seek justice from the prison authorities and second to challenge the decision of such authorities in the court. Thus, the requirement of legal aid was brought about in not only judicial proceedings but also proceedings before the prison authorities which were administrative in nature. The court has reiterated this again in Hussainara Khatoon *vs.* State of Bihar and said: "it is an essential ingredient of reasonable, fair and just procedure to a prisoner who is to seek his liberation through the court's process that he should have legal services available to him. Free legal service to the poor and the needy is an essential element of any reasonable, fair and just procedure." The court invoked Article 39-A which provides for free legal aid and has interpreted Article 21 in the light of Article 39-A. The court upheld the right to free legal aid to be provided to the poor accused persons 'not in the sense of Article 22(1) and its wider amplitude' but in the premptory sense of article 21 confined to prison situations'

In Khatri & Others *vs.* State of Bihar & Others

Right to free legal aid, just, fair and reasonable procedures is a fundamental right (Khatoon's Case). It is elementary that the jeopardy to his personal liberty arises as soon as the person is arrested and is produced before a magistrate for it is at this stage that he gets the 1st opportunity to apply for bail and obtain his release as also to resist remain to police or jail custody. This is the stage at which an accused person needs competent legal advice and representation. No procedure can be said to be just, fair and reasonable which denies legal advice representation to the accused at this stage. Thus, state is under a constitutional obligation to provide free legal aid to the accused not only at the stage of. Every individual of the society are entitled as a matter of prerogative.

In Indira Gandhi *vs.* Raj Narain the Court said: "Rule of Law is basic structure of constitution of India. Every individual is guaranteed his/her legal rights under the constitution. No one so condemn unheard. Equality of justice. There ought to be a violation to the fundamental right or prerogatives, or privileges, only then remedy go to Court of Law. But also at the stage when he first is produced before the magistrate, In absence of legal aid, trial is vitiated."

Free Legal Aid under Criminal Law

Under Section 340(1) of the Code of Criminal Procedure, 1898, it is provided that if a man was charged with an offence punishable with death, the court could provide him with a counsel upon his request. As per Tara Singh v. State (1951 AIR 441), it is not a duty of the magistrate but the privilege available to the accused if he failed to appoint advocate on his behalf.

Legal Aid by the State

The responsibility of the legal community to administer legal aid scheme and the State to fund legal representation to the accused in criminal proceedings, appeals and jails is by the state.

In 1960, the Union Government initiated the national legal aid scheme which faced financial shortages and died a natural death. In 1973, in the second phase, the Union Government constituted a committee under the chairmanship of Justice Krishna Iyer to develop a legal aid scheme for states. The Committee devised a strategy in a decentralized mode with legal aid committees in every district, state and the centre. A committee on judicature was set up under the chairmanship of Justice P. N. Bhagwati to implement the legal aid scheme. This

Committee suggested legal aid camps and nyaya-layas in rural areas and recommended the inclusion of free legal aid provision in the Constitution. In 1980, the Committee on National Implementation of Legal Aid was constituted with Justice Bhagwati was its head. Subsequently, the Parliament enacted the Legal Services Authorities Act, 1987.

NALSA Regulations

The National Legal Services Authority is a statutory body which has been set up for implementing and monitoring legal aid programs in the country. The legal aid program adopted by 'NALSA' include promoting of legal literacy, setting up of legal aid clinics in universities and law colleges, training of paralegals and holding of legal aid camps and Lok Adalats.

National Legal Services Authority is the apex body constituted to lay down policies and principles for making legal services available under the provisions of the Act and to frame most effective and economical schemes for legal services. It also disburses funds and grants to State Legal Services Authorities and NGOs for implementing legal aid schemes and programs. It has been constituted under the Legal Services Authorities Act, 1987 to monitor and evaluate implementation of legal aid pro-grammes and to lay down policies and principles for making legal services available under the Act.

National Legal Services Authority was constitu-ted on 5th December, 1995. According to Section 3 (1) under the Chapter II of the Act, the Central Government is instructed to constitute a body at the National level known as the National Legal Services Authority, to exercise powers and perform functions conferred on it or assigned to it under the Act.

Actually, Article 39A of the Constitution of India provides for free legal aid to the poor and weaker sections of the society and ensures justice for all. Articles 14 and 22(1) of the Constitution also make it obligatory for the State to ensure equality before law and a legal system which promotes justice on the basis of equal opportunity to all.

In every State, a State Legal Services Authority and in every High Court, a High Court Legal Services Committee have been constituted. District Legal Services Authorities and Taluka Legal Services Committees have been constituted in the Districts and most of the Talukas to give effect to the policies and directions of the NALSA and to provide free legal services to the people and conduct Lok Adalats in the State. Supreme Court Legal Services Commi-ttee has been constituted to administer and imple-ment the legal services programme in so far as it relates to the Supreme Court of India. It has also called upon State Legal Services Authorities to set up legal aid cells in jails so that the prisoners lodged therein are provided prompt and efficient legal aid to which they are entitled by virtue of section 12 of Legal Services Authorities Act, 1987.

NALSA lays down policies, principles, guidelines and frames effective and economical schemes for the State Legal Services Authorities to implement the Legal Services Programmes throughout the country.

Primarily, the State Legal Services Authorities, District Legal Services Authorities, Taluk Legal Services Committees, etc. have been asked to discharge the following main functions on regular basis:

- To Provide Free and Competent Legal Services to the eligible persons;
- To organise Lok Adalats for amicable settlement of disputes;
- To organise legal awareness camps in the rural areas.

Types of Legal Services

Legal Services' are of two types :
1. Pre-litigation Legal Services and
2. Post-litigation Legal Services

1. Pre-litigation Legal Services

It is rightly said that, prevention is better than cure. In these days, the number of litigation is increasing day by day, which is very dangerous for smooth administration of justice. So far, emphasis was given only on post-litigation assistance or help but now it is being realised that pre-litigation legal services are more useful than post-litigation legal services. Pre-litigation legal services include :

- Legal education
- Legal advice
- Legal Awareness
- Pre-litigation settlement.

In order to provide pre-litigation services, the voluntary organisations have been encouraged and boosted by financial support from the State. In law colleges and law faculties in the Universities, Legal aid clinics have to be established. These clinics would be of immense help in promoting legal awareness as most of the litigation is often due to ignorance of the people about their legal rights and duties.

2. Post-Litigation Legal Services

Traditionally legal aid has been provided at post-litigation stage. Post litigation legal services include – appointment of lawyer for indigent, reimbursement of process fee, witnesses' expenditure, court fee etc. by the State.

Who is Entitled to Free Legal Aid ?

The scheme of legal aid should not be based on class or status. The main test for determining whether the applicant seeking legal aid is eligible for it is :

- The means test
- The prima-facie (accepted as correct until proved otherwise) at the very first sight case test and
- The reasonableness test.

Any person, who is :

➤ a member of the scheduled castes or tribes

➤ belonging to the Schedule caste/ tribe, persons suffering from natural calamity, industrial worker, children, insane person, handicap, persons in custody and those having annual income less than ₹1 lakh were entitled to avail free legal aid

➤ a victim of trafficking in human beings or beggar;

➤ disabled, including mentally disabled

➤ a woman or child

➤ a victim of mass disaster, ethnic violence, caste atrocity, flood, drought, earth quake, industria disaster and other cases of undeserved want

➤ an industrial workman

➤ in custody, including protective custody

➤ facing a charge which might result in imprisonment

➤ unable to engage a lawyer and secure legal services on account of reasons such as poverty, indigence and incommunicado situation

➤ in cases of great public importance

➤ Special cases considered deserving of legal services.

Services Offered by the Legal Services Authority

- Payment of court and other process fee.
- Charges for preparing, drafting and filing of any legal proceedings.
- Charges of a legal practitioner or legal advisor.
- Costs of obtaining decrees, judgments, orders or any other documents in a legal proceeding.
- Costs of paper work, including printing, translation, etc.

Duties of the Police and the Courts

The police must inform the nearest Legal Aid Committee about the arrest of a person immediately after such arrest.

The Magistrates and sessions judges must inform every accused who appears before them and who is not represented by a lawyer on account of his poverty or indigence that he is entitled to free legal services at the cost of the State.

Failure to provide legal aid to an indigent accused, unless it was refused would vitiate the trial. It might even result in setting aside a conviction and sentence.

When can Legal Services be Rejected ?

If the applicant :

➤ has adequate means to access justice

➤ does not fulfill the eligibility criteria

➤ has no merits in his application requiring legal action.

Cases for which Legal Aid is not Available

- Cases in respect of defamation, malicious prosecution, contempt of court, perjury etc.
- Proceedings relating to election
- Cases where the fine imposed is not more than ₹ 50
- Economic offences and offences against social laws
- Cases where the person seeking legal aid is not directly concerned with the proceedings and whose interests will not be affected.

When can the Legal Services be Withdrawn ?

The legal services committee can withdraw the services if :

➤ the aid is obtained through misrepresentation or fraud.

➤ any material change occurs in the circumstances of the aided person.

➤ there is misconduct, misbehavior or negligence on the part of the aided person.

➤ the aided person does not cooperate with the allotted advocate

➤ the aided person appoints another legal practitioner

➤ the aided person dies, except in civil cases

➤ the proceedings amount to misusing the process of law or of legal service.

HIERARCHY OF BODIES CREATED UNDER THE ACT

A nationwide network has been envisaged under the Act for providing legal aid and assistance.

National Legal Services Authority is the apex body constituted to lay down policies and principles for making legal services available under the provisions of the Act and to frame most effective and economical schemes for legal services. It also disburses funds and grants to State Legal Services Authorities and NGOs for implementing legal aid schemes and programmes.

State Legal Services Authority is constituted to give effect to the policies and directions of the Central Authority (NALSA) and to give legal services to the people and conduct Lok Adalats in the State. State Legal Services Authority is headed by the Chief Justice of the State High Court who is its Patron-in-Chief. A serving or retired Judge of the High Court is nominated as its Executive Chairman.

District Legal Services Authority is constituted in every District to implement Legal Aid Programmes and Schemes in the District. The District Judge of the District is its ex-officio Chairman.

Taluk Legal Services Committees are also constituted for each of the Taluk or Mandal or for group of Taluk or Mandals to coordinate the activities of legal services in the Taluk and to organise Lok Adalats. Every Taluk Legal Services Committee is headed by a senior Civil Judge operating within the jurisdiction of the Committee who is its ex-officio Chairman.

Supreme Court Legal Services Committee

There is a general perception that approaching the Supreme Court of India for legal remedies is unaffordable to the lay person. This is not true. It is with a view to providing easy and inexpensive access to the Supreme Court and giving legal advice that the Supreme Court Legal Services Committee (SCLSC) has been constituted under the Legal Services Authorities Act, 1987 ('Act'), for the effective rendering of justice in the apex court. Following are the functions of Supreme Court Legal Services Committee :

(i) Lay down policies and principals for making legal services available under the provisions of this Act.

(ii) Frame the most effective and economical schemes for the purpose of making legal services available under the provisions of this Act.

(iii) Utilise the funds at its disposal and make appropriate allocation of funds to the State Authorities and District Authorities.

(iv) Take necessary steps by way of social justice litigation with regard to consumer protection, environment protection or any other matter of special concern to the weaker sections of the society.

(v) Organise legal aid camps, especially in rural areas, slums or labour colonies.

(vi) Encourage the settlement of disputes by way of negotiations arbitration and conciliation.

(vii) Undertake and promote research in the field of legal services with special reference to the need for such services among the poor.

(viii) To do all things necessary for the purpose of ensuring commitment to the fundamental duties of citizens under Part-IVA of the Constitution.

(ix) Monitor and evaluate implementation of the legal aid programmes at periodic intervals.

(x) Provide grants-in-aid for specific schemes to various voluntary social service institutions and the State and District Authorities.

(xi) Develop, in consultation with the Bar Council of India, programmes for clinical legal education and promote guidance.

(xii) Take appropriate measures for spreading legal literacy and legal awareness amongst the people and, in particular, to educate weaker sections of society.

(xiii) Make special efforts to enlist the support of voluntary social welfare institutions working at the grass-root level.

(xiv) Coordinate and monitor the functions of State Authorities, District Authorities, Supreme Court Legal Services Committee, High Court Legal Services.

(xv) Committees, Taluka Legal Services Committees and voluntary social service.

The High Court Legal Services Committee

The High Court Legal Services Committee has been constituted u/s. 8A of the Legal Services Authorities Act; 1987. The committee provides free legal aid to all entitled persons and bears the necessary incidental expenses like typing, copying, postage charges, translation etc. High Court Legal Services Committee performs following functions :

(i) Provides free legal service to persons who may have to file or defend litigations pending in the

High Court and who satisfy the eligibility criteria laid down for the purpose of receiving free legal aid under the Act.

(ii) Files Public Interest Litigation in the High Court.

(iii) Conducts, under the supervision of the State Authority, Lok Adalats for settlement of cases pending in the High Court.

(iv) Prepares and submits such reports, returns and other statistics or information as the State Authority may call for.

The State Authority

Every State Government constitutes the State Legal Services Authority (SLSA) and the High Court Legal Services Committee (HCLSC) for exercising powers and functions as determined by the State Authority. The SLSA consists of - the Chief Justice of High Court as the Patron-in-Chief, a Judge of the High Court nominated by the Governor as Executive Chairman and other members nominated by the State Government in consultation with the Chief Justice of High Court. The HCLSC consists of - Judge of the High Court as the Chairman and other members prescribed by the State Authority and nominated by the Chief Justice of High Court.

Functions of the State Authority

The State Authority is responsible for giving effect to the policy and directions of the Central Authority. It provides legal services like the Central Authority and conducts Lok Adalats. While under-taking legal aid programmes, it also performs other functions of the State Authority fixed by way of regulations. It shall be the duty of the State Authority to give effect of the policy and directions of the Central Authority. Without prejudice to the gene-rality of the functions referred to in sub-section (1), the State Authority shall perform all or any of the following functions :

(i) Give legal service to persons who satisfy the criteria laid down under this Act.

(ii) Conduct Lok Adalats, including Lok Adalates for High Court cases.

(iii) Undertake preventive and strategic legal aid programmes and

(iv) Perform such other functions as the State Authority may in consultation with the Central Authority, fix by regulations.

The District Authority

The State Government constitutes the District Legal Services Authority (DLSA) for every district for exercising powers and functions as determined by the District Authority. The DLSA consists of - the District Judge as Chairman and other members nominated by the State Government in consultation with the Chief Justice of High Court. The District Authority is responsible for performing functions of the State Authority in the District as delegated by the State Authority. It coordinates the activities of the Taluk Legal Services Committee and other legal services in the District. It organises Lok Adalats within the District. The District Authority also performs other functions fixed by way of regulations by the State Authority. The State Authority consti-tutes the Taluk Legal Services Committee (TLSC) for every taluk or mandal. The TLSC consists of senior most Judicial Officer as the ex-officio Chairman and other members prescribed by the State Government in consultation with the Chief Justice of High Court. The TLSC is responsible for organising Lok Adalats within the taluk. It coordinates the activities of legal services in the taluk. It performs other functions as assigned by District Authority. Section 9-11 of the Legal Services Authorities Act deal with the District Legal Services Authority. The State Government shall, in consultation with the Chief Justice of the High Court, constitute a District Authority for every district in the State to exercise the powers and perform the functions conferred on, or assigned to the District Authority under the Act.

Functions of the District Authority

It shall be the duty of every District Authority to perform such of the functions of the State Authority in the District as may be delegated to it from time to time by the State Authority. Without prejudice to the generality of the functions referred to in subsection (1) the District Authority may perform all or any of the following functions :

(i) Co-ordinate the activities of the Taluk Legal Services Committee and other legal services in the District,

(ii) Organised Lok Adalats within the District; and

(iii) Perform such other functions as the State Authority may fix by regulations.

Taluka Legal Services Committee

Sections 11-A and 11-B were inserted by the Act 59 of 1994 whereby provisions relating to Taluk Legal Services were added in the Legal Services Authorities Act, 1987.The Taluk Legal Services Committee work under the rules made by the different States. Relating to its composition, conditions of services in certain States some additional functions have also been assigned, e.g. in Andhra Pradesh where the functions are subject to superintendence of the District and the State Authority. Apart from the above mentioned four-tier machinery the Legal Services Authorities Act also provides for the Supreme Court Legal Services Committee to perform functions as may be determined by the Central Authority and State Authority respectively.

Functions of the Taluka Legal Services Committee

(i)   Co-ordinate the activities of legal services in the Taluk,

(ii) Organised Lok Adalats within the Taluk and

(iii) Perform such other functions as the District Authority may assign to it.

Lok Adalat (People's Courts)

'Lok' stands for 'people' and the vernacular meaning of the term 'Adalat' is the court..The introduction of Lok Adalats added a new chapter to the justice dispensation system of this country and succeeded in providing a supplementary forum to the victims for satisfactory settlement of their disputes. It is one of the components of Alternate Dispute Resolution (ADR) systems. The ancient concept of settlement of dispute through mediation, negotiation or through arbitral process known as 'Peoples' Court verdict' or decision of 'Nyaya-Panch' is conceptualized and institutionalised in the philosophy of Lok Adalat.It is an Indian contribution to the world of jurisprudence of ADR. Lok Adalat (people's courts), established by the government settles dispute by the principles of justice, equity and fair play, which are the guiding factors for decisions based on compromises to be arrived at before such Adalats.

The camps of Lok Adalats were initially started in the state of Gujarat in 1982. The first Lok Adalat was organised on 14th March 1982 at Junagarh. Maharashtra commenced the Lok Nyayalaya in 1984. The movement has now subsequently spread to the entire country. The reason to create such camps was only the pending cases and to give relief to the litigants who were in a queue to get justice.

Statutory Provisions

Legal Aid is a kind of human right in the context of conflicts and contradictory interests. The Central Government, taking note of the need for legal aid for the poor and the needy, had introduced Article 39 (A) in the Constitution in February 1977. Article 39 A of the Constitution of India provides for equal justice and free legal aid. It is, therefore clear that the State has been ordained to secure a legal system, which promotes justice on the basis of equal opportunity. The language of Article-39 A is understood in mandatory terms. This is made more than clear by the use of the word 'shall' in Article 39 A.

It is emphasised that the legal system should be able to deliver justice expeditiously on the basis of equal opportunity and provide free legal aid to ensure that opportunities for securing justice are not denied to any citizens by reasons of economic or other disabilities. It was in this context that the Legal Services Authorities Act, 1987 has been enacted by the Parliament. One of the aims of this Act is to organise Lok Adalats to secure that the operation of legal system promotes justice on the basis of equal opportunity. Chapter VI of the Act deals with Lok Adalats. The Act created National, State and District Legal Service Authorities with the power to organise Lok Adalats.

The poor and resourceless persons need justice, they require for that, for which they can access to justice. Mere recognition of rights does not help them, without providing for necessary infrastructure to secure them justice whenever needed. Even if the infrastructure is created, if he does not get the 'legal aid' to reach it, the purpose of entire justice system suffers a defeat.

*In **Hussainara Khatoon vs. State of Bihar**,* the Supreme Court observed :

Today, unfortunately, in our country the poor are priced out of the judicial system with the result that they are losing faith in the capacity of our legal system to bring about changes in their life conditions and to deliver justice to them. The poor in their contact with the legal system have always been on the wrong side of the line. They have always come across 'law for the poor' rather than 'law of the poor'. The law is regarded by them as something mysterious and forbidding always taking something away from them and not as a positive and constructive social device for changing the social economic order and improving their life conditions by conferring rights and benefits on them. The result is that the legal system has lost its credibility for the weaker section of the community. It is, therefore, necessary that we should inject equal justice into legality and that can be done only by dynamic and activist scheme of legal services.

Cases Suitable For Lok Adalats

Lok Adalats have competence to deal with a number of cases like :

- Compoundable civil, revenue and criminal cases.
- Motor accident compensation claims cases
- Partition Claims
- Damages Cases
- Matrimonial and family disputes
- Mutation of lands case
- Land Pattas cases
- Bonded Labour cases
- Land acquisition disputes
- Bank's unpaid loan cases
- Arrears of retirement benefits cases
- Family Court cases
- Cases which are not *sub-judice*

Cognizance of Cases by Lok Adalats

A Lok Adalat may take cognizance of cases, as per Section 20 of the Legal Services Authority Act where :

- The parties thereof agree.
- One of the parties thereof makes an application to the court for referring the case to the Lok Adalat for settlement and if such court is prima facie satisfied that there are chances of such settlement; cat the very first sight.
- The court is satisfied that the matter is an appropriate one to be taken cognizance of by the Lok Adalat, the court shall refer the case to the Lok Adalat provided that no case shall be referred to the Lok Adalat by such court except after giving a reasonable opportunity of being heard to the parties.

Need For Lok Adalats

Justice Ramaswamy says, "Resolving disputes through Lok Adalat not only minimises litigation expenditure, but it saves valuable time of the parties and their witnesses and also facilitates inexpensive and prompt remedy appropriately to the satisfaction of both the parties".

Lok Adalat has a positive contributory role in the administration of justice. It supplements the efforts and work of the courts. Area of contribution chosen for the purpose specially concerns and helps the common man, the poor, backward and the most needy sections of the society.

Benefits of Lok Adalat

(i) **No Court fee :** no court fee and even if the case is already filed in the regular court, the fee paid will be refunded if the dispute is settled at the Lok Adalat.

(ii) **No strict application** of the procedural laws and the Evidence Act while assessing the merits of the claim by the Lok Adalat. The parties to the disputes though represented by their advocate can interact with the Lok Adalat judge directly and explain their stand in the dispute and the reasons therefore, which is not possible in a regular court of law.

(iii) Disputes can be brought before the Lok Adalat directly instead of going to a regular court first and then to the Lok Adalat.

(iv) The decision of the Lok Adalat is binding on the parties to the dispute and its order is capable of execution through legal process.

(v) **No appeal lies** against the order of the Lok Adalat whereas in the regular law courts there is always a scope to appeal to the higher forum on the decision of the trial court, which causes delay in the settlement of the dispute finally. The reason being that in a regular court, decision goes with the court but in Lok Adalat it is mutual settlement and hence no case for appeal will arise. In every respect the scheme of Lok Adalat is a boon to the litigant public, where they can get their disputes settled fast and free of cost.

Lok Adalats, as it has been again and again iterated throughout the paper, serve very crucial functions in a country due to many factors like pending cases, illiteracy etc. The Lok Adalat was a historic necessity in a country like India where illiteracy dominated about all aspects of governance. The most desired function of lok adalats may seem to be clearing the backlog, with the latest report showing 3 crore pending cases in Indian courts but the other functions cannot be ignored. The concept of Lok Adalat has been a success in practice.

Powers of Lok Adalat

Lok Adalat has the same powers as those vested in a civil court under the code of civil procedure, 1908 while trying a suit in respect of the following matters:

(i) the summoning and enforcing the attendance of any witness and examining him on oath.

(ii) the discovery and production of any document.

(iii) the reception of evidence on affidavits.

(iv) the requisitioning of any public record or document or copy of such record or document from any court or office and

(v) Such other matters as may be prescribed.

Every Lok Adalat shall have the requisite powers to specify its own procedures for the determination of any dispute coming before it.

The Legal Services Authorities (Amendment) Act, 2012

Chapter VIA provides certain provisions dealing with pre-litigation conciliation and settlement pertaining to public utility services. Section 22A provides that in this Chapter and two the purpose of section 22 and 23 unless the context otherwise requires: 'permanent Lok Adalant' means a permanent Lok Adalat established under sub-section (1) of Section 22 B. 'Public utility service' means any :

(i)   Transport service for the carriage of passengers of goods by air, road or water or

(ii) Postal, telegraph or telephone service or

(iii) Supply of power, light or water to the public by any establishment or

(iv) System of public conservancy or sanitations or

(v) Service in hospital or dispensary or

(vi) Insurance service.

It also includes any service which the Central Government or the State Government, as the case may be, in the public interest, by notifications, declare to be a public utility service.

Legal Aid in Context of Social Justice and Human Rights

This vice of social inequality assumes a particularly reprehensible form in relation to the backward classes and communities which are treated as untouchable and so the problem of social justice is as urgent and important in India as is the problem of economic justice. Equality of opportunity to all the citizens to develop their individual personalities and to participate in the pleasures and happiness of life is the goal of economic justice. The concept of social justice thus takes within its sweep the objectives of removing all inequalities and affording equal opportunities to all citizens in social affairs as well as economic activities. The problem of poverty and unequal distribution of wealth may be confined to the bigger cities and towns in India but the problem accentuated by the vice of social inequality existing in a gross form prevails in all of our villages. For instance, the harijans constitute a large class of landless labourers who are treated as untouchables by the rest of the community, who have no house to live in, generally no clothes to wear, who do not get food to eat & sometimes even decent drinking water is beyond their reach. The poor also have no access to legal assistance. Poor people are vulnerable to injustice. Poverty fosters frustration, ill feeling and a brooding sense of injustice. Democracy realizes that this problem which concerns a large number of citizens cannot be successfully met unless law is used wisely to restore balance to the economic structure and to remove the causes of economic inequality.

The Constitution of India and Legal Service

The Constitution of India has solemnly promised to all its citizens-social, economic and political justice, liberty of thought expression, belief, faith and worship; equality of status and opportunity to promote among the all fraternity assuring the dignity of the individual and the unity of the nation. The Constitution has attempted to attune the apparently conflicting claims of socio-economic justice, individual liberty and fundamental rights by putting some relevant provisions.

- Article 14 ensures equality before the law and equal protection of law. Every individual should have the right to represent before the court of law.

- Seven sub-clauses of Article 19(1) guarantee the citizens seven different kinds of freedom and recognise them as their fundamental rights. Article 19 considered as a whole furnishes a very satisfactory and rational basis for adjusting the claims of individual rights of freedom and the claims of public good.

- Article 38 requires that the state should make an effort to promote the welfare of the people by securing and protecting as effectively as it may a social order in which social, economic and political justice shall inform all the institutions of national life.

- Article 39 clause (a) says that the State shall secure that the operation of the legal system promotes justice, on a basis of equal opportunity and shall, in particular provide free legal aid by suitable legislation or schemes, or in any other way to ensure that opportunities for securing that justice is not denied to any citizen by reason of economic or other disabilities.

- The social problem presented by the existence of a very large number of citizens who are treated as untouchables has received the special attention of the Constitution as Article 15(1) prohibits discrimination on the grounds of religion, race, caste, sex, or place of birth. The state would be entitled to make special provisions for women and children, and for advancement of any social and educationally backward class of citizens, or for the SC/STs.

- A similar exception is provided to the principle of equality of opportunity prescribed by Article 16(1) as much as Article 16(4) allows the state to make provision for the resolution of appointments or posts in favour of any backward class of citizens which, in the opinion of the state, is not adequately represented in the services under the state.

Free Legal Aid under Criminal Law

Under Section 340(1) of the Code of Criminal Procedure, 1898, it is provided that if a man was charged with an offence punishable with death, the court could provide him with a counsel upon his request. As per Tara Singh v. State (1951 AIR 441), it is not a duty of the magistrate but the privilege available to the accused if he failed to appoint advocate on his behalf.

FUNDING

The Central Government by way of grants provides funding to the Central Authority for providing legal services. Similarly, the State Government by way of grants provides funding to the State Authority and the District Authority for providing legal services.

The National Legal Aid Fund

The National Legal Aid Fund established by the Central Authority includes sums of money given as grants by the Central Government, any grant or donation made to the Central Authority by any other person for the purpose of legal services, and amounts received by the Central Authority under the orders of any court. The National Legal Aid Fund shall be utilised towards the cost of legal services provided by the SCLSC, grants made to the State Authorities and other expenses of the Central Authority.

The State Legal Aid Fund

The State Legal Aid Fund established by the State Authority includes sums of money given as grants by the Central Authority, any grant or donation made to the State Authority by any other person for the purpose of legal services, and amounts received by the State Authority under the orders of any court. The State Legal Aid Fund shall be utilised towards the cost of functions of State Authorities, cost of legal services provided by the HCLSC and other expenses of the State Authority.

The District Legal Aid Fund

The District Legal Aid Fund established by the District Authority includes sums of money given as grants by the State Authority, any grant or donation made to the District Authority by any other person for the purpose of legal services, and amounts received by the District Authority under the orders of any court. The District Legal Aid Fund shall be utilised towards the cost of functions of District Authorities, Taluk Legal Services Committee and other expenses of the District Authority.

Summary

Introduction–Legal aid may be taken to mean free legal assistance to the poor persons in any judicial proceedings before the Court. Tribunals or any authority. It intends to provide free legal assistance to the poor persons who are not able to enforce the rights given to them by law.

Legal aid in India–The adversarial system is characterized by the technical nature of law and been called as formal because it requires pleadings and court fees. Section 340(1) of the Code of Criminal Procedure, 1898, explains that if a man was charged with an offence punishable with death, the court could provide him with a counsel upon his request. Article 39-A in the Constitution which is as follows: equal justice and free legal aid -The State shall secure that the operation of the legal system promotes justice, on a basis of equal opportunity and shall, in particular, provide free legal aid, by suitable legislation or schemes or in any way, to ensure that opportunities for securing justice are not denied to any citizen by reason of economic or other disabilities.

NALSA–The National Legal Services Authority (NALSA) has been constituted under the Legal Services Authorities Act, 1987 to provide free Legal Services to the weaker sections of the society and to organise Lok Adalats for amicable settlement of disputes.

Entitlement to legal services– Section 12 and 13 of the Legal Services Authorities Act, deal with the criteria of eligibility to the legal services and its procedure. Every person who has to file or defend a case shall be entitled to legal services under this Act if that person is :

- A member of a Scheduled Caste or Scheduled Tribe;
- A victim of trafficking in human beings or beggar as referred to in Article 23 of the Constitution;
- A women or a child; mentally ill or otherwise disabled person;
- A person under circumstances of under circumstances of underserved want such as being a victim of a mass disaster, ethic violence, caste atrocity, flood, drought, earthquake or industrial disaster; or

- An industrial workman; or

- In custody, including custody in protective home within the meaning of clause (g) of Section 2 of the immoral Traffic (prevention) Act, 1956 (104 of 1956); or in a Juvenile Justice Act, 1986 (53 of 1986); or in a psychiatric hospital or psychiatric nursing home within the meaning of clause (g) of Section 2 of Mental Health Act, 1987 (14 of 1987); or

- In receipt of annual income less than rupees nine thousand or such other higher amount as may be prescribed by the State Government, if the case if before a court than the Supreme Court and less than rupees twelve thousand or such other higher amount as may be prescribed by the Central Government, if the case is before the Supreme Court.

Hierarchy of Bodies created under the Act :

- A nationwide network has been envisaged under the Act for providing legal aid and assistance. National Legal Services Autority is the apex constituted to lay down policies and principles for making legal services available under the provisions of the Act and to frame most effective and economical schemes for legal services for legal services. It also disburses funds and grants to State Legal Services Authorities and NGOs for implementing legal aid schemes and programmes.

- In every State a State Legal Services Authority is constituted to give effect to the policies and directions of the Central Authority (NALSA) and to give services to the people and conduct Lok Adalats in the State. State Legal Services Authority is headed by the Chief Justice of the State High Court who is its Patron-in-Chief. A serving or retired Judge of the High Court is nominated as its Executive Chairman.

- District Legal Services Authority is constituted in every District to implement Legal Aid Programmes and Schemes in the District. The District Judge of the District is its ex-officio Chairman.

- Taluk legal Services Committees are also constituted for each of the Taluk or Mandal or for group of Taluk or Mandals to coordinate the activities of legal services in the Taluk and to organise Lok Adalats. Every Taluk Legal Services Committee is headed by a senior Civil Judge operating within the jurisdiction of the committee who is its ex-officio Chairman.

Lok Adalat–Lok Adalat is one of the alternative dispute redressal mechanisms, it is a forum where disputes/ cases pending in the court of law or at pre-litigation stage are settled/ compromised amicably. Lok Adalats have been given statutory status under the Legal Services Authorities Act, 1987. Under the said Act, the award (decision) made by the Lok Adalats is deemed to be a decree of a civil court and is final and binding on all parties and no appeal against such an award lies before any court of law. If the parties are not satisfied with the award of the Lok Adalat though there is no provision for an appeal against such an award, but they are free to initiate litigation by approaching the court of appropriate jurisdiction by filing a case by following the required procedure, in exercise of their right to litigate.

Funding–The Central Government by way of grants provides funding to the Central Authority for providing legal services. Similarly, the State Government by way of grants provides funding to the State Authority and the District Authority for providing legal services.

Multiple Choice of Questions

1. Article 39A of the Constitution of India deals with :
   (a) Free Legal Aid
   (b) Free and Compulsory Education
   (c) Free Housing to the Poor
   (d) Free Medical Aid to the Citizen

2. Which of the following governs the conduct of advocates ?
   (a) The rules framed by the Bar Council of India.
   (b) The CPC.
   (c) The Advocates Act, 1961
   (d) The rules framed by the various High Courts
   (e) All of the above

3. Which, among the following, is an advocate not prohibited from doing ?
   (a) Personally engaging in business
   (b) Being the managing director of a company
   (c) Being a full-time salaried employee of a company
   (d) Running for political office
   (e) Participating in the management of a business that she has inherited

4. Which of the following statements about the duties of advocates is least accurate ?

    (a) An advocate must accept any brief in the Courts or Tribunals or any other authorities

    (b) The fees charged by the advocate should be consistent with the advocate's standing at the Bar and the nature of the case

    (c) If an advocate withdraws from an engagement, the advocate must refund anypart of unearned fee to the client

    (d) An advocate may never refuse to accept any briefs.

    (e) An advocate should not accept a brief or appear in a case in which an advocate has reason to believe that she will be a witness

5. Which of the following statements about the duties of advocates to their opponents is least accurate ?

    (a) An advocate must only communicate or negotiate with an opposing party through the counsel representing the opposing party

    (b) An advocate must never communicate or negotiate with an opposing party at all

    (c) An advocate must only communicate or negotiate with an opposing party regarding the controversy, through the counsel representing the opposing party

    (d) An advocate must never communicate or negotiate with an opposing party regarding the controversy

    (e) None of the above

Short Answer Questions

1. What is the history of legal aid ?

2. How was legal aid movement in India initiated ?

3. What is Nalsa regulations ?

4. Short note on the following :

    (a) Free legal aid under international law

    (b) Taluk Legal Services Committee

    (c) Supreme Court Legal Services Committee

    (d) High Court Legal Services Committee

5. Name the international conventions regarding legal aid.

Long Answer Questions

1. What is Lok adalat. Explain in detail how it works.

2. Explain in brief the Funding process.

3. Name the international conventions regarding legal aid.

Board Questions

1. Service of Mr. Varun, an officer with Water (Jal) Board was terminated by the authorities by paying him three months salary. No inquiry was conducted against Mr. Varun and also the termination order did not assign any reason of his termination. In the above situation, the action of Water (Jal) Board authority justified or not ? Give reasons to your answer.

2. What is 'Legal Aid' ? State the two kinds of Legal Services available to a person for his grievance redressal. State any one value communicated by the system of Legal Aid.

3. With regards to the responsibility of the State Government to provide legal aid service.

    (a) What is the composition of state authority ?

    (b) State any four functions of the state authority.

4. What provisions have been made in India to provide funds to the Central Authority, State Authority and District Authority for providing Legal Services to its citizens ?

NCERT Questions

Activity Based Learning

Activity based learning provides opportunities to students with direct observation and learning about some aspect of the practice of law. In this activity, students are required, in groups or individually, to provide answers to the questions below to observe their knowledge on the functioning of legal services in India. This is only a learning activity for class discussion.

1. Make a chart as to how legal aid camps are organised in your area and how frequent are they organised. List out different organisations that provide legal aid camps. See the people who come for these camps. Make a note of their

problems and the remedies available to them through the legal aid camps.

2. Go to the Court and see if there is any lawyer specifically appointed for giving legal services. Schedule a meeting to see how legal services are provided. Does the lawyer get paid for the free legal services that he provides ?

4. Apart from free legal aid, list out the other legal services provided by different organisations in your area.

Sample Questions

1. Who can avail free legal aid under the provision of Legal Services Authorities Act ?

2. 'Prevention is better than cure', in the light of above statement explain the pre-litigation legal services provided to the accused.

3. What is National Legal Services Authority (NALSA) Regulations, 2010 ? Explain its relevant features.

4. Explain the functions of Central Authority constituted for legal services.

❑❑

International Law

INTRODUCTION

'State' is a term used in international law to describe a country or nation considered to be an organised political community under one government. The Montevideo convention of 1933 lays down the following qualifications of a state as :

- A permanent population
- A defined territory
- A government
- A capacity to enter into relations with other states.

What is International Law ?

International law is a set of rules and customs that governs the relationships between countries, known as states. In a democracy, the 'rule of law' applies to everyone in society and is intended to strike a balance between individual freedoms and the needs of the society. If a member of society breaks one of these laws, she or he will be punished by the state after due process is followed. On the other hand, if the government of a state takes unfair or illegal action against a citizen or group, the states constitution may allow citizens to challenge their governments in local (domestic) courts. If this does not solve the problem, other laws, such as international human rights treaties, will sometimes allow citizens to take their complaints outside their state to international legal bodies.

The word International law was used first time by jurist Jeremy Benthem in 1780. International law is the set of rules generally regarded and accepted as binding in relations between states and between nations. It serves as a framework for the practice of stable and organised international relations. International law picks up where domestic law ends. It governs the way countries interact with one another, and in specific circumstances, also sets how and when an international government, like the United Nations, intervenes in how a government interacts with its citizens or other people within the state. Canada's relationship with another country, such as Germany, the United States, or Mexico, will be governed by international law through agreements that are bilateral (between two countries) or multilateral (among three or more countries).

Much of International law is consent-based governance. This means that a state member is not obliged to abide by this type of international law, unless it has expressly consented to a particular course of conduct.

Some of the main subjects of International law include :

Some of the main subjects of International law include :

Human rights : ensuring the fundamental rights of every individual.

Regulating the use of armed force : making universal rules so that countries resolve differences through peaceful means.

Protection and safety : of individuals during times of war.

Trade and development : making trade and development easy all over the world.

The law of the sea : helps in establishing law of the sea all over the world.

Environmental issues and climate change : creating universal rules for the preservation of natural resources and protection of the environment.

Transportation : setting safety standards for international travel by air, rail and sea.

Telecommunications : setting rules for building and maintaining communication systems that cross state borders.

EVOLUTION OF INTERNATIONAL LAW

There was little scope for an international law in the period of ancient and medieval empires and its modern beginnings coincide, therefore, with the rise of national states after the middle Ages. Rules of maritime intercourse and rules respecting diplomatic agents soon came into existence. The growth of international law came largely through treaties concluded among states accepted as members of the 'family of nations,' which first included the states of Western Europe then the states of the New World, and, finally the states of Asia and other parts of the world. The United States contributed much to the laws of neutrality and aided in securing recognition of the doctrine of freedom of the seas. The provisions of international law were ignored in the Napoleonic period, but the Congress of Vienna reestablished and added much, particularly in respect to international rivers and the classification and treatment of diplomatic agents. The Declaration of Paris abolished privateering, drew up rules of contraband and stipulated rules of blockade. The Geneva Convention (1864) provided for more humane treatment of the wounded. The last quarter of the 19th century saw many international conventions concerning prisoners of war, communication, collision and salvage at sea, protection of migrating bird and sea life and suppression of prostitution. Resort to arbitration of disputes became more frequent. In World War I, no strong nations remained on the sidelines to give effective backing to international law and the concept of third party arbitration was again endangered; many of the standing provisions of international law were violated. The end of hostilities in 1945 saw the world again faced with grave international problems, including rectification of boundaries, care of refugees, and administration of the territory of the defeated enemy. The inadequacy of the League of Nations and of such idealistic renunciations of war led to the formation of the United Nations as a body capable of compelling obedience to international law and maintaining peace. After World War II, a notable advance in international law was the definition and punishment of war crimes. Attempts at a general codification of international law, however, proceeded slowly under the International Law Commission established in 1947 by the United Nations.

The nuclear age and the space age have led to new developments in international law. The basis of space law was developed. Treaties have been signed mandating the internationalisation of outer space and other celestial bodies. The nuclear nonproliferation treaty attempted to limit the spread of nuclear weapons. The agreements of the Strategic Arms Limitation Talks led to limited defensive and offensive weapon systems. This was first of many international arms treaties signed between the two nations (US and USSR in 1972) until the dissolution of the Soviet Union. Other treaties have covered the internationalisation of Antarctica, narcotic interdiction, satellite communications, and terrorism, etc. Environmental issues have led to a number of international treaties, including agreements covering fisheries, endangered species, global warming and biodiversity. Since the signing of the General Agreement on Tariffs and Trade (GATT) in 1947, there have been numerous international trade agreements. The establishment of the International Criminal Court (2002), with jurisdiction over war crimes, crimes against humanity, and related matters, marked a major step forward in international law.

Kinds of International Law

There are two major kinds of International law :

1. Private International Law.
2. Public International Law.

1. Private International Law : The term private International law may be defined as under: 'That branch of International law which determines that which law is to be applied to a specific case containing a foreign element is called Private International law.'

Explanation : From the above definition it is evident that private international law is to regulate those cases where a foreign element involves in the matter and the difficulty arises that which law shall be applicable to the case, in other words when it becomes difficult for a domestic court that the law of which state shall be applicable to a certain case because the case contains an element of a foreign state / states law.

2. Public International Law : It may be defined as under: 'A body of legal rules which regulates the relation of states inter se as well as their relations with other non-state entities is said to be Public International law.'

Explanation : From the above definition it may be concluded that Public International law is a set of legal rules which not only regulates the relations between the Nation States but also regulates their relations with other non-state entities. In other words it is a body of rules which regulates the relationship of the international actors with each other. These international actors may be given as under: States, individuals, NGOs, IGOs, Multi-National Corporations and Movements.

There is a sheer difference between Private International Law and Public International law. Some points of distinction may be given as under :

S.No.	Private International Law	Public International Law
1.	It deals with the individuals of one, two or more countries.	It deals mainly with the relationship of states with each other.
2.	The rules of Private International law are the outcome of state or state laws.	The rules of Public International law are the outcome of International customs, treaties and other sources.
3.	It differs from state to state.	Public International law is same for all the states of the world.
4.	It has been enacted by the legislature of the state or states.	It comes into force of treaties, customs, international agreements or decisions of arbitral tribunals.
5.	It is more civil in nature.	It is both civil and criminal in nature
6.	It is enforceable by the concerned state executive.	It is enforceable by the adverse view of nation of the word and fear of war or breakage of diplomatic relations etc.

SOURCES OF INTERNATIONAL LAW

Sources of International law means those origins from where it attains its authority and coercive agency. It is not so easy to pinpoint the sources of International law. Yet, the most authoritative source of international law is Article 38(1) of the Statute of the International Court of Justice, which provides that when a court which deals with disputes relating to international law, it shall apply :

● International conventions, whether general or particular, establishing rules expressly recognized by the contesting states,

● International custom, as evidence of general practice accepted by law

● The general principles of law recognised by civilised nations.

● Subject to provisions of Article 59, judicial decisions and teachings of the most highly qualified publicists of the various nations, as subsidiary means for the determination of rules of international law".

Treaties and Conventions

The term treaty may be defined as "the agreement entered into by Nation states for their relations with each other and to undertake certain duties, obligations and rights is said to be a treaty." A treaty need not be one consolidated document but may consist of more than one related documents.

A state may express its consent to be bound by a particular treaty in certain cases, the most common of which are:

(i)   Consent by Signature

(ii) Consent by exchange of Instruments

(iii) Consent by Ratification

Customs

Customs are those habits and practices which the nation's states commonly observe and the violation of which is considered as against the courtesy of international behavior. There are certain practices which the world community observes without any express provisions but because of practice they honor the same. So if there is no treaty between the parties to a dispute then the statute binds the Court to decide the case in the light of such international customs.

Judicial /Arbitral Decisions

Usually the Judicial decisions of the International Court of Justice are not binding and they have no value in the sense that they are related and binding only to that certain case for which they have given. And they cannot be cited as strict reference in any other case. But despite the fact the Statute reveals that in case of default of all the above sources the court shall resort to the prior judicial decisions.

INTERNATIONAL INSTITUTIONS

The growth in the number of sovereign nations and increasing international relations gave rise to notions of international co-operation. The 19th century saw the commencement of international non-governmental associations such as the International Law Association, in 1873, and the International Committee of the Red Cross, in 1863. These institutions paved the way for the formation of the

League of Nations in 1919 which was the predecessor to the United Nations in 1945.

Today, there are numerous organisations established by inter-governmental agreement and having a large number of social, economic and cultural influences which have been facilitated by the United Nations. Some of the key organisations that have been set up with the aid of the League of Nations and the United Nations are mentioned below:

1. International Labour Organisation (ILO)

It stands for the International Labour Organisation. It came into existence on April 11, 1919 and was associated with the League of Nations. Now it is working in co-operation with U.N.O. as its specialised agency. All members of the U.N.O. automatically become the members of the I.L.O. Besides, the I.L.O. can admit certain nations of its own accord. It has its own Charter, which was renewed and modified in 1954.

Organisation

It consists of three main organs:

(i)   The International Labour Conference

(ii) The Governing Body

(iii) The International Labour Office

Functions

The I.L.O. seeks to promote social justice by improving the conditions of the workers all over the world. For the achievement of the purposes I.L.O. is concerned with :

(i)   Regulation of hours of work

(ii)   The prevention of unemployment

(iii)   Provision of adequate living wages

(iv)   Protection of workers against sickness, diseases and injury arising out of their employment

(v)   The protection of children and women

(vi)   Provision for old age and injury

(vii)   Organisation of technical and vocational education

(viii) Provision for child welfare and maternity protection

(ix)   Housing and other facilities for workers.

2. United Nations Educational, Scientific and Cultural Organisation (UNESCO)

In 1945, UNESCO was established in order to respond to the firm belief of nations, forged by two world wars in less than a generation that political and economic agreements are not enough to build a lasting peace. Peace must be established on the basis of moral of humanity and intellectual solidarity. UNESCO strives to build networks among nations that enable this kind of solidarity by :

Mobilising for education : So that every child, boy or girl, has access to quality education as a fundamental human right and as a prerequisite for human development.

Building intercultural understanding : It builds international understanding through protection of heritage and support for cultural diversity. UNESCO created the idea of World Heritage to protect sites of outstanding universal value.

Pursuing scientific cooperation : Such as early warning systems for tsunamis or trans-boundary water management agreements, to strengthen ties between nations and societies.

Protecting freedom of expression : An essential condition for democracy, development and human dignity.

UNESCO is known as the 'intellectual' agency of the United Nations. At a time when the world is looking for new ways to build peace and sustainable development, people must rely on the power of intelligence to innovate, expand their horizons and sustain the hope of a new humanism. UNESCO exists to bring this creative intelligence to life; for it is in the minds of men and women that the defenses of peace and the conditions for sustainable development must be built.

3. International Monetary Fund (IMF) and World Bank

The World Bank was instituted as the International Bank for Reconstruction and Development (IBRD–the World Bank) and along with the IMF were established by the delegates of the Bretton Woods Twins in 1944. These two sister institutions were started in order to aid the economies of various nations which had suffered immense losses subsequent to the Second World War. The World Bank aids member states by providing loans to member states for the purpose of development and raises its funds by way of the world's financial markets.

The World Bank focuses on poverty reduction and the improvement of living standards worldwide by providing low-interest loans, interest-free credit, and grants to developing countries for education, health, infrastructure and communications, among other things. The World Bank works in over 100 countries.

4. World Health Organisation (WHO)

The WHO was formulated in 1948 to set up an agency that would move towards aiding member states with regards to health concerns. WHO has been a core agency for setting up of norms and standards to be followed with regards to human health and research regarding the containment of diseases as well assessing worldwide health trends. It coordinates with various agencies in different countries to facilitate greater knowledge and awareness of health issues in various countries. These organisations and their counterparts are aimed to promote international cooperation between member states on a large number of issues from rights of labourers, redevelopment of countries and economies as well as monitoring health trends across the world.

INTERNATIONAL HUMAN RIGHTS

The UDHR was proclaimed in a resolution of the United Nations General Assembly on December 10, 1948, out of a strong collective desire to for peace in the aftermath of World War II. The Universal Declaration of Human Rights (UDHR) is the basic international pronouncement of the indivisible, inalienable, and inviolable rights of all human beings. It is a statement of values and principles to which the international community has promised to adhere, even though the UDHR is not by itself a human rights treaty. It is the foundational international vision for human rights and has become the best known and most often-cited human rights instrument in the world.

The UDHR contains 30 articles, or sections, that set out people's universal rights. Some of the rights are based on our physical needs, such as the right to life, right to shelter, and right to food. Other rights are to protect us, such as the right to be free from torture, inhumane treatment, or punishment. There are other rights which ensure we are able to develop to our full potential, such as the right to education, right to work, and right to participate fully in cultural life.

The rights included in the UDHR are based on values of dignity, justice, respect, and equality. The declaration affirms entitlement to human rights regardless of who you are, where you come from, what language you speak, or what your religious beliefs are. Under the Universal Declaration of Human Rights, human rights are supposed to be :

Universal : They apply to everyone in the world.

Equal : All people are entitled to have the same rights, privileges and status under the law.

Interdependent and indivisible : The rights are dependent on one another and cannot be separated.

Inalienable and inviolable : You cannot give up your rights, even if you want to, and no one should be able to violate or disregard your rights.

Declaration of Human Rights

One of the most influential documents in this regard is the Universal Declaration of Human Rights which deals with various provisions, a few of them being :

- Liberty of a person (Article 3)
- Equality before law (Article 7)
- Prohibitions on torture (Article 5)
- Socio-economic rights such as right to work and equal pay (Article 23)
- Right to social security (Article 25)

While it is not a binding document, per se, there have been many instances where it has been referred to by cases of the International Court of Justice and is an extremely important document for the purpose of international human rights.

Convention on the Elimination of All Forms of Racial Discrimination which read with provisions of the Universal Declaration of Human Rights give rise to a host of enforceable rights in both treaty and customary international law.

There are various bodies such as the Commission on Human Rights, which is known as the Human Rights Council since 2006. It looks into matters of human rights issues. However, it has faced criticisms on its political selectivity and failure to objectively review the issues in certain countries. The Human Right Council is continuing the work of the previously set up Commission by broadening its framework by spreading its area over a wider framework. Generally human rights violations are dealt with by the state in which they occur. However, there are certain human rights, established under treaty that may constitute ergaomnes meaning towards all obligations for the state parties. This means that there are some violations that are so grave, that any state may take action against such crimes, regardless of whether they occurred in their jurisdiction or not. All states have a shared interest in elimination of such grave violations. This is one of the most empowering features of international human rights law where it does away with the borders and limitations of a domestic body and allows the international community to also seek an active role to protect the rights of citizens of other countries. Given the primacy of human rights even in domestic legislatures all over the world, it is almost no surprise that international human rights law is possibly given such a high degree of importance in the world of international law.

CUSTOMARY INTERNATIONAL LAW

Article 38 of the Statute of the International Court of Justice (ICJ) defines custom as "evidence of a general practice accepted as law." According to legal scholar Anthony D'Amato: "The importance of custom is rooted in the desire of the international community for order and security aims which are indistinguishable from the meaning of law."

Traditional writings maintain that customary international law consists of two elements:

(1) Usage, states' practice, and

(2) Opinio juris, a sense of legal obligation.

Courts traditionally have ascertained custom by engaging in a detailed historical analysis of many centuries of state practice, recognising a customary international law when it reflects both a state's uniform practice over a long period of time and that state's conscious acceptance of the principle as law. International customary law is probably the most disputed and discussed source of international law. For example, it is not clear when a particular State practice becomes a legally binding State practice. It is also unclear how one can identify a rule of international custom, or how one can prove its existence.

INTERNATIONAL LAW AND MUNICIPAL LAW

The relation between international law and municipal law is of theoretical as well as practical importance because of following reasons :

(i) The law of treaties which affects the state law can be clearly understood only when the relation between the two legal systems is appreciated.

(ii) Municipal court will face a problem of giving effect to rules of international law. Therefore, it is necessary to have clear under-standing of the relation between municipal law and state law.

(iii) International court may have to determine the effect of municipal law in the internatinal sphere.

What is the relationship between International and Municipal Law?

Apparently there seems no relationship between international law and municipal law. But if examined with philosophical eye then it would be that there is a relationship between both the legal orders. The test as to observe the relationship between the two systems may be conducted in case of a conflict between the two legal orders. The situation would arise that what law shall be applicable to the case in question.

According to the followers of the Dualistic theory Municipal law and International law are two separate, distinct and self-contained legal orders, independent from each other. Both the orders enjoy its own spheres and each one is the supreme in its own sphere. According to the followers of the monistic theory International law is not distinct and autonomous body of law, rather there exists only one set of legal system *i.e.,* the domestic legal order. Harmonisation theory impliedly accepts the distinction between the two legal orders but they contend that the differences or conflicts between them may be harmonized. According to this theory, neither Municipal law nor International law has supremacy over each other. They are of the view that both the systems have been framed ultimately for the conduct of human behaviour, so both of them are supreme in that sense.

INTERNATIONAL LAW AND INDIA

The relevant and basic provisions of the Constitution of India relevant and for consideration of its interaction and inter-relationship with International Law are :

(i)   Article 51   (ii) Article 73

(iii) Article 245 and 246 (iv) Article 253

(v)   Article 260   (vi) Article 363

(vii) Article 372 and

(viii) VII schedule entries 10 to 21.

Article 51 of the Indian Constitution specifically states that the State shall endeavor to 'foster respect for international law and treaty obligations in the dealings of organised peoples with one another'.

Under Article 253 of the Constitution of India, the Parliament and the Union of India have the power to implement treaties and can even interfere in the powers of the state government in order to give power to provisions of an international treaty.

India generally follows that merely affirming a treaty by way of ratifying it by the assent of the executive unless the treaty requires ratification by way of an act of the legislature. In the land mark case of Kesavananda Bharti vs. State of Kerala, it was observed that the court must interpret the provisions of the constitution in light of Charter of the United Nations.

There has been an evolution of the philosophy of the role of international treaties to which India is party to with relation to the Indian Constitution. In the case of Magan Bhai Patel vs. Union of India, the court held that if a treaty or international agreement restricts the rights of the citizens or modifies the laws of the state would require to have a legislative measure. E.g., if India is a party to an international agreement to stop the killing of a species of turtle, it restricts the right to trade of certain fishermen by prohibiting killing of the turtle. If this treaty is to be enforced in India, the Indian Parliament needs to pass a domestic legislation regarding prohibition of the killing of such turtle species. If no such right is restricted then it does not need to have a legislative measure to enact it or give rise to some weight in domestic law in the treaty.

It is also a very clear of Indian law that international treaties cannot on their own override domestic law. Hence, these treaties which are not enabled by the legislature will not have the same force in law if there is a contradictory law provided for.

However, in the case of Sheela Barse vs. Secretary Children's Aid Society, the Supreme Court held that India had ratified conventions regarding the protection of children and this placed an obligation on the State Government to implement these principles. This was a case in which there were no contradictory laws and as they were supplementing the law already in force the court held that the treaty could be applied directly to Indian law.

The most revolutionary of these cases was the case of Vishaka vs. State of Rajasthan, in which the Indian courts used the provisions of the Convention on Elimination of all forms of Discrimination against Women, (CEDAW), to create legally binding obligations regarding sexual harassment.

In A.P. Pollution Control Board vs. Prof. M.V. Nayadu, the Supreme Court recognised and applied the International Customary Rule of "precautionary principle". The Indian Supreme Court's view about customary nature of "precautionary principle" was appreciated in a Canadian case.

India has dealt with the interplay of international law as fits the need of the day. While any restriction of rights requires the need for an amendment by legislature, enhancing or broadening the scope of such rights is allowed as long as there is nothing to the contrary or similar in domestic law.

DISPUTE RESOLUTION

In the domestic scenario disputes may be resolved by various methods by way of application to court, mediation, conciliation or even arbitration. In international law there may be disputes regarding a large number of issues relating to treaties or some basic covenants of international law. In the event such disputes arise between states or even between individuals and the state, there are certain institutions and mechanisms to resolve such disputes. There are two categories of settlement of international disputes.

1. **Peaceful /Amicable settlement**

    The following methods can be adopted

    ● Negotiation
    ● Good offices
    ● Mediation
    ● Conciliation
    ● Enquiry
    ● Arbitration
    ● Judicial settlement
    ● Settlement under auspices of the United Nation Organisation

2. **Coercive Settlement**

    ● Retorsion
    ● Reprisals
    ● Pacific Blockade
    ● Intervention
    ● War

International Court of Justice and International Criminal Courts are two important international dispute resolution centres.

INTERNATIONAL COURT OF JUSTICE

The International Court of Justice (ICJ) is termed as the main judicial branch of the United Nations. In 1946, the General Assembly of the United Nations, enacted the Statute of the ICJ which gave rise to the institution of the International Court of Justice at The Hague, Netherlands. All members of the UN are party to this statute, by default owing to Article 93 of the United Nations Charter and non-members may also become parties under this Article. It consists of 15 judges elected by the General Assembly and Security Council voting separately. It is the principal judicial organ of the U.N.O. The judges are elected for a term of 9 years. All questions are decided by a majority of the judges. The chief function of the Court is to make peaceful settlement of legal disputes between nations. The Court does not deal with political disputes as these are the charge of the Security Council. It also gives advisory opinion on matter referred to it by the General Assembly or the Security Council. The Court is successor to the Permanent Court of International Justice and the judicial organ of the League of Nations. The judges of the Court represent the different legal systems of the world. The judges, however, do not represent their states. They are appointed in their individual capacity because of their judicial eminence. All the same, they must be qualified to be appointed as a judge of the highest court of their country. The decisions of the Court are enforced by the Security Council. It may take steps it deems fit. Its decisions are binding on the parties. Even States that are not members of the U.N.O. may accede to the Charter of the Court. The Court has its own Charter.

INTERNATIONAL CRIMINAL COURT

The International Criminal Court (ICC) is the first permanent, treaty-based international criminal court established to bring to justice the perpetrators of the most serious war crimes. The jurisdiction of the ICC is more restricted than that of ordinary criminal courts. The ICC is established under the Rome Statute, a treaty that came into force in 2002 and has been signed onto by 114 countries. Unlike the tribunals for Rwanda and the former Yugoslavia, which were established by the UN Security Council and only prosecute crimes committed during specific conflicts, the ICC is a permanent court of criminal jurisdiction that is independent from the UN. The ICC only tries cases that have not been investigated or prosecuted by a national judicial system, unless those proceedings are deemed not to be genuine (for example, a trial is held for the purpose of shielding a person from criminal responsibility) and only tries persons accused of the most serious crimes, including:

- Crimes against Humanity
- Genocide
- War Crimes
- Crimes of Aggression

The ICC may prosecute criminals for crimes committed in a country which accepts the jurisdiction of the court. Thus, only if countries agree to submit to the jurisdiction can the ICC take up certain cases in which the person who has committed the crime is a national of the country or if it was committed in the territory of that country. The cases may be referred by the country directly to the ICJ or though the Prosecutor of the ICC, who is the person appointed to try cases on behalf of the ICC.

Other Dispute Resolution Mechanism

Often the treaties entered into by the States themselves lay down the procedure to be followed in case of a dispute. For instance, the General Agreement on Trade and Tariffs provides for a dispute resolution panel within its own provisions. Treaties often employ mediation, arbitration and other such dispute resolution mechanisms to arrive at an agreeable decision. The United Nations has even created its own forum to deal with issues related to investment disputes in association with the World Bank.

These are some of the dispute resolution mechanisms available with regards to international disputes available to resolve disputes in international law. There are numerous other forums that can be created which are all dependent on agreements between parties and the provisions of the treaties. The ICJ's enabling provisions are also wide enough to deal with most disputes that may arise between member states.

Summary

Introduction–International law, commonly referred to as 'public international law,' regulates relations and activities between nations. It also contains rules regarding the operations of international organisations, such as the United Nations. In addition, it governs state treatment of individuals and juridical persons (*i.e.*, non-natural persons, such as a corporation, association or partnership).

Public International Law–Public International Law is the law that regulates relations between states. Public International law is different from other types of laws because it is concerned with interstate regulation, *i.e.*, it deals in regulating the conduct of one state with another and is not concerned with the relations between private entities (legal and natural persons) and even the domestic laws of any country.

Private International Law–Private International Law, often referred to as 'Conflict of Laws', is a set of rules and principles that govern interstate interactions and transactions of private parties.

Sources of International Law–A source of law within a domestic legal system is easier to determine. they are as follows :

- Treaties and Conventions
- Customs
- General Principles of Law Recognized by Civilized Nations

- Judicial / Arbitral Decisions
- Juristic Works

International institutions :

- United Nations Organisation
- International Labour Organisation (ILO)
- United Nations Educational, Scientific and Cultural Organisation (UNESCO)
- World Bank and the International Monetary Fund (IMF)
- World Health Organisation (WHO)

The United Nations Organisations–The United Nations is an international organisation founded in 1945. It is currently made up of 193 Member States. The mission and work of the United Nations are guided by the purposes and principles contained in its founding Charter. The United Nations can take action on the issues confronting humanity in the 21st century, such as peace and security, climate change, sustainable development, human rights, disarmament, terrorism, humanitarian and health emergencies, gender equality, governance, food production and more. The UN's Chief Administrative Officer is the Secretary-General.

International Labour Organisations (ILO)–It stands for the International Labour Organization It came into existence on April 11, 1919 and was associated with the League of Nations. Now it is working in co-operation with U.N.O. as its specialised agency. All members of the U.N.O. automatically become the members of the I.L.O. Besides, the I.L.O. can admit certain nations of its own accord. It has its own Charter, which was renewed and modified in 1954.

United Nations Educational, Scientific and Cultural Organisation (UNESCO)– In 1945, UNESCO was created in order to respond to the firm belief of nations, forged by two world wars in less than a generation that political and economic agreements are not enough to build a lasting peace. Peace must be established on the basis of humanity's moral and intellectual solidarity.

International Monetary Fund (IMF)–The World Bank was instituted as the International Bank for Reconstruction and Development (IBRD-the World Bank) and along with the IMF were established by the delegates of the Bretton Woods Twins in 1944. These two sister institutions were started in order to aid the economies of various nations which had suffered immense losses subsequent to the Second World War. The World Bank aids member states by providing loans to member states for the purpose

development and raises its funds by way of the world's financial markets.

World Health Organisation (WHO)–The WHO was formulated in 1948 to set up an agency that would move towards aiding member states with regards to health concerns. WHO has been a core agency for setting up of norms and standards to be followed with regards to human health and research regarding the containment of diseases as well assessing worldwide health trends. It coordinates with various agencies in different countries to facilitate greater knowledge and awareness of health issues in various countries.

World Bank–The World Bank focuses on poverty reduction and the improvement of living standards worldwide by providing low-interest loans, interest-free credit and grants to developing countries for education, health, infrastructure and communications, among other things. The World Bank works in over 100 countries

International Human Rights–Human rights violations are dealt with by the state in which they occur. However, there are certain human rights, established under treaty that may constitute ergaomnes obligations for the state parties. This means that there are some violations that are so grave, that any state may take action against such crimes, regardless of whether they occurred in their jurisdiction or not. All states have a shared interest in elimination of such grave violations. This is one of the most empowering features of international human rights law where it does away with the borders and limitations of a domestic body and allows the international community to also seek an active role to protect the rights of citizens of other countries.

Customary International Law–Article 38 of the Statute of the International Court of Justice (ICJ) defines custom as "evidence of a general practice accepted as law." According to legal scholar Anthony D'Amato: "The importance of custom is rooted in the desire of the international community for order and security—aims which are indistinguishable from the meaning of 'law."

Traditional writings maintain that customary international law consists of two elements:

(i) *Usage*, states' practice, and

(ii) *Opinio juris*, a sense of legal obligation.

International Law and Municipal Law–The relation between international law and municipal law is of theoretical as well as practical importance because of following reasons :

(i) The law of treaties which affect the state law can be clearly understood only when the relation between the two legal systems is appreciated.

(ii) Municipal court will face a problem of giving effect to rules of international law. Therefore it is necessary to have clear understanding of the relation between municipal law and state law.

(iii) International court may have to determine the effect of municipal law in the international sphere.

Theories relating to Municipal Law and International Law :

- **Dualistic Theory :** According to the followers of this theory Municipal law and International law are two separate, distinct and self-contained legal orders, independent from each other. Both the orders enjoy its own spheres and each one is the supreme in its own sphere. They accepts the separate and independent existence because, according to them, there are following points of distinctions between both the orders.

- **Monistic Theory**–According to the followers of this theory International law is not distinct and autonomous body of law, rather there exists only one sets of legal system *i.e.*, the domestic legal order. They have criticized the view adopted by Dualists, and also rejected the alleged distinction between Municipal law and International law as pointed out by the dualists. According to them both the international law and municipal law are related with the same legal system. And it is not possible to treat them severely.

- **Harmonisation Theory**–Dualistic and Monistic both are the extreme views. They both are opposite to each other. But the Harmonisation theory impliedly accepts the distinction between the two legal orders but they contend that the differences or conflicts between them may be harmonized. They are of the view that both the systems have been framed ultimately for the conduct of human behaviour, so both of them are supreme in that sense.

Dispute Resolution–In the domestic scenario disputes may be resolved by way of various methods by way of application to court, mediation, conciliation or even arbitration. In international law there may be disputes regarding a large number of issues relating to treaties or some basic covenants of international law. In the event such disputes arise between states or even between individuals and the state, there are certain institutions and mechanisms in place to resolve such disputes. The international institutions are :

International Court of Justice–The International Court of Justice (ICJ) is termed as the main judicial branch of the United Nations. In 1946, the General Assembly of the United Nations, enacted the Statute of the ICJ which gave rise to the institution of the International Court of Justice at The Hague, Netherlands. All members of the UN are party to this statute, by default owing to Article 93 of the United Nations Charter and non-members may also become parties under this Article.

International Criminal Court–The International Criminal Court (ICC) is the first permanent, treaty-based international criminal court established to bring to justice the perpetrators of the most serious war crimes. The ICC is established under the Rome Statute, a treaty that came into force in 2002 and has been signed onto by 114 countries. Unlike the tribunals for Rwanda and the former Yugoslavia, which were established by the UN Security Council and only prosecute crimes committed during specific conflicts, the ICC is a permanent court of criminal jurisdiction that is independent from the UN.

Multiple Choice of Questions

1. Which are the formal sources of International law?
   (a) Custom, treaties and judicial decisions.
   (b) Custom, general principles of law and theory.
   (c) Treaties, custom and general principles of law.
   (d) Treaties, custom and General Assembly Resolutions.

2. What is the legal nature of the Universal Declaration of Human Rights (UDHR) ?
   (a) The UDHR is a multilateral treaty.
   (b) The UDHR is a UN General Assembly reso-lution.
   (c) The UDHR is a UN Security Council reso-lution.
   (d) The UDHR is a declaration adopted by several States at an international conference.

3. The Secretary General of the U.N. is appointed :
   (a) by the General Assembly on the recommen-dation of the Security Council.
   (b) by the Security Council on the recommen-dation of the General Assembly.
   (c) in a joint session of the Security Council and General Assembly.

    (d) by the permanent members of the Security Council.

4. Which one of the following organs of the United Nations performs legislative function ?
    (a) The Security Council
    (b) The General Assembly
    (c) The Economic and Social Council
    (d) The Trusteeship Council

5. The Judge of the International Court of Justice are elected by :
    (a) The General Assembly
    (b) The Security Council
    (c) Both the General Assembly and the Security Council independently of one another
    (d) The Secretary General

Short Answer Questions

1. What is the rule of Law ?
2. What is Domestic/Municipal Law ?
3. How has International Law evolved ?
4. Distinguish between Public International Law and Private International Law.
5. What is Customary International Law ?
6. What does I.C.C do ?

Long Answer Questions

1. What is International law and what are the main subject of International Law ? Distinguish it from Municipal Law.
2. What are the sources of International Law ? Explain.
3. What are the International Institutions? Also explain their functions.
4. What is U.D.H.R ? How does it help on a global scenario ?
5. What is the relationship between International Law and Municipal Law ?
6. What is the impact of International law on India ? Explain with cases.
7. What are the dispute resolution mechanisms under International Law ?

Board Questions

1. For adoption of International Treaties into domestic law United Kingdom (UK) follows the 'Doctrine of Transformation'. In India the constitution has the provision for implementation of treaty obligation applicable to the country.

    (a) Explain the Doctrine of Transformation and its application.

    (b) State the Indian constitution provision for the implementation of a treaty with reference of any two decided case laws.

2. There was a treaty between two neighbouring countries 'Sodoland' and 'Borway', to stop the killing of Olive Ridly Turtle. A dispute arose between them regarding fulfilment of certain terms and conditions of this treaty obligation. Sodoland became member of United Nations in the year 1946 whereas Borway is not a member of United Nations. Sodoland refused to fulfil its treaty obligations. Aggrieved by this, Borway approached International Court of Justice to resolve this dispute.

    (a) Can Borway approach International Court of Justice ? If yes, under which provision of United Nations charter ?

    (b) Explain the jurisdiction of International Court of Justice.

NCERT Questions

True/False

1. A human rights treaty (law) of the United Nations is 'domestic' law.
2. Quebec follows the Criminal Code of Canada.
3. The rule of law only applies to citizens.
4. A universal standard applies only to a few states.
5. A multilateral treaty is a legal agreement between two states.
6. The International Tribunals for Rwanda and the former Yugoslavia can prosecute cases for criminal acts during any world conflict.
7. The International Criminal Court is a part of United Nations.
8. Expand the following :
    (a) I.C.C   (b) I.C.J
    (c) H.R.C   (d) U.D.H.R
    (e) W.H.O   (f) I.M.F
    (g) U.N.E.S.C.O (h) I.L.O

Short Answer Questions

1. Name a few key international organisations and state their areas of work.
2. Distinguish between Public International Law and Private International Law.
3. What is the role of the UN High Commissioner for Human Rights ?
4. What is the treatment of human rights in International Law ?
5. State the various sources of International Law.

6. What happens in case of conflict between a treaty provision and a domestic law ?
7. Explain the existing dispute resolution mechanism in International Law.

II Class activities

1. Organise a session of Model United Nations (MUN) in your class.
2. Prepare a report (1000 words) on the relation between International Trade and International Law.
3. Emulate a Human Rights Tribunal/ War Tribunal in your class.
4. Find out whether there is any difference between International Humanitarian Law and Human Right Law.
5. Explore the online services of the Peace Palace Library.

Sample Questions

1. With regards to International Human Rights 'ICCPR' stands for:

   (a) International Covenant on Civil and Political Rights.
   (b) International Covenant on Criminal and Penal Rights.
   (c) International Charter on Civil and Political Rights.
   (d) International Committee on Civic and Public Rights.

2. The International Criminal Court was set up with a purpose of prosecuting criminals for four major crimes. Which amongst the following doesn't belong to that category ?

   (a) Genocide
   (b) War Crimes
   (c) Crimes against Humanity
   (d) Intellectual Property Piracy.

3. What is a Treaty? How can a state express its willingness to be bound by a treaty ?

❏❏

PROJECT 1

CARLILL *VS* CARBOLIC SMOKE BALL COMPANY

Fact

Carbolic Smoke Ball Company gave an advertisement in the Pall Mall Gazette stating that it will give £ 100 to any person who contracted to influenza after using the smoke ball in the specified manner for the required period. To gain the confidence of the customers the Carbolic Smoke Ball Company stated that they have deposited £ 1000 with Alliance Bank, Regent street, showing their sincerity in the matter. The plaintiff (Carlill) purchases one smoke ball as per the advertisement. Plaintiff uses the smoke ball as prescribed for the required tenure but still contracts influenza. Since in the advertisement, the company promised to pay the compensation to anyone who contacted influenza even after using their medicine, Carlill claims 100 pounds from the company for the diseases caused as she used the company's smoke ball in the specified manner for the prescribed period. The Carbolic Smoke Ball Company refuses to pay £ 100 to the plaintiff stating that they are not bound to pay any money to Carlill.

Issue

There were basically three isues in the matter. Firstly, was there any acceptance between Carbolic Smoke Ball Company and the plaintiff? Secondly, was there any legal contract between both the parties? And thirdly, was the Carbolic Smoke Ball Company bound to pay £ 100 to Carlill. The rule is very clear. A contract is formed when there is proper offer and acceptance. The acceptance must be clear and communicated. The requirements of the offeror must be fulfilled.

Conclusion

Carbolic Smoke Ball Company's advertisement stated that whoever contracts with influenza even after using the smoke ball in the prescribed manner is liable to claim £ 100 from the company, hence it can be said that the company offered a contract. Carlill the plaintiff on seeing the advertisement purchased the smoke ball, hence she accepted the offer. She used the smoke ball in the prescribed manner for the required amount of time, which shows that Carlill have met the conditions of the contract. Here the offer was open for all. This kind of offer is known as general offer. In general offer the acceptance need not to be communicated. The performance of the terms and conditions are enough to conclude that offer has been accepted. In this case, even after using the smoke ball in the prescribed manner Carlill got contracted with influenza. So Carlill had performed the terms and conditions of the offer and that's conclude that she had accepted the offer. Using the advertisement, Carlill can sue the Carbolic Smoke Ball Company for the breach of contract based on terms and conditions of the contract.

Judgment

An offer can be made to the whole world which turns into a contract with anyone who comes forward and fulfils the conditions of the offer. There was no need to aware the company about the acceptance of the contract. It is said in the advertisement that whoever uses the smoke ball in the prescribed manner and still gets influenza is liable to claim £ 100 from the Carbolic Smoke Ball Company and must be rewarded for the same. The company is bound to pay 100 pounds to Carlill.

Probable Viva Questions

1. What are the essential elements of offer and acceptance?
2. What kind of offer was given by Carbolic Smoke Ball Company?
3. What is the difference between general and specific offer?
4. What is the rule of acceptance in general offer?
5. What was the judgment in the case of Carlill vs Carbolic Smoke Ball Company ?

❑❑

PROJECT 2

DONOGHUE *VS* STEVENSON

Fact

Donoghue, the plaintiff went to a cafe with her friend. Her friend ordered a tumbler of a Scotsman ice cream float, a mix of ice cream and ginger beer for her. Initially when the beer was poured down from a brown and opaque bottle labeled in the name of respondent's company, no problem arose. But when the remaining of the beer was poured down into the tumbler, a decomposed snail also floated out of the bottle. Donoghue alleged that because of having such beer she had abdominal pain and felt ill. She was later admitted into the hospital and subsequently found to be suffering from gastroenteritis and shock. There was no contractual obligation between the plaintiff and respondent. But since damage was occurred to Donoghue, she sued the respondent, who was the manufacturer of that ginger beer, for compensation, as there was breach of duty of care from respondent's side. The respondent claimed that there was no legal basis of plantiff's claim and he had not caused the plaintiff any injury.

Issue

The main issue was regarding negligence of Stevenson, the respondent. Whether Stevenson had a duty of care or not in the absence of contractual relations was the first issue. If there was duty of care, then whether Stevenson failed to perform his duty was the second issue. Third issue was whether Donoghue was harmed because of such absence of duty of care. And lastly, any damages occurred to Donoghue or not for such breach of duty of care.

Conclusion

In Court of Session Outer House, it was held that as a general principle, there should be liability for negligent preparation of food. When the danger had been introduced by the act of negligence, the negligent manufacturer should not be released from his duty. In the appeal made by the manufacturer to the Court of Session Inner House, the court allowed the appeal on basis of Mullen *vs* AG Barr & Co. Ltd. and held that the manufacturer was not bound to pay damages to the plaintiff. Donoghue made appeal to the House of Lords. By majority of 3-2, the court held that Donoghue had a cause of action to sue against Stevenson. The court held that the manufacturer of ginger beer had a duty of reasonable care. The manufacturer had a reasonable care to avoid acts or omissions which he can reasonably foresee would be likely to injure his neighbor. This is known as neighbor principle. Thus the respondent had a duty of reasonable care which he failed to perform and as a result of such non performance it injured the plaintiff.

Judgment

The Court held that here should be a duty of care owed by all manufacturers of "articles of common household use", listing medicine, soap and cleaning products as examples. People must take reasonable care not to injure others who could foreseeably be affected by their action or inaction. The legal basis of the case being proved the plaintiff had to prove factual elements of the case so that she could receive the compensation.

Probable Viva Questions

1. What are the essential elements of negligence?
2. Was there any breach of duty by the manu-facturer?
3. What do you understand by neighbor principle?
4. In absence of any contractual obligation, was Stevenson bound to pay damages to Donoghue?
5. What was the judgment in the case of Donoghue *vs* Stevenson?

❏❏

PROJECT 3

SHANTA BAI *VS* STATE OF BOMBAY

Fact

The husband of the petitioner granted her the right by an unregistered document to take and appropriate all kinds of wood from certain forests in his Zamindary. In the meantime, Madhya Pradesh Abolition of Proprietary Rights (Estates, Mahals, Alienated Lands) Act, 1950 was passed and all proprietary rights in the above– mentioned land was vested in the State under section 3 of the Act. The petitioner could no longer cut any trees. She applied to the Deputy Commissioner for cutting trees. Under section 6(2) of the Act, the Deputy Commissioner permitted the petitioner to cut the trees from the said forest. But on the other hand the Divisional Forest Officer took action against the petitioner. He passed an order by which the petitioner's name was cancelled and the cut materials were forfeited. The petitioner moved to the State Government against this order. But the State Government rejected her application. Thereafter she filed writ petition to the Supreme Court under article 32 of the Constitution and contended that the order of Forest Officer infringed her fundamental rights under articles. 19(1)(f) and 19(1)(g).

Issue

The main issue was whether the fundamental rights of the petitioner was violated. Secondly, what was the status of the petitioner – whether she was leasee, licensee or she had rights of profits-a-prendre. Thirdly, what kind of property is a tree – is it a movable or immovable property?

Conclusion

If the document was made with an intention to transfer any proprietary interest in the land, such transfer would be ineffective as the document was not registered under the Registration Act. Moreover, the transfer was ineffective as under section 3 of the Madhya Pradesh Abolition of Proprietary Rights Act as it vested such proprietary interest of the forest in the State. If it was a profits-a-prendre that was sought to be transferred by it, then again the document was needed to be compulsorily registered. Profits-a-prendre means grant of the produce of the soil "like grass, or turves or trees". By nature the property proved to be immovable and needed to be registered as it was held in the case of Ananda Behera *vs* the State of Orissa. If it was a contract that gave rise to a purely personal right, the petitioner could not complain as the State had not acquired or taken possession of the contract which remained her property, and she was free to dispose of it in any way she liked. The State not being a party to that contract would not be bound by it. Even if for some reason or other the State became bound, the petitioner should have filed a suit for enforcement of the contract and compensation for any possible breach of it. No question of infringement of any fundamental right could arise. On the other hand whether tree is movable or immovable property, it was found that as per Transfer of Property Act, 1882, Registration Act, 1908 and General Clauses Act, 1897 trees (except standing timber) are immoveable property. Those trees which could fall at an early date and were intended to be cut down could be regarded as standing timber and moveable property. The remaining trees will be considered as immoveable property.

Judgment

The Court held that the writ petition must fail as no fundamental right of the petitioner was violated in absence of any registered document. The status of the petitioner was not answered as it was not a necessary question to be answered in this writ petition. On the question of whether tree is a movable property or not, it was held that if the intention was to cut down the tree and use as timber, it is a movable property. Otherwise, tree is an immovable property under Transfer of Property Act, 1882, Registration Act, 1908 and General Clauses Act, 1897.

Probable Viva Questions

1. What do you understand by movable and immovable property?
2. Why did the petitioner fail to succeed?
3. What do you understand by profits-a-pendre?
4. Is tree a movable or immovable property?
5. What was the judgment in the case of Shanta Bai *vs* State of Bombay?

❑❑

Bibliography

Unit-1
Judiciary

◆ Common refrence in all the chapters was the CBSE book available online.
1. https://en.wikipedia.org/wiki/**Judiciary**>of>India
2. www.mapsofindia.com _ Government of India _ Judiciary
3. indiancourts.nic.in/
4. www.silf.org.in/16/**indian-judicial**-system.htm
5. www.yourarticlelibrary.com/essay/**judiciary**-in-**india**-11...**indian-judiciary**/40371/
◆ Books reffered
◆ Judicial Accountability – Kalraj Mishra

Unit-2 (1)
Law of Property

1. https://en.wikipedia.org/wiki/Transfer of **Property Act** 1882
2. ecourts.gov.in/sites/default/files/TRANSFER%20OF%20**PROPERTY**%20**ACT**.pdf
3. mayank-**lawnotes**.blogspot.in/2007/01/transfer-of-**property**.html
4. www.legalservices**india**.com/article/.../definition-&-concept-of-**property**-502-1.html
5. www.grrajeshkumar.com/class-**notes**-on-**property-law**-unit-iii-2nd-sem-3-year-ll-b/
◆ Books referred
◆ Transfer of property act – S. N. Shukla
◆ Textbook on the Transfer of Property Act, - by Avtar Singh
◆ Transfer of Property Act, 1882 - by Universal Law Publishing

Unit-2 (2)
Law of Contract

1. www.**law**teacher.net/lecture-**notes**/**contract-law**/
2. www.mbaexam**notes**.com/**law-of-contracts-notes**.html
3. www.slideshare.net/ramonavansluytman/study-**notes-contract-law**
4. www.lawnotes.in > Home > Indian Law > Indian Acts
◆ Books referred
◆ Mulla's Indian Contract Act- by Mulla
◆ Contract and Specfic Relief 2013 -by Avtar Singh
◆ Contract law – by R.K. Bangia

Unit-2 (3)
Law of Torts

1. study.com/academy/lesson/what-is-**tort-law**-definition-and-examples.html
2. www.lawnotes.in/**Law of Torts**
3. www.legalserviceindia.com/articles/**torts** s.htm
4. www.lawteacher.net > Lecture Notes
5. www.grrajeshkumar.com/class-**notes**-on-**law-of-torts**-1st-sem-3-year-ll-b/
6. www.slideshare.net/augustineferdinand1/**law-notes-tort**
7. www.academia.edu/.../**TORT**-TOPIC-1-INTRODUCTION Definition Nature and...
8. www.studynama.com
◆ Book referred
◆ Introduction to the Law of Torts and Consumer Protection Paperback – by Avtar Singh

Unit-2 (4)
Criminal Laws in India

1. https://en.wikipedia.org/wiki/**Indian_criminal_law**
2. https://en.wikipedia.org/wiki/**Criminal_Law_**(Amendment)**_Act,_**2013
3. www.legalservice**india**.com/**Criminallaws/criminal_law**.htm
4. www.ili.ac.in/1_**criminal**%20**law**.pdf
◆ Books refrred
◆ The Indian Penal Code - As Amended by the Criminal Law (Amendment) Act, - by Ratanlal and Dhirajlal
◆ The Code of Criminal Procedure - by Ratanlal and Dhirajlal

Unit-2 (5)
Administrative Law

1. mayank-**lawnotes**.blogspot.in/2007/01/**administrative-law**.html
2. www.**lawnotes**.in/**Administrative_Law**
3. www.lawnotes.in _ Home _ Administrative Law
4. www.slideshare.net/AbhijithMuralisudha/**administrative-law**
5. publicadministrationtheone.blogspot.com/.../**administrative-law**-meaning-scope-and.ht...
◆ Books referred
◆ Indian Administrative Law - by Kagzi M.C. Jain
◆ ADMINISTRATIVE LAW - b y MASSEY I. P.

Unit-3
Arbitration

1. https://en.wikipedia.org/wiki/**Arbitration**
2. www.wipo.int/amc/en/**arbitration**/what-is-arb.html
3. https://ipba.org/media/fck/files/**Arbitration**%20in%20India.pdf
4. www.citehr.com _ ... _ Human Resource Management
5. https://legaldesk.com/general/different-**types-of-arbitration**-and-their-importance

Unit-4
Human Rights

1. www.un.org/en/universal-declaration-**human-rights**/
2. www.ohchr.org _ OHCHR _ English
3. www.**humanrights**.com
4. www.important**india**.com
5. www.yourarticlelibrary.com/**essay**/**human-rights-in-india**-and-its-protection/47124/

Unit-5
Legal Profession in India

1. www.uianet.org _ Home _ Actions _ The legal profession worldwide
2. www.barcouncilofindia.org _ About the profession
3. www.lawctopus.com/academike/history-**legal-profession-india**
4. https://www.scribd.com/doc/60313754/History-of-**Legal-Profession-in-India**

Unit-6
Legal Services in India

1. www.**legalserviceindia**.com
2. nalsa.gov.in/
3. https://en.wikipedia.org/wiki/**Legal_aid**
4. www.**legalserviceindia**.com/articles/laid.htm

Unit-7
International Law

1. https://en.wikipedia.org/wiki/**International_law**
2. www.ohchr.org _ OHCHR _ English
◆ Books referred
◆ Textbook on Public International Law -by Rakesh Kumar Singh
◆ Public International Law - by V. K. Ahuja